THE THREAD-SPIRIT

The Symbolism of Knotting & the Fiber Arts

Mark Siegeltuch

FONS VITAE

Fons Vitae
49 Mockingbird Valley Drive
Louisville, Kentucky 40207-1366 USA
fonsvitaeky@aol.com • www.fonsvitae.com

Cover design by Aileen Winter Mostel
Layout and design, Aileen Winter Mostel

ISBN 9781891785450
Library of Congress Control Number: 2009937738

Printed in Canada

TABLE OF CONTENTS

ACKNOWLEDGMENTS

This book arose from a long period of study and reflection, much of it under the guidance of Dr. Edmund Carpenter, who first introduced me to the work of A. K. Coomaraswamy and who let me assist him in his prolonged efforts to bring the work of Carl Schuster to print. Ted has been both a teacher and a friend and his work in the fields of anthropology and communications has been a source of inspiration to me and to many others. He encouraged me to apply the wide-ranging work of Carl Schuster to a more narrowly focused topic.

I would also like to express my particular gratitude to Aileen Winter Mostel, who put so much of her time and skill into the design and layout of this book. The images included in this work are such an important part of the story that their presentation required as much thought as the text. Aileen was the natural choice both because of her talent and because she helped design the Carl Schuster volumes on which this work is based.

Thanks also to Tobias Mostel, Aileen's husband, for his many years of friendship and encouragement, as well as for editorial assistance. I told him about my plans for the book years ago and we have spent many hours discussing the ideas contained here.

I should also mention Laurin Raiken for his continuing interest in my work and for allowing me to lecture every year on this material at New York University. The best way to learn a subject is to teach it.

Thanks also to Bernard Peirani, who reviewed some of this material in an early stage of development and made many good suggestions; and to Paul Schroeder for his introduction to Rama Coomaraswamy and for the fine example he set by editing Coomaraswamy's *Yaksas*, which had been out of print for many years.

Lastly, my gratitude to Virginia Gray-Henry and Fons Vitae Press for publishing a work that has such a restricted audience. Her enthusiasm for the subject was clear from the outset.

This book is dedicated to the memory of my sister, Abby Siegeltuch, who shared my scholarly interests and who grappled as well as anyone with the mysteries of symbolic expression.

PREFACE

There is no value in being original when writing about traditional symbolism unless one means a return to origins. My task was to collect those images and stories that best allow the reader to understand the enduring continuity of the doctrine supporting this symbolism. A great deal of material was available but what cannot be demonstrated in a few pages is unlikely to be convincing in many.

I stand firmly upon the shoulders of giants—scholars of the highest distinction like René Guénon, Ananda Coomaraswamy, and Carl Schuster. Many other writers, less profound in their understanding, have nonetheless contributed greatly to the materials presented here by their thoughtful collection and evaluation of the evidence.

Scholarship of this sort is a great work of translation in which the metaphorical and analogical must be reduced and reordered to meet the dictates of expository writing. The beauty and power of these stories and images are normally the first casualties. It is a mighty labor to recover what was once a living tradition anchored in the highest realities—spoken, heard, danced, sung. I chose to deal with this problem by piling example upon example as is common in works of this kind, and to use footnotes when related motifs were suggested, as they were at every turn. What Rabbi Adin Steinsaltz writes about the Talmud applies equally well to the study of traditional symbolism: "When a man begins to study Talmud, he always finds himself in the middle of things, no matter where he starts. Only through study and a combination of facts can he arrive at the ability to understand."

I start by documenting the evidence before moving on to discuss the metaphysical doctrines that support it, excavated with such remarkable precision and clarity by Ananda Coomaraswamy and René Guénon. The work of Carl Schuster represents the continuation and culmination of Dr. Coomaraswamy's work in that he was able to demonstrate the prehistoric origins of these ideas, something Coomaraswamy predicted.

If the reader believes in the doctrines expressed here, then this is truly "the greatest story ever told"; or, as is written in the *Upanishads*, "All else is but a tale of knots."

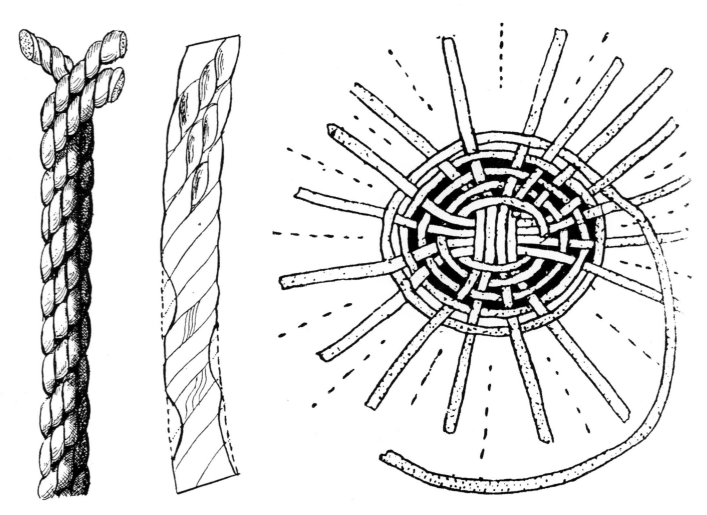

Fig. F.1: Reconstruction of a prehistoric cord from a clay imprint.   Fig. F.2: Külko basketry technique.

FOREWORD

We will never know who tied the first knot. Animals are capable of making and using tools, but only humans create symbols. When we find the first evidence of human culture, in early Paleolithic times, it is already fully developed and shows intelligence as great as our own. What distinguishes early man from us is a different mode of thought; one in which the practical and symbolic are united in a way we cannot manage. Our obsessive pragmatism reduces this integrated vision to a series of problems that require solutions: how to attach a spearhead to a shaft or construct a net for catching game. I suspect that they looked at their own bodies as a model. "The knee bone connected to the leg bone," as the song reminds us. The practical value of knots and their crucial role in the development of human culture cannot be separated from the way in which they were conceived, including all the related associations they had, and continue to have.

Historically, knotting is closely allied with the fiber technologies. Our first evidence of cordage comes from the caves of Lascaux in France (c. 15,000 B.C.) where the remains of a fiber cord composed of three two-ply strings were found fossilized in lumps of clay[1] (Fig. F.1). We find sewing needles as early as 25,000 B.C.[2] and more recently, evidence of a simple form of weaving dating from 27,000 B.C.[3]

Knotting is also integral to sewing, the oldest of the fiber technologies. Carl Schuster, whose work will be addressed later, believed that tailored fur garments were the first human clothes and that the patterns that decorated these garments survived because they were carved on bone, ivory and stone.[4]

Sewing, netting, wickerwork, basketry, weaving, and rug making—whatever their developmental sequence—have common roots, an interlacing or tying of materials.[5] Simple weaving or "twining" resembles sewing. Wicker and basketry techniques often resemble flax weaving both in technique and in the manner in which the fibers are wetted to keep them pliable (Fig. F.2).[6] Further, many primitive shuttles look like darning needles.[7] The boundaries separating these arts are hard to define:

> In the prehistoric Southwest, there were many objects which were produced in techniques and materials closer to the same in basketing than in true textiles. Also some were made of vegetable fibers reduced to fine cordage or thread elements, and employed techniques in their production more like those used in textile

weaving. In essence, these woven pieces belong to neither basketry nor to true loomed textiles.[8]

The Greek word, *peirar* (a piece of rope, a woof thread) is related to the Sanskrit word *parvan* (knot, link or joint), which suggests that the act of knotting lies at the root of weaving and its allied arts.[9]

Aside from the scant archeological evidence, we know little about the history of knotting and fiber technology because sinew, thread, rope and cloth are perishable.[10] Where physical evidence is scarce, however, we may profitably turn our attention to the realms of art, language and folklore. Here we can find the remnants of ancient beliefs that illuminate the subject from another angle.

By Neolithic times, knots were being used for a variety of specialized functions such as counting and record keeping (Fig. F.3). These forms developed from common meanings and assumptions. Our taxonomy should not be allowed to obscure this fact.

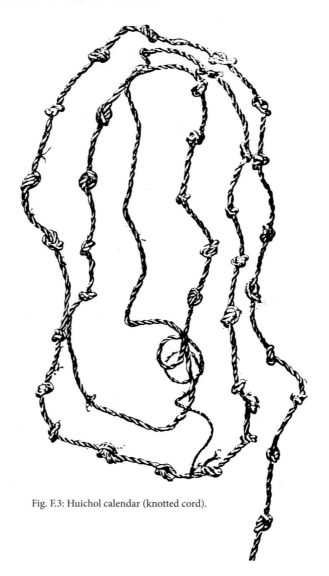

Fig. F.3: Huichol calendar (knotted cord).

THE THREAD-SPIRIT
The Symbolism of Knotting & the Fiber Arts

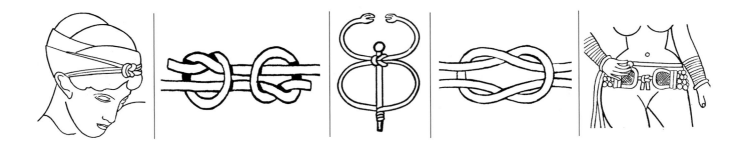

Olaus Magnus, Wind Knots

MAGIC KNOTS

The folk has thus preserved, without understanding, the remains of old traditions that go back sometimes to the indeterminably distant past, to which we can only refer as "prehistoric".... Had the folk beliefs not indeed been once understood, we could not now speak of them as metaphysically intelligible, or explain the accuracy of their formulations.

Ananda K. Coomaraswamy

The symbolic use of the knot and the ceremony of tying and untying have a long history and a worldwide distribution. In addition to their role as instruments for binding objects or restraining physical activity, knots have a concomitant spiritual significance. It is widely believed that they possess magical power to work good and evil. As a form of restraint, they may be tied to prevent illness or misfortune. Conversely, they may be untied to free someone from a difficulty, or to allow an event—such as the birth of a child—to proceed smoothly.

LOVE KNOTS

In ancient times it was believed that magic knots, accompanied by the appropriate spell, could win or retain a lover. In his Eighth Eclogue, Virgil writes of a lovesick maiden:

> Around his waxen image first I wind
> Three woolen fillets of three colors join'd;
> Thrice bind about his thrice-devoted head,
> Which round the sacred altar thrice is led.
> Unequal numbers please the gods.—My charms,
> Restore my lovely Daphnis to my longing arms.
> Knit with three knots the fillets; knit'em straight; And say, "these knots to love I consecrate."[11]

Such practices were not unique to the Romans. Sorcerers in 18th century Scotland employed a similar method to work their love magic.[12] Frazer records the case of an Arab girl, who, having lost her heart to a certain man, tries to regain his love by tying knots in his whip; she is outdone by a rival who unties all the knots.[13]

There are further examples from literature. In John Gay's *Shepherds Week* (1714) we read:

As Lubberkin once slept beneath a Tree,
I twitched his dangling Garter from his knee;
He wist not when the hempen String I drew,
Now mine I quickly doff of Inkle Blue;
Together fast I tye the Garters twain,
And while I knit the knot repeat this strain.
Three times a true-love's knot I tye secure,
Firm be the knot, firm may his love endure.
With my sharp Heel I three times mark the Ground,
And turn me thrice around, around, around.

Shakespeare's Two Gentlemen of Verona and Oliver Goldsmith's The Vicar of Wakefield (1766) also contain references to love knots.[14]

Heraklas, a Greek physician and author of the first century A.D., was the first writer to describe the Love knot. He called it the single *karkhesios*, which authorities, such as the Swedish physiologist Hjalmar Ohrvall, have identified as the Englishman's knot.[15]

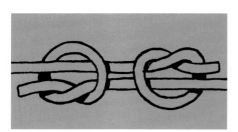

Fig. 1.1: Fisherman's knot.

The Love knot is known worldwide by a variety of names including the Fisherman's knot (Fig. 1.1), True-Lovers knot, and Middleman's knot. It is formed from a loop and two overhand knots that can be pulled together or tightened separately. Ohrvall relates that Swedish sailors would send these knots to their sweethearts, leaving the overhands separated. If the man was still in favor, the knots would be returned with the overhands joined.

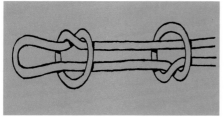

Fig. 1.2: Lover's knot.

There are several varieties of Love knot (Fig. 1.2). The Swedish distinguish between the Love knot, the Friendship knot and the Betrothal knot, which plays an important role in many marriage ceremonies.[16]

MARRIAGE KNOTS

The English colloquial expressions "getting hitched" and "tying the knot" are both reminders of the importance once attributed to knots in the marriage ceremony, where a number of diverse associations are brought together. Knots are related to procreation as well as to the protection and future well being of the bride and groom. Further, the knot is a symbol for the union of two lives, or more properly, two families. Lastly, knots are often equated with vows—"with this ring I do thee wed."

The bridal veil is one custom that has survived; it served originally as a source of protection for the married couple. In 19th century Russia, a net was thrown over the bride and bridegroom. The groom's attendants were given nets or girdles to wear. Anyone seeking to harm the married couple would have to untie all the knots in the net.[17]

In Macedonia, a bride had a girdle tied around her waist with three knots.[18] Similarly, brides in ancient Israel wore knotted cords as amulets.[19]

On the East Indian island of Rotti, once a man paid his bride price, a cord was fastened around the waist of his bride, but only if she was a virgin. Then, as Frazer describes:

Nine knots are tied in the cord, and in order to make them harder
to unloose, they are smeared with wax. Bride and bridegroom are
then secluded in a chamber, where he has to untie the knots with the
thumb and forefinger of his left hand only. It may be from one to
twelve months before he succeeds in undoing them all. Until he has
done so he may not look on the woman as his wife. In no case may
the cord be broken, or the bridegroom would render himself liable
to any fine that the bride's father might choose to impose. When all
the knots are loosed, the woman is his wife, and he shews the cord
to her father, and generally presents his wife with a golden or silver
necklace instead of the cord.[20]

The physical attachment of the bride and groom is another common feature found in marriage ceremonies.

In the Parsi marriage ceremony, a curtain is held up to screen the
bride and groom from each other; under this they grasp each other's
right hand, after which another piece of cloth is placed around them
so as to encircle them, and the ends of the cloth are tied together by
a double knot. In the same way, raw twist is taken and wound round
the pair seven times over the joined hands of the couple as well as
round the double knot of the ends of the cloth around them.[21]

Among the Karans of Bengal, the hands of the bride and groom are tied
together; while in Northern India, their clothes are knotted together as
they revolve around the sacred fire.[22] The bride and groom are not just two
people getting married, but participants in a ritual drama.

A second and more evident point is that any marriage is the joining of two
families. The expression, "family ties" registers this idea clearly.

Among the Brahmans, towards the end of the marriage ceremony,
the husband advances towards his young wife, who is seated facing
the east, and while reciting mantras, he fastens the *tali*—a little gold
ornament which all married women wear —around her neck, securing it with three knots; before these knots are tied the father of the
bride may refuse his consent, but after they are tied the marriage is
indissoluble. A cord is also tied round the bride's waist, and when
she departs from the house, the verse "I loosen thee" is said.[23]

If the practice of tying or joining the bride and groom is common, so too
is the ceremony of untying. Here the act may signify the bride's impending loss of virginity. Any knot present at the ceremony is seen as preventing the consummation of the marriage. In Perthshire, Scotland, during
the 18th century, the minister of Logierait left the following account of
a local custom:

Immediately before the celebration of the marriage ceremony every
knot about the bride and bridegroom (garters, shoe-strings, strings
of petticoats, etc.) is carefully loosened. After leaving the church,
the whole company walk round it, keeping the church walls always
upon the right hand. The bridegroom, however, first retires one way

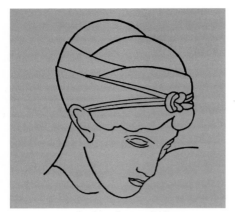

Fig. 1.3: Roman bride with Hercules knot.

Fig. 1.4: Square knot.

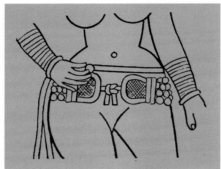

Fig. 1.5: Goddess at Lucknow (Buddhist).

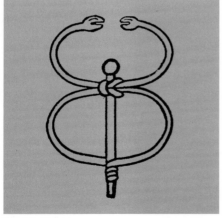

Fig. 1.6: Caduceus.

with some young men to tie the knots that were loosened about him, while the young married woman in the same manner retires somewhere else to adjust the disorder of her dress.[24]

In other parts of Scotland it was common for the bride and groom to have one or both shoes untied during the marriage ceremony, a practice also found in Syria and North Africa.[25]

In classical times, a Roman bride wore garments bound with a girdle of sheep's wool and tied with a knot called a Hercules knot (Fig. 1.3). After the marriage, the couple proceeded to the groom's house, where the bride would tie woolen fillets to the doorpost. Once in the bridal chamber, the husband untied the knot and removed his wife's girdle.[26]

The Roman *nodus Herculis* (also *Herculeus* and *Herculaneus*) has been identified as the Square knot, known to every scout (Fig. 1.4).

Throughout the ancient world, special amuletic powers were attributed to this knot. It is often shown serving as a shoulder, girdle or necklace knot. We also find the knot in amuletic form, in wood or gold, where it serves as a clasp or necklace. Both the Greeks and Romans believed that the Hercules knot could heal wounds. Pliny wrote:

> To tie up wounds with the Hercules knot makes the healing wonderfully more rapid, and even to tie daily the girdle with this knot is said to have a certain usefulness...[27]

The invention of the knot was attributed to Hercules who was worshipped as a savior and protector.

The Hercules knot is a local adaptation of much older beliefs, and not the product of classical civilization (Fig. 1.5). Many knots, and the Hercules knot in particular, are connected with fertility and procreation. This is what gives them such a central role in the marriage ceremony.

That familiar symbol, the caduceus, is sometimes depicted with a Hercules knot uniting two snakes (Fig. 1.6).

Knots are also related to marriage vows. There is ample evidence to show that knots were once equated with words. In the Old Testament we read:

> If a man vow a vow unto the Lord or swear an oath to bind his soul with a bond (literally: to tie a knot against himself) he shall not break his word, he shall do according to all that proceedeth out of his mouth.[28]

Here a vow of self-restraint is described as a knot tied against oneself. It is possible that the swearing of an oath was accompanied, at one time, by the ritual tying of a knot.

The connection between knots and oaths is a close one. In Hebrew, to bind and loose (*asur, muttar*) mean respectively, to prohibit and allow. In one sense the knot represents the restraint of emotion or action. There are parallels among the ancient Greeks where restrained desires or ambitions are characterized as bonds or cords placed around men by the gods.[29] We will find support for this relationship in the *sutratman* (thread-spirit) doctrine in which the thread or rope represents the cosmic breath, and the knots individual names or existences. The connection between words and knots persists in such expressions as, "a knotty argument," or the "threads of a discussion."

BIRTH KNOTS

Birth, marriage and death are the most important events in the life of any community. We have seen how knots are associated with procreation in the marriage ceremony. The role of the knot in the rituals connected with birth is more clearly defined and the same conceptions are shared by widely divergent groups of people.

Generally, birth is associated with the idea of unloosing and various customs are observed to facilitate delivery, such as unbraiding hair, untying knots on clothing or shoelaces, removing locks, or even uncrossing legs, arms or fingers.

Both the Greeks and the Romans believed in the magical power of knots to aid or obstruct the birth of a child. Pliny warns against interlacing one's fingers or crossing or clasping one's knees in front of a pregnant woman.[30] Elsewhere in the *Natural History* he writes:

> If the man by whom a woman has conceived unties his girdle and puts it round her waist, and then unties it with the ritual formula; "I bound, and I too will unloose," then taking his departure, child-birth is made more rapid.[31]

Roman women who took part in the rites of Juno Lucina, goddess of child-birth, had all the knots on their person untied[32] (Fig. 1.7):

> Say ye, "Thou Lucina, hast bestowed on us the light of life;" say ye "Thou dost hear the prayer of women in travail." But let her who is with child unbind her hair before she prays, in order that the goddess may gently unbind her teeming womb.[33]

According to legend, Alcmena, the mother of Hercules, was in labor for seven days and seven nights because Juno Lucina sat in front of the house with clasped hands and crossed legs. The child was born only after the goddess was charmed into a change of heart.[34]

The same prohibitions uttered by Ovid were observed in Bilaspur in India, where a woman's hair was unknotted before the birth of a child.[35] Rumanian Jews once followed a similar custom.[36]

In the Toumbuluh tribe of North Celebes, a pregnant woman's husband was forbidden from tying knots or sitting with crossed legs.[37] Among the Hos of Togoland, West Africa, the following practice was employed in the event of a difficult birth:

> When a woman is in hard labor and cannot bring forth they call in a magician to her aid. He looks at her and says, "The child is bound

Fig. 1.7: Juno Lucina, goddess of childbirth.

in the womb, that is why she cannot be delivered." On the entreaties of her female relations he then promises to loose the bond so that she may bring forth. For that purpose he orders them to fetch a tough creeper from the forest, and with it he binds the hands and feet of the sufferer on her back. Then he takes out a knife and calls out the woman's name, and when she answers he cuts through the creeper with a knife, saying, "I cut through to-day thy bonds and thy child's bonds." After that he chops up the creeper small, puts the bits in a vessel of water, and bathes the woman with the water.[38]

Similar practices were found among the Kaitish of Australia, the Dyaks of Borneo, the Mandelings and Battas of Sumatra, in Java, Cochin-China, and among the Sinhalese.[39]

In Western Europe such beliefs existed among the 19th century Saxons of Transylvania; they untied all knots when a woman was in labor, as well as unlocking all the doors and boxes in the house.[40] Similar ideas were found among the Bulgarians, Lapps, Scots and Danes.[41] In the same regard, Ohrvall relates that the Scandinavian name Knut (knot) was originally given to boys whose parents no longer wished to have children. It was thought that the name would prevent further conception.[42]

SORCERER'S KNOTS
Given the symbolic value attached to knots in the rituals attending birth, marriage and death, it is only natural that they should become objects of power in and of themselves. Here we enter the province of the magician and witch and the beliefs of the common folk. The movement from ritual to magic involves a devolution into superstition. Ananda Coomaraswamy explains:

> The notion that "old folklore ideas" are taken over into scriptural contexts, which are thus contaminated by the popular superstitions, reverses the order of events; the reality is that the folklore ideas are the form in which the metaphysical doctrines are received by the people and transmitted by them. In its popular form, a given doctrine may not always have been understood, but for so long as the formula is faithfully transmitted it remains understandable; "superstitions" for the most part, are no mere delusions, but formulae of which the meaning has been forgotten and are therefore called meaningless – often, indeed, because the doctrine itself has been forgotten.[43]

In this sense, the use of knots as weapons of magic, or their mutation into gold or wooden amulets or bracelets, marks a continuation and elaboration of their original ritual functions. What is of interest is the stability of certain themes and images through time, even where their true significance has been lost or misconstrued.

Robert Burns wrote:

> Thence, mystic knots mak great abuse
> On young guidman (husbands), fond, keen an'

croose (confident);
When the best wark-lume i' the house,
By contraip wit (magic)
Is instant made no worth a louse,
Just at the bit (nick of time).[44]

Burns gives expression to the long-held belief that magic knots may be tied against a married couple to prevent conception. What is of greater interest is the symbolism of the loom and its juxtaposition with the sexual problems of the bewitched husband. The Scottish expression, "just at the bit" means at the exact or critical moment. (The word "bit" is related to the word "bite," with the attendant idea of a closing jaw.)[45] The equivalent English expression, "the nick of time," means an opening or opportunity (a "nick" is a hollow or slot), which describes the opening between the warp and woof threads on a loom. It is only during this brief interval of separation that the weaver may "shoot" the spool or shuttle through to secure another thread in the fabric. There is an analogy here with the process of impregnation, with the nick or slot serving as the vagina and the shuttle (ME *sceotan*, to shoot) as the ejaculate. The underlying idea is that there is a propitious moment for conception that must not be missed, another widespread belief among primitive peoples. This imagery is paralleled precisely in Homer.[46]

Weaving and magic were closely associated in classical and medieval times. A number of medieval penitentials and church decrees refer to the supernatural powers of those involved in textile work to weave curses into garments.

> Have you been present at, or consented to, the vanities which women practice in their woolen work, in their weaving, who when they begin their weaving, hope to be able to bring it about that with incantations and with their actions that the threads of the warp and of the woof become so intertwined that unless (someone) makes use of these other diabolical counter-incantations he will perish totally. If you have been present or have consented, you must do penance for thirty days on bread and water.[47]

Errors made during weaving were regarded as unlucky or were deliberately introduced to harm someone magically. The term "louse" which appears in the Burn's poem may refer to a defect that occurs when the weaver forgets to change the shed, causing the warp threads to creep up and show between the weft threads.[48]

The use of magic knots to kill or injure people has a long history. Solomon Gandz wrote:

> In Hebrew literature the "charmer" or "enchanter" is also called *hober haber* which means literally: "a man who ties magic knots." Babylonia is characterized by "the multitude of its sorceries and the great abundance of its enchantments," literally: "by the great abundance of its knots," and from other sources we learn indeed that "knots were largely employed by the Assyrians in their spells

for removing illness . . . and to prevent the spirits of the dead from annoying the living."[49]

In ancient Babylonia sorcerers believed that they could strangle their victims, wrack their limbs, and tear their entrails, by merely tying knots in a cord.[50] In the Koran we learn of women who practice magic by tying knots in cords and blowing and spitting on them.[51]

Often the tying of knots is not intended to kill the victim but to render him impotent as we saw in the Burn's poem. This particular kind of magic was well known in Europe and was called *nestelknupten* in Germany, *nouer l'aiguillette* in France, *nalknytning* in Sweden, and *asur* in medieval Hebrew. The practice was even given a legal definition:

> The legal term was *ligatura*. To make a ligature was held to be a serious crime under Salic law in the fifth century, and Theodore of Tarsus pronounced the practice detestable in the seventh century. It was made punishable by excommunication in 1208, and by death according to a decree of the Council of Regensburg.[52]

Prosecution for such crimes lasted into the 18th century according to J.G. Dalyell. In 1718, the parliament of Bordeaux sentenced someone to be burned alive, for the "desolation of a family by means of knotted cords."[53] Dalyell quotes the French jurist and political philosopher, Jean Bodin:

> Yet Bodin, who takes special cognizance of the subject, observes, that while at Pictou, in the year 1567, his hostess, "being well skilled in the matter," explained to him that there was above fifty modes of casting the knot, so as to affect either spouse: that it might be devised, so as to operate for a day, for a year,—for ever.[54]

The English word, "spellbound," expresses the same idea. These reports provide evidence of the longevity of the belief in the harmful effects of knots.

KNOT AMULETS

If knots can be employed to harm people, they can be used to protect them. As an apotropaic device, the knot takes on new forms and moves from the medium of string or fiber into wood, metal, jade and ivory. It is possible that rings and bracelets are descended from knotted cords or fiber amulets.

In postbiblical Aramaic literature, the amulet is called *quami'a*, meaning originally a knot, and then something suspended from a knot.[55] In Russia, the words for amulet (*nauzu*) and knot (*uzelu*) are etymologically related; while the Greek *desmos* signifies "knot," and also "spell" or "charm."[56] In English we speak of "charms" or "charm bracelets," preserving the link between the object and its intended effect.

Egyptian hieroglyphic writing has thirty or more signs that represent string, cord or rope.[57] The familiar *ankh*, which is a tie or strap, represents "life" or "living," while the *tyet*, a variant of the ankh, signifies "life" or "welfare." The names of Egyptian kings were normally surrounded by cartouches —round or oblong spaces —encircled by double ropes; a form of amuletic protection for the name.[58]

Several ancient Egyptian string amulets have survived; one consists of seven overhand knots with a Square knot joining their ends.[59] Cyrus Day noted how similar this ancient artifact is to the modern Egyptian *ukad*, a knotted cord used as a charm to cure fevers and colds.[60] The tomb of Tut-Ankh-Amen contained a number of gold and wood representations of the Square or Hercules knot. Similar gold knots were found at Dahshur (12th Dynasty, 2000 B.C.) and Deir el Bahri (1500 B.C.).[61]

Amulets are employed worldwide for a variety of purposes, the most common being the cure of illness. The ancient Hindus believed that knots tied in the garments of a traveler would insure a safe trip.[62] The sacred thread or *janeu* whose knots are called *Brahma-granthi* (the knots of the Creator) is still worn today and features in the Upanayana ceremony in which young men are initiated into Hinduism. The rite goes back to at least Vedic times and preserves the character of tribal initiation from which it may have developed.

> Before the ceremony the boy is regarded as once-born and after the ceremony he becomes *dvija* (twice-born), and is admitted to the privileges of his society and has access to the sacred books. The sacred thread is usually worn over the left shoulder, going diagonally across the breast, and under the right arm by the right hip.[63]

In pre-revolution Russia, it was thought that knots could protect a man from weapons, acting to restrain or "tie up" his enemies.[64] Similarly, the Armenians believed that they could protect their cattle by symbolically "binding up" the mouths of wolves by means of knotted shoelaces.[65]

ILLNESS AND DEATH

The use of knots to prevent illness and death is rooted in the belief, once common to all Indo-European peoples, that evil fortune is a bond or fetter placed on a man by the gods. Thus a man's fate is "spun" or "woven" by the gods, be they Norse Norns, Slavic Siwa, Greek Moira, or Roman Parcae.[66] Death is the ultimate bond. In medieval illustrations, Death is pictured carrying a rope or noose to bind his victims and carry them off. We find the same image in Homer, Saxo Grammaticus, and the *Satapatha Brahamana*.[67] Similar beliefs were found among the ancient Iranians:

> The old Persian war-god Verethragna fetters the hands of the foeman behind his back. The death-demon Astovidotus binds the dying. According to the Iranian Epic Ahriman has a Net. While Tus and Feribur seize the castle of the Deva Bahman, the mighty Ahriman spreads out his air-like net. Likewise the god of fate is equipped with noose and net.[68]

In the Hindu pantheon, Yama carries a foot fetter (*padbisa*) while his messenger, Mrtyu, carries a noose (*pasa*) and fetters to inflict illness or death. Varuna, an older Indo-Iranian god also carries a noose[69] (Fig. 1.8).

The gods or fates also show their power by binding men with disease or ill fortune. It is the function of prayer and sacrifice to remove these bonds.

Fig. 1.8: Granite statue of Varuna, 12th century, India.

As we have seen, ατε, "sin, infatuation," is in Homer a bond in which Zeus binds men; such also is it in the *Rg Veda*. "Unloose sin from me as a cord, unloose evil from me like a cord which holds captive a calf" (II, 28, 5). "Unloose, unbind the error committed which is attached to my body" (I, 24, 9). Such prayers are exceedingly frequent.[70]

Illness is conceived quite graphically as a binding, so that the Hebrew word *hebhel* (pain), means "bond." Or, as we read in Job 30:18: "By the great force of my disease is my garment changed; it bindeth me about as the collar of my coat."

In Babylon and Assyria we find: "Headache like a garment will envelop him and pain and shivering like a net." And, "the evil spirit hath set a net… the wanderer has fallen sick of a headache."[71] The purpose of knots and knot amulets may be to act in place of the gods. To undo the work of the gods requires an untying.

We find these beliefs incorporated into the iconography and language of all the major religions. Thus we find in Psalms (18:32): "It is God that girdeth me with strength and maketh my way straight." The equation of a man's fate with a garment placed upon him is frequent throughout the Old Testament: "For he put on righteousness as a breastplate, and a helmet of salvation upon his head; and he put on the garments of vengeance for clothing, and was clad with zeal as a cloak."[72] In English we still speak of "investing" someone with ecclesiastic dignity.[73]

In the New Testament the power to "bind" and "loose," once wielded by the magician, is now handed to the Apostles.[74] The word religion itself derives from the Latin *ligare* (to tie). We are bound to our gods and we bind them to us. So says the proverb, "ungirt, unblessed."

In 18th century Scotland, Satan was asked to unloosen a knot to restore a person's health, a practice varying little from those of the ancient Greeks; Christianity has merely changed the cast of characters.[75] A Scottish cure for a sprained leg or arm involved the casting of nine knots in a black thread that was then tied around the suffering limb. The following rhyme was spoken:

> The Lord rade
> And the foal slade;
> He lighted
> And he righted,
> Set joint to joint,
> Bone to bone,
> And sinew to sinew.
> Heal, in the Holy Ghost's name![76]

J. Grimm, in his *Deutsche Mythologie*, showed this rhyme to be based on the myth of the ancient Norse god, Balder, whose lame horse was healed by the god Woden.[77] Christ has been substituted for Woden in the Scottish version. The story is older than Grimm supposed and bears a certain resemblance to the Old Testament story of Ezekial in the Valley of the Bones.[78]

Cuneiform tablets from the 8th century B.C. record Babylonian and Assyrian knot "cures" for headaches and other ailments.[79] Knotted cords were tied around the head, neck and limbs of the patient, and after a time, were thrown away. These activities were accompanied by the proper spells.

In Rumania, knots tied to cure an illness were removed from the patient and cast into running water.[80] The Germans and the Dutch tied strings to trees, or tied knots in the branches, to transfer the illness.[81]

Ceremonies involving the dead and the dying are also common. In 17th century Italy it was forbidden to place knots in the hands of the dead.[82] It was thought they would impede the passage of the soul into heaven. Frazer writes of a similar case:

> When they brought a woman to the stake at St. Andrews in 1572 to burn her alive for a witch, they found on her a white cloth like a collar, with strings and many knots on the strings. They took it from her, sorely against her will, for she seemed to think that she could not die in the fire, if only the cloth with the knotted strings was on her. When it was taken away, she said, "Now I have no hope of myself."[83]

Here the knot preserves life, much as the knots in a fabric or rope keep it from coming unraveled or untied.

WIND KNOTS

The symbolism connected with wind knots is an outgrowth of an ancient cosmological scheme shared by a great number of ancient cultures. It is a commonplace in folklore that there are four winds that blow from the four quarters of the earth. The idea that the world is divided into four quarters— our cardinal points: north, south, east and west—may be an extrapolation from the structure of the human body. In Hebrew, east, west, north and south are referred to by expressions meaning, "in front," "behind," "left," and "right." Persian, Arabic, and several other languages follow this mode of expression.

Pliny, in discussing the Hercules knot, remarks that "Demetrius (a physician, circa 200 B.C.) wrote a treatise in which he states that the number four is one of the prerogatives of Hercules"[84], probably a reference to the fact that the knot has four corners, with a cord extending from each. This may explain its association with the *omphalos*, the sacred stone representing the center (literally, "navel") of the world. Representations of the *omphalos* were common in ancient Greece, the best known in the temple of Delphi, the spiritual center of Greece. The stone is generally depicted with a netlike cover with knots that resemble the Hercules knot.[85]

Another related point is the frequent equation in ancient writings between the wind and the divine breath. The Hebrew *ruah* signifies both "wind," "blast" and "breath," though the true meaning may be closer to "Spirit."

(The Greek *pneuma* and the Latin *animus* are equivalent terms.) The writer William Least Heat Moon remarks:

> People of the Old Testament heard the voice of God in desert whirl-winds, but Southwestern Indians saw evil spirits in the spumes and sang aloud if one crossed their path; that's why, in New Mexico and Arizona today, the little thermals are "dust devils."[86]

God makes the winds his messengers in both the Old Testament and the Koran and in this sense they may be said to represent angels.[87]

The microcosmic/macrocosmic relationship involved in this symbolism is important. The universe has a navel and four quarters just as the human body does. The wind and the breath are related by the same analogy. The human body is a fertile source of symbolism.

In Book Ten of the *Odyssey* we find a reference to wind knots. As Ulysses is about to leave the island of Aiolos, he is given a gift to speed his journey.

> When in return I asked his leave to sail and asked
> provisioning, he stinted nothing,
> adding a bull's hide sewn from neck to tail
> into a mighty bag, bottling storm winds;
> for Zeus had long ago made Aiolos warden of the
> winds, to rouse or calm at will.
> He wedged this bag under my after deck, lashing
> the neck with shining silver wire
>
> so not a breath got through; only the west wind he
> lofted for me in a quartering breeze
> to take my squadron spanking home.[88]

Notice again the equation of the wind with the breath and the expression, "quartering breeze." The three witches in Macbeth express the same belief in the same language:

> 2 Witch. I'll give thee a wind.
> 1 Witch. Th'art kind.
> 3 Witch. And I another.
> 1 Witch. I myself have all the other,
>   And the very ports they blow,
>   All the quarters that they know,
>   I'th'shipman's card (mariner's chart).[89]

Such ideas were common in the Renaissance. Thomas Nashe wrote that the witches of Ireland and Denmark would sell a man a wind that will "blow him safe unto what coast he will"; while the *Daemonologie* (1597) of James I expressed the opinion that witches used wind knots to "rayse stormes and tempestes in the aire, either upon sea or land."[90]

Fig. 1.9: Olaus Magnus, Wind Knots.

Fig. 1.10: Olaus Magnus, Four Winds.

It was usually the northern peoples, the Lapps, Finns or Norse that were associated with wind knots (Figs. 1.9 and 1.10). Olaus Magnus, cartographer and chronicler of the northern tribes wrote in 1555:

> The Finlanders were wont formerly amongst their other Errors of Gentilisme, to sell Winds to Merchants, that were stopt on their Coasts by contrary Weather; and when they had their price, they knit three magical knots, not like to the Laws of Cassius, bound up with a Thong, and they gave them unto the Merchants; observing the rule, that when they unloosed the first, they should have a good Gale of Wind: when the second, a stronger wind: but when they untied the third, they should have such cruel Tempests, that they should not be able to look out of the Forecastle to avoid the Rocks, nor move a foot to pull down the sails, nor stand at the Helm to govern the ship; and they made an unhappy trial of the truth of it, who denied that there was any such power in those knots.[91]

The belief in wind knots, once common throughout Europe, seems to have survived longer in the north. An ancient Norse myth tells us of the lame smith Volundr, who kept a supply of wind knots in his smithy.

> A long rope of bast hung there, with knots in it at regular intervals. In each and every knot a storm wind was bound. Each week he untied a knot and freed the wind that was bound in it, and sent it south with his mad song, charged with clouds and hail.[92]

ENDNOTES

1. Abbot Glory, "Debris de corde paleolithique à la Grotte de Lascaux." For a description in English, see Elizabeth Barber, *Women's Work*, pp. 51-53.

2. Jolly, C. and White, R., *Physical Anthropology and Archeology*, p. 380; specimens in ivory and bone from western Russia.

3. "Find Suggests Weaving Preceded Settled Life," *New York Times*, May 9, 1995. Elizabeth Barber suggests that the term 'weaving' should only be applied to a mechanized process. These early forms are really interlacing of one kind or another.

4. See Edmund Carpenter and Carl Schuster, *Social Symbolism in Ancient and Tribal Art*.

5. Charles Amsden, *Navaho Weaving*, discusses many of the techniques used in the Americas.

6. See Otis Mason, *Aboriginal Indian Basketry*.

7. See H. Ling Roth, *Ancient Egyptian and Greek Looms*.

8. Clara Lee Tanner, *Prehistoric Southwestern Craft Art*, p. 49.

9. R. B. Onians, The *Origins of European Thought*, p. 314.

10. See Turner and van Griend, editors, *History and Science of Knots*. This volume contains a variety of articles on knotting, lace making, macramé, and crocheting, including studies of knotting in the Pleistocene period, Mesolithic and Neolithic Scandinavia, in Ancient Egypt, in China, and among the Eskimo. The articles cover diverse subjects including mathematical theories of knotting and are of uneven quality.

11. *Eclogues*, trans. John Dryden.

12. J. G. Dalyell, *The Darker Superstitions of Scotland*, p. 306.

13. J. G. Frazer, *The Golden Bough*, III, p. 305.

14. Day, *Quipus and Witches' Knots*, p. 75.

15. For a discussion of the works of Heraklas and Ohrvall, see Day, ibid., p. 86.

16. For a fuller discussion of Love knots, see Turner & van de Griend, "On the Love Knot," op. cit., pp. 397-417.

17. W. J. Dilling, "Knots," *Hastings Encyclopedia of Religion and Ethics*, Vol. 7, p. 749.

18. Ibid., p. 749.

19. Ibid., pp. 748-749.

20. Frazer, p. 301.

21. Dilling, p. 749.

22. Ibid., p. 749.

23. Ibid., p. 748.

24. Ibid., p. 749. cf. Dalyell, p. 302. The cosmic symbolism is more apparent in Dalyell's account: "Next, the whole community quitting the church, environed it according to the course of the sun."

25. Dilling, p. 749. cf. *Aeneid*, IV, 517. The wearing of one shoe is another common ritual seen in many parts of the world.

26. Ibid., p. 749.

27. Pliny, *Natural History*, XXVIII.xvii.63-4.

28. Numbers, 30:2.

29. Onians, Chapter 5, passim.

30. Pliny, *Natural History*, XXVIII.xvii.60.

31. Ibid., XXVIII.ix.39-42.

32. Frazer, p. 294.

33. Ovid, *Fasti*, III.255-258.

34. Ovid, *Metamorphosis*, IX.281-315. Another version of the story places the blame with the Fates and Eileithyia, goddess of childbirth. See Frazer, p. 299, ft. 1.

35. Dilling, p. 750. These same practices were observed in ancient India, where all knots were unloosened before the birth of a child.

36. Frazer, p. 298.

37. Ibid., p. 295.

38. Ibid., p. 295.

39. Ibid., p. 294.

40. Ibid., p. 294.

41. Dilling, p. 750 and Frazer, pp. 294-298.

42. Day, p. 73.

43. Coomaraswamy, *Collected Works*, Vol. I, p. 306.

44. Robert Burns, "Address to the Deil," XI (1794). *The Complete Poetical Works of Robert Burns*, p. 1214.

45. There is a connection here with the "jaws of death" that guard the entrance into heaven. For a discussion of this motif, see Coomaraswamy's "Symplegades" in *Collected Works*, Vol. 1.

46. Onians, pp. 346-347. In an equivalent formulation, the shed of the loom is the narrow path to heaven and the shuttle an arrow. Many ancient shuttles resemble arrows and are referred to as such. The Greek word *kairos* refers both to the shed of a loom and to the target or mark used by archers. What we call a narrow "window of opportunity" was traditionally conceived as a door (Latin *porta*, as in opportunity) that opens for an instant and allows entry only to the worthy. There is also the figure of Kairos, the youngest son of Zeus, who balances on the razor's edge, representing eternity (the nick of time). See A. B. Cook, *Zeus*, Vol. 2, Part 2, pp. 859-868.

47. Valerie Flint, *The Rise of Magic in Medieval Europe*, p. 227. The quote is from the *Decretum of Bishop Burchard of Worms* (11th century). Flint documents a number of the beliefs associated with knots, weaving, and tying that are mentioned here.

48. See Marta Hoffman, *The Warp Weighted Loom*, p. 40.

49. Solomon Gandz, "The Knot in Hebrew Literature or From the Knot to the Alphabet," p. 192.

50. Frazer, p. 302.

51. Ibid., p. 302.

52. Day, p. 71.

53. Dalyell, p. 307.

54. Ibid., p. 306.

55. Gandz, p. 192. He suggests that the English word "cameo" derives from this root.

56. Day, pp. 51-52. A Russian wizard is an *uzol'nik* (knot-tier).

57. Ibid. On Egyptian knotting, see Wilemina Wendrich, "Ancient Egyptian Rope and Knots" in Turner & van de Griend, *History and Science of Knots*, pp. 43-68.

58. A similar protective framework is formed by the Chinese character *heng* used during the rite of fixation or stabilization. See René Guénon, *Fundamental Symbols*, p. 272.

59. Day, p. 52.

60. Ibid., p. 49.

61. Ibid., p. 53.

62. Frazer, p. 306.

63. Dogra & Dogra, *Hindu and Sikh Wedding Ceremonies*, p. 87. Elements of the Upanayana have also been incorporated in the modern Hindu marriage ceremonies.

64. Frazer, pp. 306-307.

65. Ibid., p. 308.

66. Onians, p. 352.

67. Ibid., p. 354 and passim. Cf., Mircea Eliade, *Images and Symbols*, III.

68. Onians, p. 363.

69. See Merh, *Yama—The Glorious Lord of the Other World*, pp. 60-61, 79-83.

70. Onians, op. cit., p. 359.

71. Ibid., p. 364, ft. 2.

72. Isaiah 59:17, *cf.*, Isaiah 11:5; 61:10;.Psalms 30:11.

73. Onians, p. 360, ft. 7.

74. Matthew 16:19; 28:18; Luke 13:16.

75. Dalyell, p. 307.

76. Frazer, pp. 304-305.

77. Ibid., p. 305, ft. 1.

78. Carlo Ginzburg in *Ecstasies: Deciphering the Witches' Sabbath*, Part 3, Section 2, "Bones and Skin" discusses myths and rituals associated with the reconstruction of the bones of dead animals. See also, Mircea Eliade, *Shamanism*, pp. 160-164.

79. Day, p. 46.

80. Ibid., p. 48.

81. Ibid., p. 49.

82. Dalyell, p. 309.

83. Frazer, p. 309.

84. Pliny, *Natural History*, XXVIII.XVII.63-4.

85. See Day, op. cit., p. 56 and pp. 61-61, note 1.

86. William Least Heat Moon, *Blue Highways*, p. 160.

87. See Réne Guénon, *Fundamental Symbols*, p. 187.

88. *Odyssey*, X.19-29.

89. *Macbeth*, I.III.

90. Day, p. 44.

91. Ibid., pp. 44-45.

92. Ibid., p. 45.

Chapter 2   **MNEMONIC KNOTS**

The Distribution of Mnemonic Knots

Knot Calendars

Knot Records

The Quipu

Biblical and Talmudic Evidence

The Abacus

Finger Counting and Calculation

Rosaries

Musical Knots

Fig. 2.1: Kogi man using mnemonic device.

Fig. 2.2: Maori mnemonic device.

MNEMONIC KNOTS

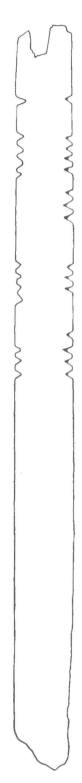

My Lord embraces all things in His knowledge; will you not remember?
Koran vi.80

It would be difficult to overestimate the role that memory plays in a traditional society where what is known is synonymous with what can be remembered. We have only to think of Homer's "winged words" to realize that in the absence of writing, culture must be constantly reiterated if it is to survive. Language cannot bear the burden of memory by itself so traditional societies must bring to bear the collective powers of music, dance, architecture and the plastic arts in the battle to preserve their inheritance. A story presented in several media has a better chance of survival.

Mnemonic knots are one method of aiding recall. Knotted cords, notched sticks or rosaries, used in conjunction with speech, provide visual and tactile counterparts to the evanescent world of sound. In this way, a name or event can be bound in time and remembered (Figs. 2.1, 2.2, and 2.3). Just as an effigy may be nailed or tied to produce a desired effect, nailing or tying can preserve a memory or mark the passage of time.[1] The Romans used *bulla* (tacks) to mark important days on the calendar much like our "bulletin" board.[2] The notion of binding or fixing an event survives in such expressions as "fixing the date" or "nailing down a deal."

As memory devices, knots have invited comparison with writing and we find representations of knots in Egyptian hieroglyphs and in Chinese script; a case of a new medium borrowing its symbolism from an older established one.[3]

Despite these continuities, knots clearly lack the intrinsic power of script. Any mnemonic device is only useful in conjunction with the memory of the user and it cannot convey any more than can be remembered. No mnemonic device can overcome this limitation.

If mnemonic devices have limitations as historical records, there is another arena where they achieved greater success—as enumerators and calculators. Knots or pebbles, once freed from their associations with specific names and events, can take on an abstract character that lends itself to mathematical manipulation. Devices like the bead-frame and the counting board, which once had ritual functions, developed into counting and calculating devices. These forms outlasted the other memory devices we shall be discussing.

Fig. 2.3: Bamboo tally stick, Burma.

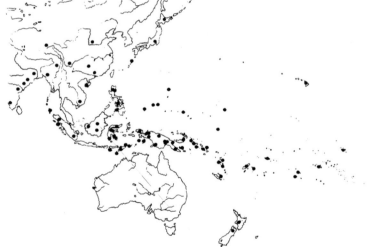

Fig. 2.4: Distribution of mnemonic knots in North and South America.

THE DISTRIBUTION OF MNEMONIC KNOTS

If we can judge by their widespread distribution, the use of mnemonic knots must be very old. The Danish anthropologist Kaj Birket-Smith assembled much of the existing evidence in an article titled "The Circumpacific Distribution of Knot Records."[4] Following the work of the Finnish ethnologist, Erland Nordenskiöld, he noted the extensive use of knot records throughout South America and added an equally large list of North American tribes, mostly on the West Coast but with one outlying group on the Great Plains and several more in the Southeast (Fig. 2.4).

Thus, Spier's supposition is corroborated that we have to do with "a continuous distribution from Peru to Canada" and, it may be added even to Alaska. As to the northern Amazon area it is a well-known fact that there have been considerable influences from Columbia. Under the circumstances, the occurrence of knot records among the Powhatan, may seem remarkable. They were used however, also by the Monacan, one of the adjacent Siouan tribes of Virginia, and Mooney asserts that "this system proved so convenient in dealing with the Indians that it was adopted for that purpose by a governor of South Carolina," which seems to show that it was generally known throughout the region, not only by the Algonkian and Siouan tribes but also by the Creek.[5]

Fig. 2.5: Distribution of mnemonic knots in Asia and the Pacific.

Moving into Asia, their use is attested in ancient China, Japan, Tibet, Vietnam, India, and Indonesia. Island hopping into the Pacific examples are found in the Philippines, New Zealand, New Guinea, and throughout Melanesia, Micronesia, and Polynesia (Fig. 2.5). They are notably absent in Australia.

While the survey doesn't pay as much to attention to Europe and Africa, Birket-Smith provides references for both continents. As to the question of age, he makes the following observations:

> In China, they must, at any rate, be older than the first script, i.e. at least date from the Late Neolithic in the early 2nd millennium B.C. This agrees with the fact that they were obviously known to the

Proto-Austronesians, who probably started to spread over Indonesia and the Pacific in roughly the same period. However perhaps we have to go still further back in time, to the Early Neolithic, since they are common also among the Papuans. On the other hand, they are hardly older, for they are apparently wholly lacking in Australia where the culture is basically mesolithic.[6]

KNOT CALENDARS

In Book Four of *The Histories*, Herodotus relates a story about the Persian king, Darius. Having crossed the Danube in pursuit of his Scythian enemies, Darius orders his men to destroy a bridge they have used. He is dissuaded from this course of action by Coes, the son of one of his commanders, who urges him to leave some men behind to defend the bridge so that the army may have a safe means of return. Darius is pleased with the advice.

> Soon after, he called a meeting of the Ionian commanders and showed them a long leather strap in which he had tied sixty knots. "Men of Iona," he said, "my orders to you about the bridge are now cancelled; I want you to take this strap, and every day undo one of the knots, beginning with the day on which you see me start my march against the Scythians. Should I fail to return before all the knots have given out, you are at liberty to sail home; meanwhile, in accordance with my change of plans, guard the bridge with every possible care for its safety. This will be the greatest service you can do me."[7]

Here is an early reference to the simple knot calendar. Each knot represents one measurable unit—a day, full moon, etc.—that can be added to, or subtracted from the cord.

In 18th century India, the inhabitants of the hills near Rajmahal, in Bengal, sent knotted strings to guests invited to their festivals. One knot was excised each day. When no knots remained, the guests knew the festival day had arrived.[8] Similarly:

> When a marriage was being arranged among the Khonds, a Dravidian tribe of Southern India, knotted strings were given (perhaps still are given) to the family of the bride and to the representatives of the groom ("searchers of the bride"), and the date of the betrothal ceremony was kept in mind by the untying, in both strings, of a knot a day.[9]

These examples bear a close resemblance to practices of the ancient Hebrews. In Jeremiah (2:32) we read: "Can a maid forget her ornaments, or a bride her attire? Yet my people have forgotten me days without number." The Hebrew word for attire, *qishshurim*, signifies a knot or knotted cord. The bride untied one knot each day in anticipation of the wedding. Solomon Gandz interprets the passage:

> Yet the Israelites, the Lord's bride, have forgotten their Lord days without number. They were like the faithless bride, that does not care for the approach of the wedding day, that forgets to untie the knots and thus lets several days pass without number.[10]

The use of knots to keep track of time was observed by Dr. Karl Weule when he traveled among the Makonde in German East Africa in 1906.

> With a courteous gesture the Makonde handed me a piece of bark string about a foot long, with eleven knots at regular intervals, proceeding to explain, with Sefu's help, that the string was intended to serve as a kind of calendar. Supposing he was going on an eleven days' journey, he would say to his wife, "This knot," (touching the first) "is to-day, when I am starting; to-morrow" (touching the second) "I shall be on the road, and I shall be walking the whole of the second and third day, but here" (seizing the fifth knot) "I shall reach the end of the journey. I shall stay there the sixth day, and start for home on the seventh. Do not forget, wife, to undo a knot every day, and on the tenth you will have to cook for me; for, see, this is the eleventh day when I shall come back."[11]

In North America we have the testimony of John Lederer who made three exploratory journeys from the tidewater settlements of Virginia into the interior in 1670. Describing the manners and customs of the Indians of Western Carolina and Virginia, he writes: "An account of Time, and other things, they keep on a string or leather throng tied in knots of several colours."[12]

A knotted cord can also serve as a means for organizing a revolt or conspiracy.

> Many passages in the Bible tell of conspiracy, treason and rebellion. But while reading it in the modern translations, and even in the original Hebrew, we do not realize that the phrase *qashar'al* used for conspiracy, means verbally, "to make a knot against someone." For instance: "Zimri hath conspired," literally: "Zimri hath made a knot;" "and his treason that he wrought," literally: "and his knot that he tied." "Amos hath conspired against thee," verbally: "hath made a knot against thee."[13]

Such practices may have originated as rituals designed to injure the enemy or as a covenant among the plotters.[14] Whatever the case, the cord came to be useful in coordinating the activities of the conspirators. One other example will suffice.

In New Mexico, in 1675, Pope, a celebrated Tewa medicine man, led a revolt against the Spanish.

> The plot quickly spread among the Pueblos, meeting with enthusiasm as it went. Aug. 13, 1680 was the day set for the onslaught, and the news was communicated by runners, even to the far-off Hopi in Arizona, by means of knotted strings....[15]

The Pueblos were still using knots to coordinate their activities as late as 1920.[16] Knot calendars were also known among the Yakima, the Choctaws, the Huichol Indians of Mexico, and the Solomon, Palau, and Marquesan Islanders of the Pacific.[17]

KNOT RECORDS

Before men put knots to work recording time, they used them to remember songs, stories and genealogies. Still later, knotted cords served to keep accounts for the census taker or the tax collector.

Assuming that the concrete precedes the abstract, genealogical knots are the oldest form, each knot representing an ancestor. Songs and stories are remembered in connection with ancestors and are a natural extension of genealogical knots. Time keeping and accounting can be connected to the increased need for record keeping which arose with the growth of cities and city-states.

Two visitors to the Marquesas Islands, Paul Claverie (1881) and Karl von den Steinen (1928) witnessed the use of genealogical knots.[18] Claverie was shown a knotted cord and told that each knot represented an ancestor of a certain high priest, going back to the first man and woman. Karl von den Steinen collected examples of these cords that were said to represent the earth and the history of the gods, containing both songs and genealogies. Several were elaborate affairs, containing many strings and in one case, almost 290 knots.

As Lord Raglan has shown, the historical value of these devices is suspect.[19] They rely primarily on human memory and their accuracy is doubtful beyond three or four generations. Like the complex genealogies in Genesis, they are part of oral lore, where the past quickly becomes part of the shadowy world of the ancestors, when the earth was formed and great deeds were done.

Joseph Needham, in his monumental work, *Science and Civilization in China*, brings to light evidence concerning the use of knot records in China.

> A very simple device, used rather for recording numbers than for calculating, was the system of knotted strings best known in the form of the Peruvian quipu, which is described in detail by Locke. Ancient Chinese literature contains a number of distinct references to the use of the quipu. The locus classicus is perhaps the *I Ching* (Book of Changes), where the reference may date from the -3rd century: "In the most ancient times the people were governed by the aid of the quipu (*chieh sheng*)." But there is also a mention in Chuang Tzu, and in a famous chapter of the *Tao Te Ching*. Li Nien gives several later references. Of particular interest is the description by Simon of the use of the quipu by the aboriginal inhabitants of the Liu-Chhiu Islands: quite possibly it might still be found in China among the tribesfolk such as the Miao or the Yi. Here is another of those strange similarities between East Asian and Amerindian culture.[20]

In the *I Ching* we read, "In ancient times people tied knots to record events. Later sages changed (this method) and recorded events through writing." More specifically, "Great events are recorded and remembered by large knots, minor events by small knots."[21] We don't know the antiquity of knot records in China, but they were beginning to be replaced by writing as early as the 6th century B.C.[22] Legend attributes the invention of writing to Fo-hi (2800 B.C.), who is said to have invented eight symbols that were pictorial representations of knotted cords. This would put the invention of writing in the same period as similar developments in the Near East.

Needham makes reference to an article by Edmund Simon, which concerns the knot records employed by the inhabitants of the Ryukyu Islands in Japan.[23] According to Simon, the islanders used knots for recording tax receipts, census counts, the size of the harvest, and other activities requiring enumeration (Fig. 2.6). This system was used until the First World War, when it was replaced by writing.

Daniel Tyerman and George Bennet were sent to the Pacific in 1822 at the behest of the London Missionary Society. They were fascinated by a complex record-keeping device that they observed in the Hawaiian Islands.

> The tax-gatherers, though they can neither read nor write, keep very exact accounts of all the articles, of all kinds, collected from the inhabitants throughout the island. This is done principally by one man, and the register is nothing more than a line of cordage from four to five fathoms in length. Distinct portions of this are allotted to the various districts, which are known one from another by knots, loops and tufts, of different shapes, sizes and colors. Each tax-payer in the district has his part in the string, and the number of dollars, hogs, dogs, pieces of sandalwood, quantity of taro, &c., at which he is rated, is well defined by means of marks, of the above kinds, most ingeniously diversified. It is probable that the famous quippos, or system of knots, whereby the records of the Peruvian empire are said to have been kept, were a similar, and perhaps not much more comprehensive, mode of reckoning dates and associating names with historical events.[24]

Bronze Age fleets sailing from Southeast Asia may have disseminated these technologies across the Pacific.

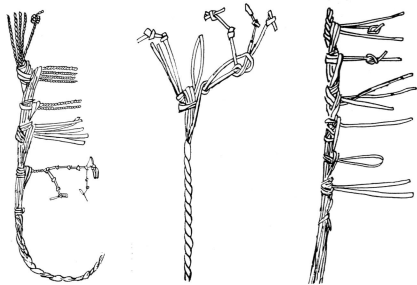

Fig. 2.6: Knot record, Ryukyu Islands.

THE QUIPU

Quipu is the Quechua word for knot, and the quipus were knotted cords used by the Incas for record keeping (Fig. 2.7). Over 700 of these mnemonic devices have survived, forty-two of them belonging to the American Museum of Natural History.

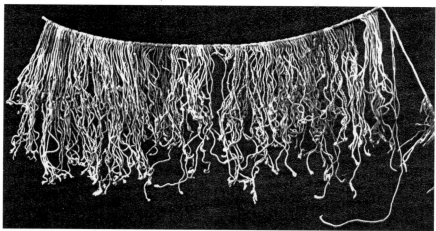

Fig. 2.7: Incan quipu from Medialima.

The Incas had no system of writing and used the quipus to administer an empire that extended over 3000 miles.

> The government, on one hand, was an absolute monarchy, and on the other, partook of the nature of a highly developed communism, involving taxes, tributes, census, records of crops and herds, governmental construction of bridges, temples, and irrigation canals, to render hospitable and productive the mountain fastness surrounding Cuzco.[25]

The quipu was used primarily to record numbers, although it also served as a memory device for the preservation and transmission of royal orders, orations, poems, traditions, and historical data. There is also some evidence to suggest that it was employed to record the movements of heavenly bodies.

Our knowledge of the quipu is aided by the accounts of 16th century chroniclers like the mestizo writer, Garcilaso de la Vega, whose *Royal Commentaries of the Incas* provides valuable background information. Garcilaso was the son of a conquistador and an Inca princess. He learned the traditions of his mother's race from his relatives and his account of the quipu is the best we have.

Another mestizo writer, Felipe Huaman Poma de Ayala, provided additional material in his *La Nueva Chrónica y Buen Gobierno*, though he lacked the critical intelligence of Garcilaso.

The first work of scholarship was L. Leyland Locke's, *The Ancient Quipu or Peruvian Knot Record* (1923), which analyzed several specimens in light of the literary evidence. In 1925, Erland Nordenskiöld published his *Secret of the Peruvian Quipus* in which he argued that the quipus were used to record the movements of the sun, moon and planets. More recently, the subject has been reviewed and expanded by Cyrus Day, William J. Conklin, and others.[26]

Fig. 2.8: Quipu keeper with quipu & counting board.

Fig. 2.9: Quipu keeper with two quipus.

Although we are told that the quipus were used to record numbers it is unlikely that they were used for calculation, though Garcilaso is a little unclear on this point.[27] It seems that the Incas used a counting board or abacus for this purpose.[28] The situation was the same in Asia and Europe where calculation and record keeping were separate activities.

Like the scribes of Egypt, the office of quipu-keeper was given over to a class of men call the *quipucamayus* (Figs. 2.8 and 2.9). Each village had from four to thirty of these officers, in keeping with the population.

> These men recorded on their knots all the tribute brought annually to the Inca, specifying everything by kind, species, and quality. They recorded the number of men who went to the wars, how many died in them, and how many were born and died every year, month by month. In short they may be said to have recorded on their knots everything that could be counted, even mentioning battles and fights, all the embassies that had come to visit the Inca, and all the speeches and arguments the king uttered.[29]

It is easy to imagine knots being used to record numbers but more difficult to see them recording history, law, speeches and the like. In fact, the knots were only part of a larger arsenal of memory techniques employed by the Incas.

> But the purpose of the embassies or the contents of the speeches, or any other descriptive matter could not be recorded on the knots, consisting as it did of continuous spoken or written prose, which cannot be expressed by means of knots, since these can give only numbers and not words. To supply this want they used signs that indicated historical events or facts or the existence of any embassy, speech, or discussion in time of peace or war. Such speeches were preserved by the *quipucamayus* by memory in a summarized form of a few words: they were committed to memory and taught by tradition to their successors and descendants from father to son.[30]

The encoding of events in songs and stories was not restricted to the *quipucamayus*, but served the society at large.

> Another method too was used for keeping alive in the memory of the people their deeds and the embassies they sent to the Inca and the replies he gave them. The *amautas* who were their philosophers and sages took the trouble to turn them into stories, no longer than fables, suitable for telling to children, young people and the rustics of the countryside: they were thus passed from hand to hand and age to age, and preserved in the memories of all. Their stories were also recounted in the form of fables of an allegorical nature, some of which we have mentioned, while others will be referred to later. Similarly the *harauicus*, who were their poets, wrote short, compressed poems, embracing a history, or an embassy, or the king's reply. In short, everything that could not be recorded on knots was included in these poems, which were sung at their triumphs and on the occasion of their greater festivals, and recited to the young Incas when they were armed knights. Thus they remembered their history.[31]

If the Inca's sense of history was not our own, their accounting practices were as efficient and accurate as those of their Spanish conquerors. The *quipucamayus* could provide the government with statistics on a variety of subjects (taxes, crops, population, etc.) at a moment's notice. There was an army of these men, who often checked each other's work for maximum accuracy. A system of runners, *chasqui*, served as a postal system, transmitting verbal and coded messages throughout the empire. They too, carried quipus.

> Other messages were carried not orally, but written down, so to speak, though, as we have said, they had no letters. These were knots in different threads of various colors, which were placed in order, though not always in the same order: sometimes one color came before another, and on other occasions they were reversed. This type of communication was a system of cyphers by which the Inca and his governors agreed on what was to be done, and the knots and colors of the threads implied the number of men, arms, or clothes or supplies or whatever it was that had to be made or sent or prepared.[32]

Fig. 2.10: Quipu from Chancay.

The quipu is a cotton or wool cord, varying in length from a few centimeters to a meter or more, with smaller pendant cords attached (Fig. 2.10). From 1 to 100 of these smaller cords may be secured, few exceeding half a meter in length. Records are kept by tying knots at varying distances from the main cord. Different types of knots are employed, as well as a variety of colored threads.

The Incas used a decimal system, indicating ones, tens, hundreds, and the like, by the position of each knot on the pendant cords (Fig. 2.11). Pendant cords were then grouped by fours and sixes, by passing another cord through their top loops. These top cords summed the pendant cords, allowing the entire quipu to be "read" more quickly.

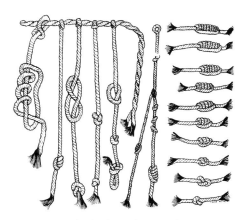

Fig. 2.11: Methods of tying knots in the quipu.

The quipu survived the Spanish conquest and lasted many centuries in Bolivia and Ecuador. A similar device, the *chimpu* was still in use in recent times among the Indians of Bolivia and Peru.

> In the nineteenth century, on the high Peruvian plateaus and on some farms and ranches, herdmen still counted by means of quipus. In a group of white strings, they noted the sheep and goats, usually putting rams on the first string, lambs on the second, goats on the third, kids on the fourth, ewes on the fifth, and so on. They used a group of green strings for cattle, with bulls on the first, milch cows on the second, barren cows on the third, then calves according to age and sex.[33]

The quipu is unique in that literary and physical evidence have permitted a reconstruction of the mnemonic system that it supported. Although there are features of the device we may never fully understand, the quipu shows how far a simple device like the mnemonic knot can be extended in the absence of writing.

BIBLICAL AND TALMUDIC EVIDENCE

Aside from the reference in the *I Ching*, which may indicate the use of mnemonic knots in China as early as 2800 B.C., our earliest evidence is found in the Bible. Solomon Gandz, in his article, "The Knot in Hebrew Literature or from the Knot to the Alphabet," gathers the existing scriptural references, some of which were noted earlier by Herz Homberg (1749-1841) and M. Gaster (1914).[34]

First, we have the phylacteries (*tephillin*) or frontlets, which serve as an aid to prayer (Fig. 2.12). Phylacteries are small leather boxes that contain strips of parchment on which passages of Hebrew scripture are written. They are attached to the forehead or left hand with knots shaped in the fashion of the Hebrew letters *daleth* and *yod*, respectively. The function of these devices is made clear in Deuteronomy where it is stressed that the commandments must be repeated and remembered: "And thou shalt bind them for a sign upon thine hand, and they shall be as frontlets between thine eyes."

In this fashion the commandments are memorized and passed on from generation to generation. Tradition has it that God showed Moses the knot of the phylacteries of the head, indicating that the knot was an important part of the device. It is clear from Proverbs that mnemonic knots were used concurrently with writing and Gandz suggests that certain letter and number forms may be imitations of knots.[35] We noted earlier how this was true of Egyptian hieroglyphs and Chinese ideograms.

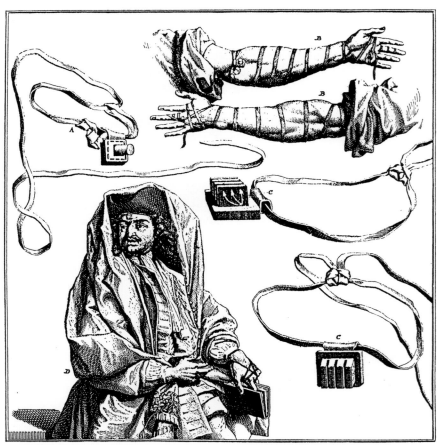

Fig. 2.12: Phylacteries of the hand and head.

The fringes are the second mnemonic device mentioned in the Bible.

> According to the school of SHAMMAI, the fringes consisted of four threads of white wool and four threads of blue, but according to the school of HILLEL they consisted of two threads of each. Those threads are fastened to the four corners of the garment (*Tallith*, or *Arba'kanphoth*), twisted to a cord in which five double knots are tied – the knots are to have different distances from each other – and tapering off in the form of loose fringes.[36]

In Hebrew, these threads are alternately call *tzitzith* (fringes, tassels or locks, as in a lock of hair)[37] and *gedilim*[38] (Fig. 2.13). The latter usage is derived from the Hebrew, Aramaic and Syriac *gedila*, signifying a thread, cord or rope.[39] The Sifre, the oldest Midrashic commentary on the Bible, defines the *gedilim* as the twisted, knotted threads attached to the borders of the garment, and the *tzitzith* as the loose fringes in which they end.[40] The function of these quipu-like fringes is explained in Numbers.

> Speak unto the children of Israel, and bid them that they make them fringes in the borders of their garments, throughout their generations, and that they put upon the fringe of the borders a ribband of blue:

> And it shall be unto you for a fringe, that ye may look upon it, and remember all the commandments of the LORD, and do them; and that ye seek not after your own heart and your own eyes, after which ye use to go a whoring.[41]

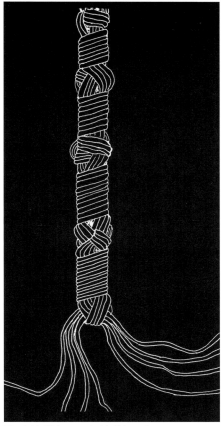

Fig. 2.13: Hebrew *tzitzith* (fringes).

The existence of such memory devices helps to explain certain obscure passages in Scripture that have been translated in a manner that hides their true significance. Thus we read in Isaiah (8:16), "Bind up the testimony, seal the law among my disciples." The testimony is bound by means of a mnemonic knot.

Similarly in Hosea (13:12), "The iniquity of Ephraim is bound up; his sin is hid." The literal sense is that the sin of Ephraim will never be forgotten because it is recorded by means of a knotted cord. The same idea is found in Job (14:17) who cries, "My transgression is sealed up in a bag, and thou sewest up mine iniquity." The King James Bible translates the Hebrew *se-ror* as bag, but the literal meaning is a knot or bundle. Again, in Isaiah 28:10 and 28:13, the "precept upon precept; line upon line" is really "knot upon knot; cord upon cord." For those who mock the Lord, his precepts are merely so many knotted cords.

The third mnemonic device is the cord register, mentioned in both the Bible and the Talmud. In Genesis we read the story of Judah and Tamar.

> And he said, What pledge shall I give thee? And she said, Thy signet, and thy bracelets, and thy staff that is in thine hand. And he gave it to her, and came in unto her, and she conceived by him.[42]

When it became known that Tamar was pregnant she was accused of harlotry and was to be burnt; at which point, she presented the signet, bracelets and staff, saying, "By the man, whose these are, am I with child"[43] This was sufficient to identify Judah. The "bracelets" of the King James Bible are really cords (*patil*). Gentlemen in ancient Babylon and Syria carried the signet or seal, the staff and the cord. The cords were used to keep accounts and records or receipts of business transactions.

In Roman Palestine the publican's knots were used to register tax collections in much the same manner as the quipu. The Talmud contains the following story:

> One woman married first a religious scholar and used to tie the phylacteries around his hand. Later on she married a publican and used to tie the knotted strings of the publican around his hand.[44]

As representatives of Roman rule, the publicans were despised by the Hebrews. Gandz maintains that the publicans used knotted cords to record taxes and carried small knots that they handed out as receipts. We find evidence for this contention in Jewish law, which forbids the carrying of these receipts on the Sabbath.[45] As time went on, these knots were replaced by written receipts that were given the same name, "publican's knots."

THE ABACUS

The connection between the abacus and the knot is not immediately evident yet the two are closely related. Most of us are familiar with the wood-frame abacus on which buttons or counters slide along wooden or wire guides. The Russian *s'choty*, the Chinese *suan-pan*, the Japanese *soroban*, and the French *boulier-compteur* are examples of this form of abacus, still in use in many parts of the world (Fig. 2.14).

It is likely that the less well known "counting board" or "sand tray" is the older form of abacus. In its simplest form it consists of a series of a parallel lines drawn in the dirt or incised in wood or stone. Pebbles or counters are placed on, or between the lines, each line representing a different value. Thus, if the decimal system is employed, the first line holds "units," the second "tens," the third "hundreds," and so on. To represent the figure 612, the user would place two counters in the first column, one in the second, and six in the third.

Because this system is positional, any number base can be employed. Each counter can stand for any value—a sheep, a soldier, a dollar, a nickel, etc.—a point remarked on by the Greek historian Polybius.

> Like counters on the abacus which at the pleasure of the calculator may at one moment be worth a talent and the next moment a chalcus, so are the courtiers at their king's nod at one moment at the height of prosperity and at the next objects of human pity.[46]

A skilled abacist can perform the four basic mathematical operations with great speed and accuracy.

Fig. 2.14: Chinese *suan-pan*.

The origin of the abacus is uncertain. The word itself is generally thought to derive from the Semitic *abq* (dust) or the Greek *abx* (slab, board), references to the fact that the earliest form of the abacus was drawn in the dust or incised on a board.

We know very little about Indian, Babylonian and Egyptian methods of calculation though their numbering systems suggest that counting boards were used. Herodotus tells us that the Egyptians reckoned with pebbles, but he does not tell us how.[47] Both the Greeks and the Romans employed the abacus as is evident from their language; to count or calculate—the Greek *psephizen* and the Latin *calculare*—both refer to small stones or pebbles (*psephoi*, *calculi*) used with the counting board.

We also possess physical evidence. The famous Salamis counting board (4th century B.C.?), in the National Museum in Athens, is a white marble slab incised with eleven parallel lines (Fig. 2.15). Along the sides of the board are letters that have been identified as Greek numerals.

We know how the device was used thanks to an artistic representation painted on the Darius Vase (3rd century B.C.?) in the Museo Nationale in Naples (Fig. 2.16). The vase depicts the Emperor Darius before his expedition against the Greeks. In one of the scenes, his treasurer sits with a counting board in front of him. He handles the calculi with his right hand while holding a writing tablet in his left. The symbols on the tablet may indicate 100 talents (*talanta hekaton*) while those on the table range from 10,000 drachma to a quarter–obol.

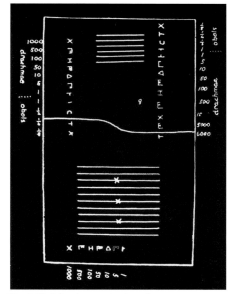

Fig. 2.15: Salamis counting board.

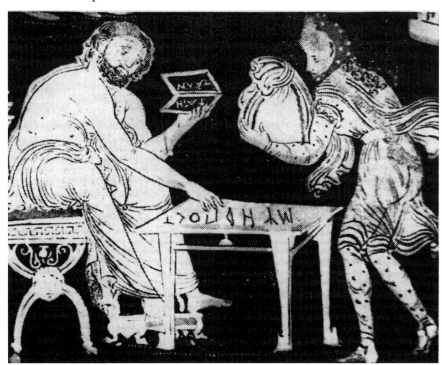

Fig. 2.16: Detail of the Darius vase showing a counting board.

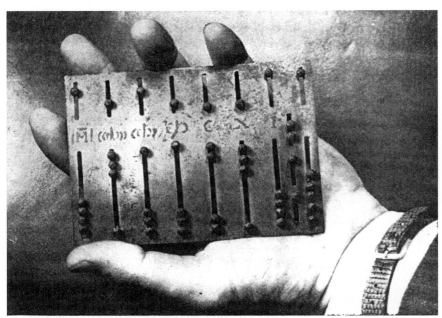

Fig. 2.17: Roman hand-held abacus.

We also have several portable abaci that have survived from Roman times. One, in the British Museum, is a hand-size metal plate with small counters that slide in grooves (Fig. 2.17). It bears some resemblance to the bead-frame abacus commonly found in the East. Is it possible that the Roman abacus found its way to China during the Han Dynasty (c. 200 B.C. to A.D. 200)? Chinese trade with the Mediterranean area began as early as the 5th century B.C.

Joseph Needham provides the Chinese perspective in his discussion of the *suan-phan* (calculating plate). The earliest reference to this abacus-like device is found in the *Shu Shu Chi I* (Memoir on some Traditions of Mathematical Art). The work is attributed to Hsu Yo and may date from A.D. 190, but may have been composed by its commentator, Chen Luan (c. A.D. 570). In the passage under consideration, Liu Hui-Chi, a Taoist master, is explaining "ball arithmetic" (*chu suan*), one of the fourteen old methods of calculation.

> (Text) The ball arithmetic (method) holds and threads together (*kung tai*) the Four Seasons, and fixes the Three Powers (heaven, earth, man) like the warp and weft of a fabric.

> (Commentary) A board is carved with three horizontal divisions, the upper one and the lower one for suspending the travelling balls (*yu chu*), and the middle one for fixing the digit (*ting suan wei*). Each digit (column) has five balls. The color of the ball in the upper division is different from the color of the four in the lower ones. The upper one corresponds to five units, and each of the four lower balls corresponds to one unit. Because of the way in which the four balls are led (to and fro) it is called 'holding and threading together the Four Seasons.' Because there are three divisions among which the balls travel, so it is called 'fixing the Three Powers like the warp and weft of a fabric.'[48]

Needham suggests that the Chinese *suan-phan* may antedate the European abacus though he concedes that definitive proof is lacking.

It is more likely that both the Roman and Chinese abaci have a common ancestor which was not developed originally for calculation. The cosmic symbolism employed in the *Shu Shu Chi I* would suggest a ritual source. The origins of mathematics are closely related to astrology and divination, be the culture Chinese, Indian, Babylonian, Egyptian or Incan. The Pythagorean and Hermetic traditions reflect similar ideas, as do the Greek and Hebrew practice of *gematria*, and medieval and Renaissance numerology. The earliest mathematicians may have been priests occupied with the movements of the heavens and the fate of men. Metaphors like the four seasons, three powers, and warp and weft of fate, are very ancient and not exclusively Chinese. The abacus, in board or bead-frame form, may represent a working out of certain cosmological ideas that also find expression in other media. There is some similarity between the abacus and board games like hopscotch and *mancala* (also known as *wari*). The bead-frame abacus also bears some resemblance to the rosary.

Solomon Gandz had another theory about the origin of the abacus. He noted that the Hebrew-Aramaic word *abq* has two roots, one signifying "dust": and the other a "knot" or "loop." Are the pebbles on the counting board and the sliding balls on wires descendants of the knot? Gandz believed this to be so and suggested that the quipu was a primitive form of the knot-abacus. He noted that in Arabic, tens and hundreds are called *uqud*, "knots."

> ALKHOWARIZMI (c. 825) says that the numbers consist of units (*ahad*), knots and composites. This still reminds of the old method of representing the tens by knots. The same division of the numbers into three classes is generally found among the late Roman writers under the classification in digits, articles and composites.[49]

The problem is subtle, however, for the Latin *articulus* can mean both "knot" and "joint." In later Hebrew, the joints are called "the knots of the fingers."[50] This may explain the Latin suffix for ten, *ginta*—as in *viginta* (20), *triginta* (30), and so forth.

> There is no satisfactory etymology for the words *konta, ginta, kosi, ginti*, indicating the tens. The writer would suggest that the word *konta, ginta*, comes from the Greek, *gony, gonata*, meaning "knee, joint, knot". *Triakonta* = *triginta* means three knots, *tettarakonta* = *quadraginta* means four knots, etc.[51]

Was the knotted cord ever used for calculating? It could serve to add numbers but how would one subtract, divide or multiply? In all the cultures that employed the abacus, calculation and record keeping were separate affairs. The Incas used some form of abacus for calculation and recorded the results on a quipu. In Europe, from ancient times through the Renaissance, results were normally recorded in ledger books using Roman numerals. Hindu-Arabic numerals were known in Europe from about A.D. 1000, but centuries elapsed before computations were done without a counting board (Fig. 2.18).

Fig. 2.18: Dame Arithmetic from Margarita Philosophica.

It is likely that the knotted cord never played much of a role as a calculating device. However, if we interpret the word *articulus* to mean "joint" we may be on more solid ground, for both the abacus and the knot record may be derived from the oldest form of calculation, finger counting.

FINGER COUNTING AND CALCULATION

Our ancestors developed a number of methods for calculating that involved counting fingers, toes, body parts, joints, or some combination of these units. Georges Ifrah analyzed these methods and suggested that before people developed an abstract concept of numbers they counted by naming body parts, touching them in a fixed order.[52] He cites several examples from New Guinea including the islanders of the Torres Strait, along the Musa River.

> The words used were simply names of parts of the body, not true number words. Most of them designated more than one part of the body and were associated with several different numbers. *Doro*, for example, designated the third finger, middle finger, or forefinger of either hand, and was associated with 2, 3, 4, 19, 20, and 21. It would have been impossible to know which of those six numbers it indicated if, when it was spoken, the act of touching one of those six fingers had not specified its meaning.[53]

In time, a correspondence was created between the body part and the number it represented and touching was no longer required.

> In some languages the original meanings of the number words are still discernible and they often reveal a relation to such techniques. Here, for example, are the number words of the Bugilai in New Guinea, with their original meanings:
>
> 1. *tarangesa*, left hand: little finger
> 2. *meta kina*, next finger
> 3. *guigimeta kina*, middle finger
> 4. *topea*, forefinger
> 5. *manda*, thumb
> 6. *gaben*, wrist
> 7. *trankgimbe*, elbow
> 8. *podei*, shoulder
> 9. *ngama*, left breast
> 10. *dala*, right breast[54]

Once a concept of number exists, larger aggregations can be formed through grouping. The body parts once used in counting are reflected in the grouping used for numeration in a given society. According to Karl Menninger, the basic models are hand (grouping by fives), hands (grouping by ten), and man, meaning fingers and toes (grouping by twenty).[55]

The Api language of the New Hebrides follows the "hand" model, grouping by fives.

1. *tai*
2. *lua*
3. *tolu*
4. *vari*
5. *luna* "hand"
6 *otai* "other one"
7. *olua* "other two"
8. *otolu* "other three"
9. *ovari* "other four"
10. *lua luna* "two hands" [56]

A quinary system can grow in complexity once the right hand is used to register each group of five, allowing larger numbers to be counted (Fig. 2.19). Merchants in the Bombay region of India once used such a system.[57]

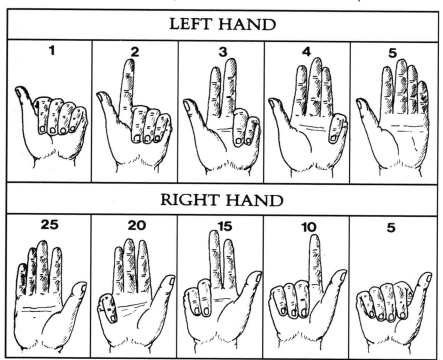

Fig. 2.19: Counting by five.

In the *Odyssey*, Homer's Old Man of the Sea counts his seals by fives, although this is not apparent in translation.

> the old one has strange powers, I must tell you.
> He goes amid the seals to check their number,
> and when he sees them all, and counts them all,
> he lies down like a shepherd with his flock.[58]

The Greek *pempázein* means to count by five, so the third line literally reads, "when he sees them all and counts them all by fives." [59]

Counting by fives is an easy way to begin numeration because the fingers themselves form a small group that is ready at hand, so to speak. The problem in using this method, as Menninger notes, is that you can't aggregate quickly enough when you wish to count larger numbers. In fact, there appear to be no true quinary number systems in the world though certain more developed number systems may have started this way. The Aztecs, for example, used a vigesimal (base 20) system but their words for the numbers one through fifteen indicate a grouping by fives, suggesting that the group of twenty developed from an earlier and simpler quinary system.[60]

There are other examples. The complex Sumerian sexagesimal (base 60) number system shows traces of an earlier quinary grouping as does the Irish language, in which the number ten (*deec*) means "two fives."[61]

> Some linguists believe that most oral numeration probably had an early quinary stage and that the Indo-European words for the first ten numbers must have been originally formed during that stage; they cite the example of the Persian word *panche*, "five," which has the same root as *panchá*, "hand." But this is only a hypothesis.[62]

Counting the fingers of two hands results in a decimal system, the most widespread method of numeration. The Chinese use this method as do most Mongolian, Semitic, and Indo-European peoples. Ten is a convenient grouping because it aggregates rapidly yet can be easily represented on two hands.

Counting the fingers and toes yields a vigesimal system, which was once more widespread than it is today (Fig. 2.20). An example from the Enggano people of Indonesia will show how it works.

kahaii ekaka	*ariba ekaka*	*kahaii edudodoka*
one man (20)	hand man (100)	one our body (400)

> There is no special word for 100, and 100 is not a stage or gradation in counting — so strongly is the 20-step felt; *ariba* is derived from *lima*, "hand," which is the number for "five" throughout the whole Austronesian linguistic region. The last number word for 400 may be explained as "so many times man as our body yields by its fingers and toes," and hence "man times man" (20 x 20 = 20^2).[63]

Celtic languages show evidence of vigesimal roots in their number words, as does Danish. In French, the number 80 (*quatre-vingt*), 4 x 20, appears unexpectedly in what is otherwise a decimal system of Roman origin. Menninger attributes this to Norman influence.

> The 20-gradation suddenly appeared in the 11th century in northern France, spread from there to the south and until well into the 17th century formed a number sequence that ran from 60, *trois-vingt* (old form *vint*), through 120, *six-vingt*, and 140 *sept-vingt*, all the way to 360, *dix-hit-vingt* (18'20). It is also remarkable that whereas old Provençal regularly counted upward by tens, the modern dialect has adopted the vigesimal count, from *tres-vint* (60 = 3'20) up to 380, *dès-e-nou-vint*, (10+9)'20.[64]

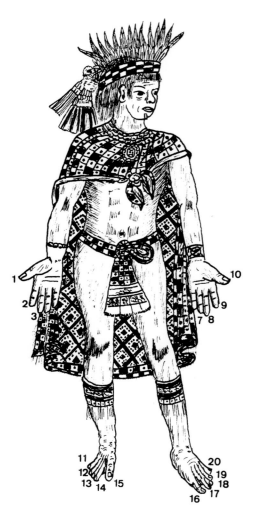

Fig. 2.20: Counting by twenty.

Other peoples who employed vigesimal systems include the Maya, the Aztecs, the Eskimos of Greenland, the Tamanas of Venezuela, and the Ainus of Japan. "For 53, for example, the Greenland Eskimos use the expression *inup pingajugsane arkanek-pingasut*, 'of the third man, three on the first foot....'"[65]

The number twenty is also used as a common measure of quantity for counting specific objects.

> The expression for an indefinite quantity, "as many fishes as will go on a stick," very early became associated with a 20-group, "20-fishes," and then detached itself from this to become an expression for the abstract number "twenty." A *schnasse Zwiefel* (*Schneise Zwiebel*) "a string of onions" slang for a twist of straw with 20 onions attached. In addition to fish, eggs are still counted in Holland by *snees*, and the Swedish farmer often says *fyra sneser*, "four *snes*," when he means eighty.[66]

In the same way, the English word "score" is used both as an expression of indefinite quantity ("scores of people") and for the number twenty ("four score and seven years ago").

If number systems are based on counting fingers and toes, what are we to make of base 12? It has never served as the basis for any number system but it is widely used for measurement and time keeping in matters commercial and astronomical.

> In his novel "The Vagabond," the Norwegian writer Knut Hamson says: "They counted a so-called great hundred for every 120 fishes." This term still measures quantities of fish, even in Germany, where it is used for other things as well. In Lubeck there was a *Hundert Bretter* = 120 items = 10 *Zwolfter* ("twelves") or, as they said in Mecklenburg, 10 *Tult*. English differentiates between the long hundred of 120 units and the short hundred which has only 100. Today, however, we recognize "hundred" only in its meaning of 100.[67]

In English we measure certain items by the dozen and by the gross (twelve dozen).

It is the number of divisors that make base 12 so convenient. In the Roman system of fractions, for example, one *as* (or pound) equaled 12 *unciae* (ounces). Thus the coin known as the *quadrans* (quarter) represented 3 ounces while the *sextans* was one-sixth or 2 ounces. Measures of distance were divided in the same way with one *pes* (foot) equaling 12 *pollices* (thumbs) or 16 *digiti* (fingers).

In a duodecimal system, it is not the fingers that are counted but the joints of the fingers (Fig. 2.21). In a system used in India, Indochina, and throughout the Middle East, the thumb is used to count the joints (or bones) of the same hand. If two hands are employed, the user can count to 24.

Georges Ifrah asks an important question about his particular method of finger counting.

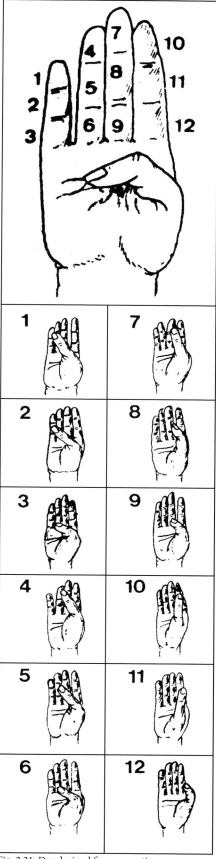

Fig. 2.21: Duodecimal finger counting.

41

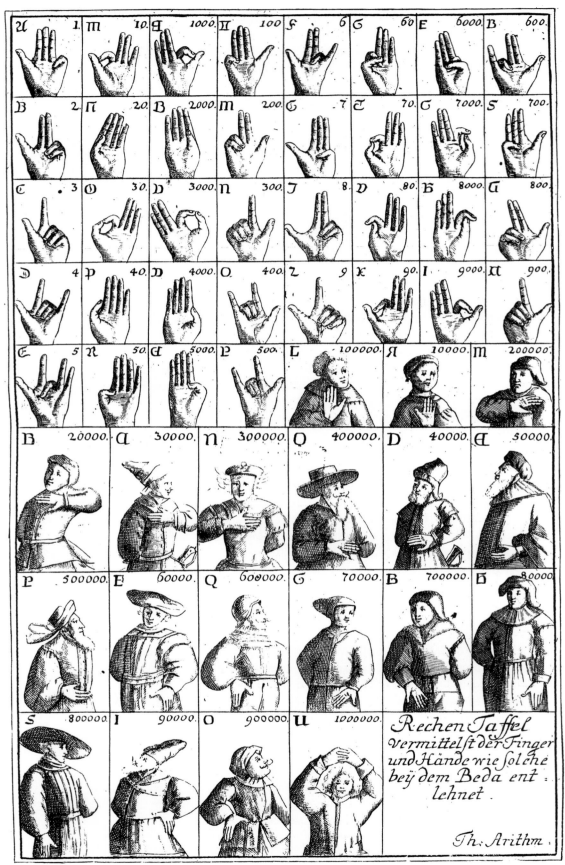

Fig. 2.22: Finger reckoning in the 18th century.

Was it this system that led the ancient Egyptians to divide day and night into twelve "hours" of light and twelve of darkness ("hours" whose length changed with seasonal variations in the duration of day and night)? Was it what led the Sumerians, and the Assyrians and Babylonians after them, to divide the cycle of day and night into twelve equal parts (call *danna*, each equivalent to two of our hours, to adopt for the ecliptic and the circle a division of twelve *beru* (30° each), and to give the number 12, as well as its divisors and multiples, a preponderant place in their measurements?[68]

Evidence for finger counting can be found among the Egyptians, Greeks and Romans. In the West, the use of the fingers for counting and calculating was taught as part of the rhetorical apparatus that supported education throughout the Middle Ages, Renaissance, and later (Fig. 2.22). We have ample literary evidence, including Aristophanes, Quintilian, Pliny the Elder, Macrobius, St. Augustine, and St. Jerome, as well as illustrated manuscripts.[69]

Most notable is the Venerable Bede's (d. A.D. 735) *De Loquela per Gestum Digitorum* (On Calculating and Speaking with the Fingers), which formed an introduction to his *De Tempora Ratione* (On the Computation of Time). Bede was a Benedictine monk whose system of "finger-bending," was intended to help in the calculation of the variable date of Easter. Bede's ingenious method was based on position or place value, like our modern system of numeric notation. It worked as follows.

The pinkie, ring, and middle fingers of the left hand were used to represent the units 1 to 9 (Fig. 2.23). For example, he writes, "If you wish to say 'one,' you must bend the little finger of your left hand and place its tip on the palm; for 'two,' lay down the ring finger next to it."[70]

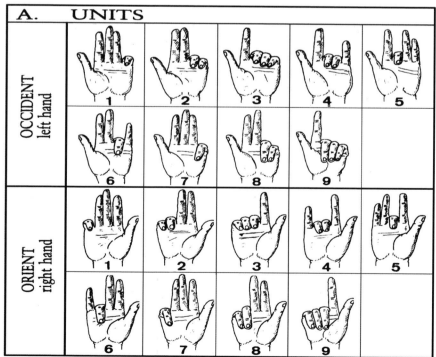

Fig. 2.23: Counting units in Bede's system.

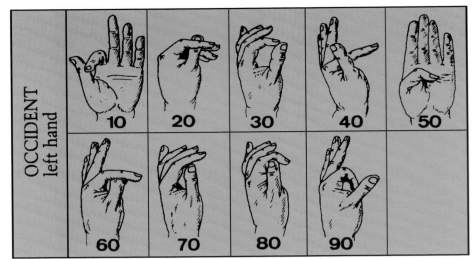

Fig. 2.24: Counting tens in Bede's system.

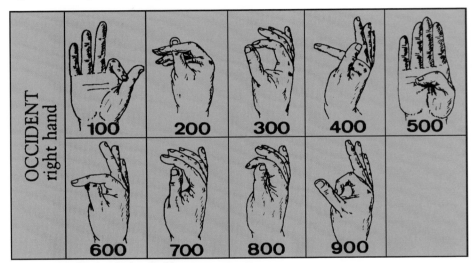

Fig. 2.25: Counting hundreds in Bede's system.

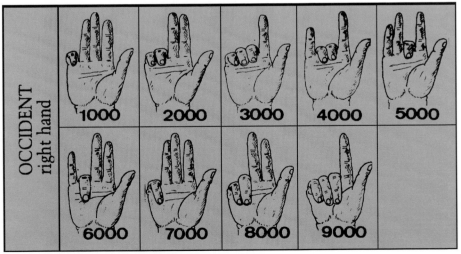

Fig. 2.26: Counting thousands in Bede's system.

The index finger and thumb of the left hand were used to designate the tens (10-90) by pointing to the joints, rather than using finger combinations (Fig. 2.24). For example, "For 40, place the thumb beside or on top of the index finger and extend them both."[71] The procedure for the right hand used the same technique.

The thumb and index finger were used to indicate the hundreds (100-900) by pointing to the joints, while the pinkie, ring, and middle fingers of the right hand represented the thousands (1000-9000) by finger flexing (Figs. 2.25 and 2.26).

> In this arrangement the person making the numbers worked backward, whereas the person opposite or facing him read the numbers in ascending order from right to left, thousands, hundreds, — tens, units, as we write them today.[72]

This explains the common terms used to indicate numbers in the Middle Ages. *Digiti* (fingers) referred to the numbers one through nine, which were formed with the fingers, while *articuli* (joints) meant all the numbers divisible by ten (10, 120, 580, etc.). A third term, *numeri compositi* (combined numbers) denoted combinations of units and of numbers divisible by ten (53, 101, 238, etc.).

In the *De Tempora Ratione* Bede explains how to calculate the twenty-eight years of the solar cycle, used in the Julian calendar to determine the variable date of Easter (Fig. 2.27).

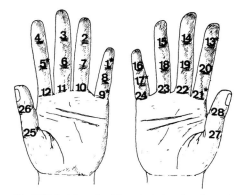

Fig. 2.27: Bede's method for calculating the solar cycle.

> To count the twenty-eight years of the solar cycle, Bede used the twenty-eight joints (or bones) of both hands and began with a leap year. Starting at the upper joint of the left little finger, he counted in descending rows of joints till he came to the twelfth year of the solar cycle, represented by the lower joint of the left forefinger. He then continued counting on the right hand in the same way, except that he began with the upper joint of the forefinger. Finally, the count was completed with the thumbs, going from the lower joint of the left one to the upper joint of the right one.[73]

Next, he calculated the nineteen-year lunar cycle, which is the period of time it takes for the phases of the moon to return to the same dates (Fig. 2.28).

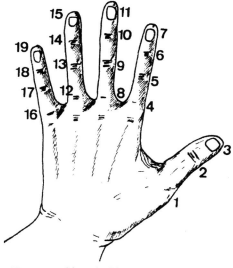

Fig. 2.28: Bede's method for counting the lunar cycle.

> Bede used the fourteen joints and five fingernails of the left hand. He began with the base of the thumb and ended with the nail of the little finger, moving upward along each finger.[74]

The evidence from China indicates that several systems of finger counting were developed at different stages in time.

> Lemoine distinguishes three type of finger-reckoning, one using only the fingers of the extended hand, a second in which the joints of the fingers are allotted numbers, and a third the most complicated, in which numbers are indicated by various positions

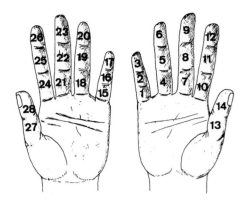

Fig. 2.29: Counting by finger joints.

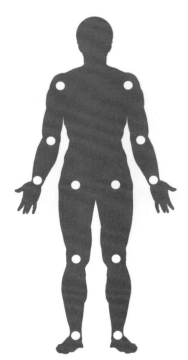

Fig. 2.30: Counting body joints.

of fingers flexed or extended in various combinations. The first is used in bargaining, and must be connected with the famous finger-game (*huo chhuan* or *tshai chhuan*), so familiar to everyone who has been present at convivial entertainments in China. This seems to be identical with the *micatio digitis* of the Romans (Ar. *mukharaja*; It. *morra*; Fr. *mourre*).

The second method, widely used in China, is connected with early calendrical calculations, since the number of joints on the hands may be made, according to the convention adopted, 19, 28, etc. The third method, which is found over the greater part of Asia, seems to be Babylonian in origin, and Lemoine has shown a detailed correspondence between its description in Bede and in a number of Persian and Arabic writings. But there was a Chinese system which differed from these. One late form, given in the *Suan Fa Thung Tsung*, represented decimals and powers of ten by the different fingers.[75]

Georges Ifrah provides more details about the second method (Fig. 2.29).

> In a system that is common in India, Indochina, and southern China, each finger bone counts as a unit, beginning with the lower bone of the little finger and going to the upper bone of the thumb. Both hands are used, each being touched with a finger of the other. Numbers 1 to 14 can be counted on one hand, 1 to 28 on both.[76]

In addition to the joints of the hand, the number twelve can also be derived from counting the major joints of the body (Fig. 2.30). The principle is simple; the body is a unity comprising twelve parts. The twelve divisions are indicated by the major body joints: ankles, knees, hips, shoulders, elbows, wrists. Should we choose to divide the body at the waist, we are left with six joints above and six below; or if we divide it bilaterally, we achieve the same result with six joints on the left side and six on the right side. Or we can quarter the body and have three joints in each quarter. We are really dealing with patterns here rather than abstract numbers, but this may have been how it was in the beginning when geometry and arithmetic were more closely linked.

The number twelve has always had mystical significance and division of the body into twelves brings to mind figures like Dionysius or Osiris who were dismembered at the joints. Ideas related to dismemberment are common to many cultures and in some cases the death of such a figure is correlated with the twelve months of the World Year or the signs of the zodiac, reinforcing the connection we have seen between counting systems, be they knots or joints, and calendrical and astronomical matters.

ROSARIES
The rosary is familiar to many of us as a religious ornament worn by Catholics, but equivalents can be found in the Arab world as well as among Hindus and Buddhists. Non-religious variants such as Turkish or Greek "worry beads" are also common (2.31).

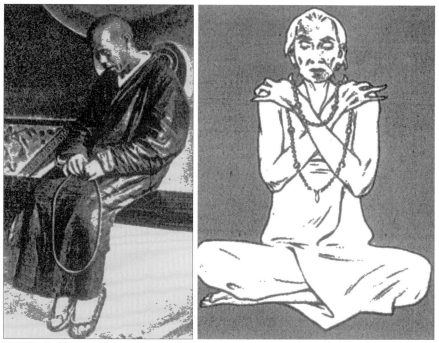

Fig. 2.31: Buddhist monk and priest from Bali with rosaries.

A rosary is a string of knots or beads that serve as a mnemonic device aiding in the recitation of prayers or the names and attributes of the deity, generally as a support for contemplation (Fig. 2.32).

The origin of the device is uncertain though there is some evidence to suggest that it was first used in Asia.[77] The term "rosary" was first associated with the device in late medieval times.[78] The rose is a traditional Christian symbol of both Mary and of Christ, with an ancient pedigree.[79] The greeting of the Angel Gabriel, "Hail Mary, full of grace, the Lord is with thee; blessed art thou among women," a commonly recited prayer then and now, became associated with the flower.

Fig. 2.32: Rosary of St. James of Galicia (Spain).

> A popular legend of the thirteenth century describes how the words of the salutation are transformed into roses that form a garland or chaplet for the Virgin. Thus the practice of weaving symbolic chaplets or wreaths of verbal roses as gifts to Mary became a favorite gesture of devotion and the term rosary, from rose garland (*Rosenkranz*), came into use.[80]

The Latin term *rosarium* ("rose garden") incorporates an even more ancient and complex symbolism centered on procreation and the renewal of life, which achieved maximum literary and visual expression in the Middle Ages and Renaissance. The ancient Roman *rosalia* was a spring festival honoring the dead during which rose blossoms were placed on the graves of ancestors. The ancient Greeks associated the red rose with the blood of a god. It was a symbol of Aphrodite and of her Roman counterpart, Venus.[81] This association with the physical aspects of sexuality was continued in medieval times in works like the *Romance of the Rose* where the rose symbolized the vagina. On the spiritual plane, it also represented the womb of Mary, often depicted as an enclosed garden (*hortus conclusus*).

The symbolism of the garden was in itself derived from the Old Testament Song of Songs, that famous dialogue between bride and groom, a similar celebration of physical and spiritual love.

Another important analogy to creation and renewal can be found in the equation of Christ to a rose (Fig. 2.33).

> In Christian tradition the rose stands not for Mary alone but also for Christ. The familiar sixteenth-century advent hymn, "Lo, How a Rose Ere Blooming," relates how both Mary and her son are roses that sprang from the Tree of Jesse. A fourteenth-century German song discloses the name of the rose, saying: "The rose is named Christ, / Mary, the garden so fair." Accordingly, sculptures from the thirteenth and fourteenth centuries place Mary and the infant Christ beside a rosetree…[82]

Fig. 2.33: Virgin and Child with Rosetree (German).

What all this symbolism has to do with the mnemonic device may not be immediately evident but it will become clearer when we discuss the thread-spirit doctrine and the symbolism of the Tree of Life. What is clear is that the mnemonic device we call the rosary is far older than the particular prayers from which it derives its name and that this association is more than incidental.

13th century documents refer to the beaded string as a *paternoster* or *patriloquium*, again in reference to the prayers associated with it. The English word "bead," not surprisingly, is the Anglo-Saxon *beade* or *bede* meaning prayer. Earlier terms include *serta* (thread, rope or wreath), *numeralia* (counters), and *calculi*, the last familiar to us from the abacus.[83]

The rosary, like the abacus, is a counting device, only here one counts spiritual exercises, be they vocal (prayers) or physical (genuflections).

> The case of the Egyptian abbot Paul, who died in 341, is related by Sozomen (c. 400-450) in his *Ecclesiastical History*, where it is stated that the saint daily recited 300 prayers, keeping count by means of pebbles gathered in his cloak, dropping one of them at the end of each prayer. Here is seen a much earlier and more primitive system of record-keeping which suggests that the rosary had evolved independently in some centres, and had not been taken over from others, where presumably it was already in a fairly developed form.[84]

In the West, the device appears to have been in continuous use from at least late Roman times.

> At Nevilles in Belgium another chain has been preserved that reputedly belonged to Abbess Gertrude (d. 659), daughter of Pippin I. Still older accounts tell of how Christian hermits Paul of Thebes (c. 234-347) and Saint Anthony (251-356) in the deserts of Egypt and Syria employed pebbles and knotted strings to keep track of the prayers they chanted unceasingly.[85]

Anne Winston-Smith chronicles the growing popularity of the rosary in later medieval times and notes that London had a number of establishments making paternosters as early as 1277 (Fig. 2.34). By the 15th century, religious confraternities that encouraged devotional practices among the laity that involved the use of the rosary had grown enormously. One such group at Cologne had over 100,000 members.[86]

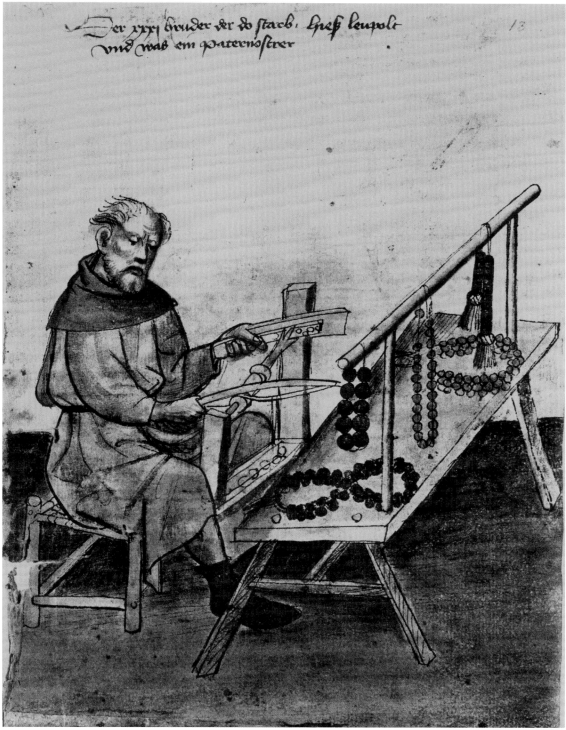

Fig. 2.34: Paternoster maker.

Fig. 2.35: Charles V with rosary.

Religious considerations aside, the device itself had a number of attractions that helped make it popular.

> From its inception, the rosary devotion was intimately tied to the string of beads that came to represent it. The many uses and attractiveness of rosary beads were conducive to the prayer's success. Indeed, they lent the devotion an added aesthetic dimension and a certain concreteness, even as simple as the tactile comfort of something to grasp onto in times of trouble and especially in the final hours [Fig. 2.35].[87]

The earliest literary reference to a rosary-like device is found in the Jain canon, where it is listed as one of the necessary articles carried by Brahmanical monks.[88] Article 10 from the Buddhist *Forty-two Points of Doctrine* reads:

> The man who, in the practice of virtue, applies himself to the extirpation of all his vices is like one who is rolling between his fingers the beads of the chaplet. If he continues taking hold of them one by one, he arrives speedily at the end. By extirpating his bad inclinations one by one, a man arrives at perfection.[89]

Here are the common themes that underlie all the traditions associated with the use of the rosary: repetition of certain prayers and actions to store up merit and the notion of advancement by gradation. As one moves from bead to bead, he or she progresses, as if climbing a ladder or pacing off a journey; the journey is an inward quest for identification with God. The goal at the end of the cycle of repetitions is release from the bondage of the self.

The Sikhs employ a knot rosary made of wool, as do Greek Orthodox monks.

> The Greeks call the knotted cord a *komroschinion*; the Russians give it the Old Slavic name of *vervitsa* ("string"). In popular language it bears the name *lestovka* because of its resemblance to a ladder (*lestnitsa*). There is also a string of beads called *komvologion* by the Greeks and *chotki* by the Russians. This does not appear to be a religious appliance, it being used by ecclesiastics and laity alike merely as an ornament or as something to hold in the hand.[90]

Note again the analogy between the rosary and the ladder, suggesting a graded ascent into spiritual realms.

The rosary is clearly related to the knotted cord as most commentators have remarked.

> Once this principle has been recognized of the substitution of some lasting sign by means of stones, bones, or kernels for the temporary knot, easily frayed out or broken, we have the rosary fully explained. The beads serve then the same purpose as mnemonic signs, and are far better suited for use than knots with their necessary monotony and monochrony, unless threads of various colours are used, — for

many coloured and variegated shaped stones can be used, — some round, some long, some flat, some in one colour, some in a different colour, — as can be seen in some of the rosaries.[91]

Fig. 2.36: Moslem *subha*.

At a more primitive level, the correlation between rosaries and joints can be seen in the case of the Moslem rosary or *subha*, used to count the 99 attributes of Allah (Fig. 2.36). Georges Ifrah explains:

> These are composed of strung beads, made of wood, mother-of-pearl, or bone, which are slipped between the fingers. They are often divided into three groups separated by two larger beads and a much larger one which serves as a handle. The number of beads is usually 100 (33 + 33 + 33 +1), but this may vary.[92]

A parallel, and probably older method used in the Islamic world for the same purpose employs the joints of the hands (Fig. 2.37).

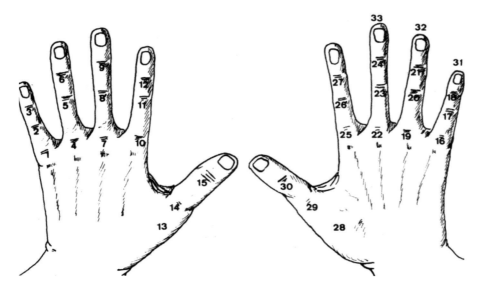

Fig. 2.37: Islamic method of finger counting.

> In this religious practice, a Moslem counts as follows. He successively touches each finger joint and the ball of the thumb on each hand, beginning with the lower joint of the left little finger and ending with the upper joint of the left thumb, which brings him to 15. He reaches 30 by proceeding in the same way with his right hand. He reaches 33 by touching the tips of the little finger, third finger, and middle finger on his right hand, or by returning to the three joints of his right forefinger. And finally he reaches 99 by repeating the whole procedure twice.[93]

It is more than likely that the earliest form of the rosary was a string of human bones, used to count and remember ancestors.

Fig. 2.38: John Cargill.

MUSICAL KNOTS

If a string of knots can represent a ladder (Latin *scala*) it can also represent a musical scale. The Celtic use of mnemonic knots to record music was first noted by John Cargill (Fig. 2.38), a memorial designer for the Charles G. Blake Company in Chicago.[94] Cargill had a keen interest in all aspects of Celtic culture and was clearly a man of uncommon intelligence whose work has been sadly neglected.

> The statement must at first seem fantastic that musical compositions may be deciphered from a number of designs that ornament Celtic works of art, especially sculptures. Nevertheless, the proper analysis of these designs discloses Celtic melodies that were current during the ninth, tenth, and eleventh centuries. These melodies, locked in design, have waited a thousand years for the necromancer that would unbind them, and lay them open once more for the living ear. Ironically, though the necromancer appeared, his discoveries have passed unnoticed; it is forty years since John Cargill published his brief pamphlet titled *Notes on the Old Cross at Canna*.[95]

Cargill had made a study of Celtic stone crosses and reached the conclusion that their designers used "the intervals of the musical string to fix the outlines of monuments."[96] These rectilinear crosses exhibited the same regularities of proportion observed in Greek temple architecture, both having been derived from the numeric intervals of the diatonic scale (Fig. 2.39).

> Take the stretched string for example. Everyone knows that the shorter the string the higher the pitch and each note requires its appropriate length and the differences between the various lengths are called intervals. If the full string measures 90 (inches, quarters or halves) then the intervals of the Diatonic scale would be 10, 8, 4 1/2, 7 1/2, 6, 6, and 3, and these sizes have been used in the construction of rectangles, Fig. 6. These rectangles have been used in cross design to give the ratio of width to height of the shaft.[97]

All of this "music in stone" was in keeping with the principles of Pythagoras, who saw numbers as the basic principle of order in the universe. How the Celts came into possession of these ideas is a matter of some debate, but it can be argued that the practical applications of geometry upon which Pythagorean speculation was based are older than the philosophy itself. John Burnett makes the point that the Greeks excelled at developing theories from the practices of others.

> …and we can see how far the Greeks soon surpassed their teachers from a remark by Demokritos. It runs (fr. 299): "I have listened to many learned men, but no one has yet surpassed me in the construction of figures out of lines accompanied by demonstrations, not even the Egyptian *arpedonapts*, as they call them." Now the word αρπεδοναπτησ is not Egyptian but Greek. It means "cord fastener," and it is a striking coincidence that the oldest Indian geometrical treatise is called the *Sulvasutras* or "rules of the cord."[98]

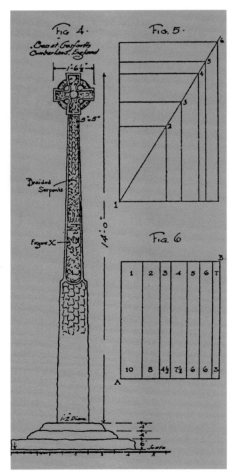

Fig. 2.39: Metrical proportions of the Celtic cross.

Once knotted, a cord can be chalked, hung by a weight, and then snapped like a stringed instrument to mark a stone for cutting.

Once Cargill had determined the principles involved in the design of stone crosses, he reasoned quite astutely that the designs on these stones might also contain musical symbolism. The idea came to him when he was considering a 10th century Celtic cross situated in the bottom of a glen on the Island of Canna, off the coast of Invernesshire, Scotland (Fig. 2.40). The cross's central panel contained two crossed animals with interlaced lines coming from their mouths. Cargill recognized the animals as panthers, typifying the resurrection of Christ. He noted a Saxon Bestiary of the period that contained the following poem of the Panther:

When the bold animal
rises up
gloriously endowed,
on the third day
suddenly from sleep,
a sound comes
of voices sweetest through the
wild beast's mouth."[99]

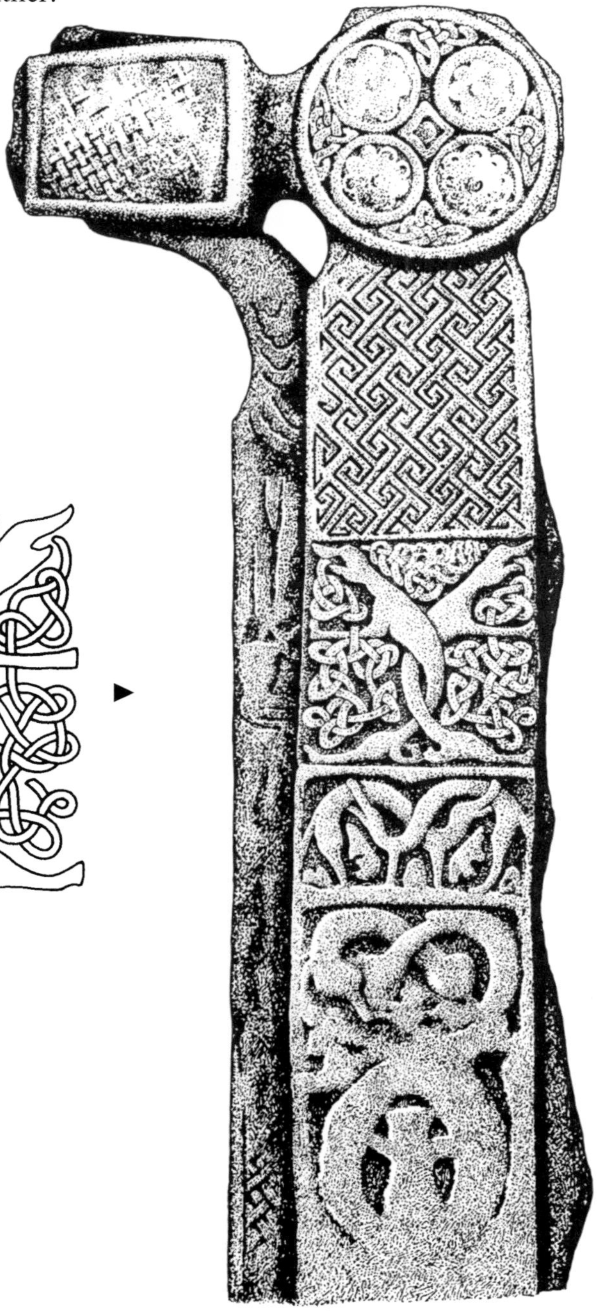

Fig. 2.40: The cross at Canna.

Fig. 2.41: Knotted cords translated as encoded music.

Beneath the panthers, a panel depicted two intertwined dragons, symbols of discord and strife. Cargill reasoned that the design as a whole was meant to illustrate the power of sacred song to overcome evil. Then, in a moment of insight, he realized the interlaced lines were musical notation (Fig. 2.41).

> Now, if, at either panther, we trace along the line which springs from the animal's mouth and count each intersection where this ornamental line crosses itself or another ornamental line as a musical note, and arrange the resulting progression of notes as a song, we may feel assured we are simply carrying out the old artist's intention.[100]

And music it was, a recognizably Celtic melody intended for Easter according to the musicologist James Travis. Several other examples of this form of musical encoding were found subsequently in the British Isles.[101] Certainly such practices were not common but it is worth noting that knotted cords were used in India and elsewhere as mnemonic devices to teach sacred music.

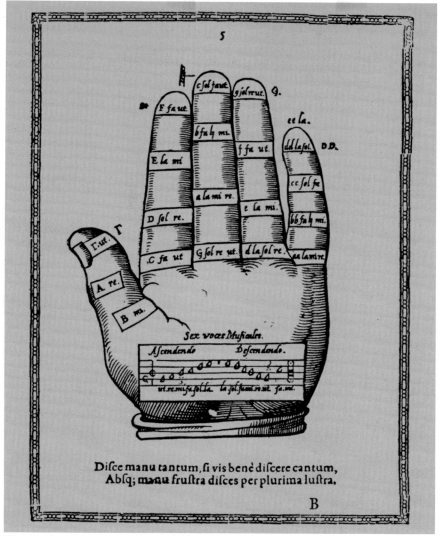

Fig. 2.42: Finger joints used to depict syllables used in singing.

The human hand was also used as an aid for teaching music in China, Japan, India, and among the Arabs and Jews. References to the practice in Europe date from classical times and numerous illustrations of the different techniques employed are preserved in manuscripts and early printed works.[102]

> But one of the most ubiquitous images of the Middle Ages and Renaissance relating to memory and the learning of music is the so-called Guidonian hand, associated with the eleventh-century music theorist and pedagogue, Guido of Arezzo, who is credited with developing modern staff notation where lines signify pitches a third apart and a method of sight-singing (solmization) that became associated with a hand that later bore his name.[103]

A 17th century German manuscript, written in Latin, uses the joints as well as the tips of the fingers and thumb to depict the syllables used in solmization (Fig. 2.42)

ENDNOTES

1. For a discussion of the related acts of tying, nailing, locking and pinning, see Onians, *The Origins of European Thought,* Ch. 5.

2. See Petronius, *The Satyricon,* XV.30.

3. See Solomon Gandz, "The Knot in Hebrew Literature or From the Knot to the Alphabet," p. 213.

4. *Folk,* Vol. 8-9, 1966-67, pp. 15-24.

5. Ibid., p. 16. He attributes their use in the eastern United States to the influence of Mexico on the late Pre-Columbian cultures of the Southeast.

6. Ibid., p. 20.

7. Herodotus, *The Histories,* IV.98.

8. Cyrus Day, *Quipus and Witches' Knots,* p. 3.

9. Ibid., p.3.

10. Gandz, p. 204.

11. Dr. Karl Weule, *Native Life in East Africa,* p. 329.

12. William Cumming, ed., *The Discoveries of John Lederer,* pp. 12-13.

13. Gandz, p. 202. Cf., I Kings, 16:16; 16:20; II Kings, 15:15; Amos, 7:10. See also, I Sam, 22:8; 22:13; II Sam, 15:31; I Kings, 15:27; 16:9; II Kings, 10:9; 21:23; 21:24; and passim.

14. The French word for weft (*la trame*) also means a plot or conspiracy. The verb *tramer* means to weave, to plot, to contrive, to hatch. These ideas are related to the notion that each man's fate is a thread woven by the gods.

15. Frederick Hodge, ed., *Handbook of American Indians North of Mexico,* p. 281.

16. Day, op. cit., p. 4.

17. Ibid., pp. 3-5.

18. Ibid., p. 7.

19. Raglan, *The Hero,* Ch. 1, and passim.

20. Joseph Needham, *Science and Civilization in China,* Vol. 3, p. 69.

21. Hsia-sheng Chen, *The Art of Chinese Knotting,* p. 11.

22. L. L. Locke, *The Ancient Quipu,* p. 60. Cf., Gandz, p. 214.

23. Edmund Simon, "Uber Knotenschriften und ahnliche Knotenschnure der Riukiu-Inseln."

24. *Journal of the Voyages and Travels by the Rev. Daniel Tyerman and George Bennet, Esq.,* pp. 71-72.

25. Locke, op. cit., p. 9.

26. Cyrus Day, *Quipus and Witches' Knots*; William J. Conklin, "The Information System of Middle Horizon Quipus"; and Antje Christensen, "The Peruvian Quipu." See also, Wired magazine, January 2007, "Untangling the Mystery of the Inca."

27. "They added, subtracted, and multiplied with these knots, and ascertained the dues of each town by dividing grains of maize and pebbles so that their account was accurate." "…everything was recorded on threads and knots, which were like notebooks." Garcilaso de la Vega, *Royal Commentaries of the Incas,* p. 124-125.

28. The Incan abacus is discussed in Cyrus Day's *Quipus and Witches' Knots,* pp. 31-37 and in Antje Christensen, "The Peruvian Quipu."

29. Garcilaso de la Vega, op. cit., p. 331.

30. Ibid., p. 332.

31. Garcilaso de la Vega, p. 332.

32. Ibid., p. 329.

33. Ifrah, *From One to Zero,* p. 93.

34. Gandz gives credit to Homberg in a footnote (p. 200, nt. 47), but was apparently unaware of the letter sent by M. Gaster to *Folklore* (XXV, pp. 254-258) that deals with some of these matters.

35. Proverbs, 3:1; 3:3; 7:1-3.

36. Gandz, op. cit., p. 199.

37. Numbers, 15:38 and Ezekial, 8:3.

38. Deut., 22:12.

39. The root is the Arabic *jadal* (to twist a cord or rope). The Babylonian *gidlu* means a cord or rope on which onions are strung. The similarity to knots is clear.

40. Gandz, op. cit., p. 199. The *midrashim* (explanations) are any of the rabbinical commentaries on the Scriptures written between the beginning of the Exile and circa A.D. 1200.

41. Numbers, 15:38-9.

42. Genesis, 38:18.

43. Ibid., 38:24-6.

44. Gandz, p. 210.

45. Ibid., p. 211.

46. T. Danzig, *Number—The Language of Science*, p. 29.

47. Needham, p. 79. One of the Pyramid Texts dating from the 6th Dynasty reads: "O ye two Scribe-gods, reckon up your registers, make calculations on your number-sticks, search (?) your rolls." (E. A. Wallis Budge, *Osiris*, vol.1, pg. 166.) This could be a reference to tally sticks, common in many cultures, which are normally used to record numbers but not to calculate.

48. Ibid., p. 77.

49. Gandz, p. 206.

50. Ibid., p. 207.

51. Ibid., p. 207. Karl Menninger believes that the suffixes *-ginta* and *-konta* merely signify a group of ten units. Karl Menninger, *Number Words and Number Symbols*.

52. Georges Ifrah, *From One to Zero*, p. 15.

53. Ibid., p. 16.

54. Ibid., p. 17.

55. K. Menninger, op. cit., p. 36.

56. Ifrah, op. cit., p. 37-38.

57. Ibid., p. 36.

58. *The Odyssey*, trans. by Robert Fitzgerald, p. 65.

59. K. Menninger, op. cit., p. 41.

60. Ibid., pp. 62-63.

61. Ifrah, op. cit., p. 47 (Sumerian) and K. Menninger, op. cit., p. 64 (Irish).

62. Ibid., pp. 37-38. Compare the Greek prefix *pan* ("all").

63. Menninger, op. cit., p. 52.

64. Ibid., p. 66.

65. Ifrah, op. cit., p. 46.

66. Menninger, op. cit., p. 51.

67. Ibid., p. 154.

68. Ifrah, op. cit, p. 65.

69. Menninger, op. cit., pp. 201-220.

70. Ibid., p. 203.

71. Ibid., p. 204

72. Ibid., p.204.

73. Ifrah, op. cit., p. 62.

74. Ibid., p. 63.

75. Needham, pp. 68-69. For a discussion of the game of *micatio* or *morra*, see Ifrah, op. cit., pp. 67-70.

76. Ifrah, op. cit., pp. 61-62.

77. W. Blackman, *Encyclopedia of Religion and Ethics*, p. 848.

78. For the history and development of these prayers and their association with the mnemonic device and with early printing, see Anne Winston-Allen, *Stories of the Rose*.

79. Ibid., p. 82, for a discussion of the symbolism of the rose in pre-Christian and Germanic traditions.

80. Ibid., pp. xi-xii.

81. Ibid., p. 82.

82. Ibid., p. 89. More can be said about the symbolism of the rose but it would take us far from our subject. We have left aside, among other matters, the association of the red rose with blood—both menstrual blood and the blood of Christ, and the thorns of the rose. For the symbolism of horns, thorns, and crowns, see Réne Guénon's essay "The Symbolism of Horns," in *Fundamental Symbols*, p. 135.

83. W. Blackman, *Encyclopedia of Religion and Ethics*, p. 854.

84. Ibid., p. 853.

85. Winston-Smith, op. cit., p. 14.

86. Ibid., p. 4.

87. Ibid., p. 111.

88. W. Blackman, op. cit., p. 848.

89. Ibid., p. 848.

90. M. Gaster, *Folklore*, XXV, pp. 257-258.

91. Ibid., pp. 257-258.

92. Ifrah, op. cit., p. 64.

93. Ibid., p. 63-64.

94. John Cargill, *The Celtic Cross and Greek Proportion*.

95. James Travis, "Old Celtic Design Music", p. 66.

96. James Cargill, op. cit., p. 1.

97. Ibid., pp. 9-10.

98. John Burnett, *Early Greek Philosophy*, p. 20. Burnett also notes that the word hypotenuse means "the cord stretching over against" (p. 105). More recent scholarship on the history of algebra and geometry has identified the use of Pythagorean triples in India, China, Babylonia, Egypt, and Neolithic Europe, suggesting a common origin in the 4th millennia B.C. See the work of the American mathematician Abraham Seidenberg and corroborating evidence from B. L van der Waerden and others.

99. James Cargill, op. cit., p. 2.

100. James Cargill, op. cit., pp. 2-4.

101. See James Travis, op. cit., p. 2.

102. A good overview of the subject including a short bibliography is provided in "The Singing Hand," in Richter, *Writing on Hands. Memory and Knowledge in Early Modern Europe*.

103. Ibid., p. 35.

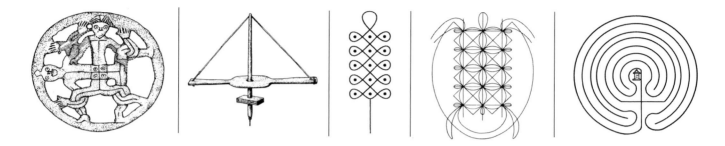

One of Dürer's "Sechs Knoten".

THE SUTRATMAN

Symbolism is a language and a precise form of thought; a hieratic and metaphysical language and not a language determined by somatic or psychological categories.
                                                                    Ananda K. Coomaraswamy

Titus Burckhardt writes:

> Ornaments in the form of a knot, which are widely distributed in nomad art, comprise an especially suggestive symbolism, based on the fact that the different parts of the knot are opposed to one another, at the same time they are united by the continuity of the string. The knot resolves for whoever understands the principles of knotting of which the invention is, so to say, itself a symbol of the hidden principles of things.[1]

It is these "hidden principles" of knotting that interest us here.

POLARITY

In the words of René Guénon, "a bond can be conceived as that which fetters or as that which unites, and even in ordinary language the word has both these meanings."[2] The polarities we discussed earlier in regard to knots—binding and loosing, illness and health, life and death, apotropaic and destructive—are all rooted in the nature of traditional symbolism in which the opposing forces found in the physical world are derived from a unity preexisting *in divinis.*

> Just as for Heracleitus "reality is a 'αρμονια of opposite tensions, a single nature which develops itself in the twofold directions" (132), so for Philo the "Monad" [Plato's 'One' as distinct from the 'others'] is not a number at all, but a premise (στοιχειον) and a principle" (αρχη, *Heres* 190—and as such, of course, "ungenerated and indestructible" and "without beginning or end" Plato, *Phaedrus* 245D + Aristotle, *Phys.* 8.1, 252 B, cf. 3.4.203 B).[3]

In the same way, Philo Judeus explains the created world "as consisting of an almost infinite series of opposites [Gr. εναντια, Sk. *dvandvau*] held together in harmony by the very creative impulse or agent that had originally separated them out from primitive and unformed matter by a series of bisections."[4] That is to say, the Logos itself is both a unifying bond and a divider, embodying the twin powers of life and death.[5]

The ritual or magic use of knots to help or harm emphasizes one side of the equation only, often because the supporting principle has been forgotten. The same devolution may be found in language:

An important example of the metaphysical bias inherent in language itself can be cited in the fact that in many of the oldest vocabularies (and with survivals in modern language, where, however, the tendency is to give an exclusively good or bad meaning to such words as "reward," which are properly neutral) a single root so often embodies opposite meanings; for example, in Egyptian the sign "strong-weak" must be qualified by determinants if we are to know which is meant, while in Sanskrit the same word can mean either zero or plenum; one infers that the movement of primitive logic is not abstractive from an observed multiplicity but deductive from an axiomatic unity.[6]

To pursue the matter further, we must imagine a state of mind that underlies both language and visual expression.

As Philo says: "Spoken words contain the symbols of things apprehended by the understanding only" (*De Abrahamo* 119). Hence the word "contain" is proper, because the real symbols are the concrete things to which the words refer by first intention. At the same time, it must always be remembered that the verbal symbols are a species rather than the genus of language, and that the connotations of things can be as well (or sometimes even better) communicated by visual symbols.[7]

From these considerations it is clear that the symbolism of knotting implicitly contains the more rationalized philosophies of later periods. Problems such as the unity of opposites or the one and the many, commonplace in Vedic, Neo-Platonic, Gnostic, Kabalistic, Scholastic and Hermetic thought, are prefigured here. What begins as an image becomes a philosophy under the influence of writing, which confers the power to separate the simultaneous into the sequential, the implicit into the explicit.

While we cannot observe "hidden principles" we can understand them by analogy from those things that are made in accordance with them. The knot is both a symbol of a veiled or hidden reality while functioning simultaneously as a device of the most profound utility. Its utility is an inseparable product of its being "well made;" that is, made according to higher principles.

THE THREAD-SPIRIT

The symbolism of knots has received some attention from folklorists and anthropologists and Mircea Eliade and others have catalogued beliefs connected with tying and binding in Indo-European and other cultures.[8] The great expositor and interpreter of these matters, however, was the art historian, folklorist, and metaphysician, Ananda K. Coomaraswamy. It was Coomaraswamy who first identified the doctrine that underlies the symbolism of knots and of thread and it was he who applied the Sanskrit term *sutratman* to the entire tradition. He wrote, "to have lost the art of thinking in images is precisely to have lost the proper linguistic of metaphysics and to have descended to the verbal logic of 'philosophy.'"[9] He also believed that traditional symbolism constituted a form of language that communicated the beliefs of ancient peoples. The symbolism of knots is but one expression of these "figures of thought" which in later periods were reduced to figures of speech.

The sutratman or "thread-spirit" doctrine, despite its Sanskrit name, belongs to many cultures—Hindu, Islamic, European, Chinese, Amer-Indian—suggesting great antiquity. The doctrine, once understood, gives meaning to the varied symbolism derived from the related arts of knotting, sewing, spinning and weaving. The doctrine is expressed both in language and art and appears in various forms in the folktales of the world as well as in the sacred writings of the world's major religions.

In the *Rg Veda* (1.115.1) we read: "The Sun is the Spirit (*atman*) of all that is in motion or at rest" and that the Sun connects all things to Himself by means of a thread of spiritual light.[10] It is important to understand that these are symbolic, not scientific statements. The Sun refers to God, and not the sun we see with our eyes.

> In all the contexts in which "Sun" has been capitalized the reference is, of course, to the "inward Sun" as distinguished from the "outward sun, which receives its power and lustre from the inward"—Boehme, Jacob, *Signatura Rerum* XI:75, to the "Sun of the Angels" as distinguished from the "sun of sense"—Dante, *Paradiso* X:53:54; compare *Convito* III:12, 50-60. This "Sun of the sun" — Philo Judeus, *De specialis legibus* I:279; compare *De cherubim* 97—Apollo as distinguished from Helios — Plato, *Laws* 898D, Plutarch, *Moralia* 393D, 400C, D—is not "the sun whom all men see" but "the Sun whom not all know with the mind"—*Atharva Veda* X:8.14, "whose body the sun is"—*Brhadaranyaka Upanisad* III:7.9. The traditional distinction of intelligible from sensible, invisible from visible "suns" is essential to any adequate understanding of "solar mythologies" and "solar cults."[11]

In the *Jaiminiya Upanishad Brahmana* (III.4.13-III.5.1) we find, "By the Gale, indeed, O Gautama, as by a thread, are this and yonder world and all beings strung together."[12] The Spirit or Gale (*atman, prana, vata, vayo*), conceived as both a breath and a ray of light—depending on the context—is the source of our being, our essence.

The progenitive power of the breath is most familiar to us from the Old Testament, beginning with Genesis 2:7: "And the Lord God formed man of the dust of the ground, and breathed into his nostrils the breath of life; and man became a living soul." This "solar breath" is not to be identified with our physical breath that depends upon it. The invisible world of the Spirit can only be explained by analogies rooted in the world of the senses. Plotinus expresses the same vision in the *Enneads* (vi.4.3):

> But are we to think of this Authentic Being as, itself, present, or does it remain detached, omnipresent in the sense only that powers from it enter everywhere?

> Under the theory of presence of powers, souls are described as rays; the source remains self-locked and these are flung forth to impinge upon particular living things.[13]

God is connected to each of his own by a ray or thread of pneumatic light upon which life depends. This ray is bestowed at birth as a gift and revoked at death, while abiding eternally *in divinis*. All things under the Sun are in the power of death. In the Upanishads we find that the "Sun's light has many rays (sons)" and that "He fills the world by a division of his essence."[14] More succinctly: "God is one in himself, many in his children" and "He divides himself while remaining undivided." We alone experience the division. The solar ray is our guide to salvation, the road back to the Source.

The generative power of the Sun is central to many traditions from the Pharaoh who "came forth from the Rays" to the French Sun King. Here the life-giving blessing of the Sun is extended like a hand toward Pharaoh Akhenaten and his family (Fig. 3.1).

Fig. 3.1: Akhnaten and his family.

The leader embodies the power of Heaven and his radiance allows his people to prosper (Fig. 3.2). As we live and breathe, we are God's children, or more correctly, it is not we who breathe, but God. The world is a vast conspiracy, a "breathing together."

It is our Solar paternity that is reflected in Aristotle's statement, "man and the Sun generate man" (*Physics* II.2), in which the metaphysical and scientific outlooks are combined. Similarly, we find in Aquinas, "The power of the soul, which is in the semen through the Spirit enclosed therein, fashions the body" (*ST* III.II), a view apparently shared by Pythagoras.[15] Coomaraswamy was able to find evidence for the idea of Solar paternity in a wide variety of cultures including Indian, ancient Greek, medieval Scholastic, Sufi, American Indian, and aboriginal Australian.[16]

The symbolism of the *sutratman* has correspondences at every level of existence, both human and divine. Cosmologically, the Sun is spoken of as a fastener or button (Sk. *asanjanam*) to which these worlds are linked by

Fig. 3.2: Portrait of the Roman Emperor Caracalla with solar rays.

means of the four quarters. This motif is familiar to us from folklore where the archer-hero sends a threaded arrow through four marks placed at the corners of an arena and it returns to his hand.[17] Often the archer is elevated and "sees the field," signifying God's omniscience and omnipresence.

In the traditional Vedic cosmology, the Sun is seven-rayed, comprising the zenith, nadir, four cardinal points, and the all-important seventh ray that alone passes through the sun to the super-solar Brahma world. This world can only be reached by the Spirit or central ray, often referred to as the Sun's "best ray," "best foot," or "light of lights."[18] This ray or central beam (*axis mundi*) pierces the center or navel of the world and unites the three worlds — an idea found in many traditions.

Architecturally, the *axis mundi* is symbolized by a central post (king post) that supports the house or temple and serves as the point of juncture for the roof beams. In the human body, the center post is the spine.

There is also a theory of cognition inherent in the symbolism. Just as the kingpost supports the building and unites the roof beams, so too our senses are unified in the single Solar breath. It is the goal of the yogi or adept to withdraw his senses from their various attachments back to the source from which all perception arises. Our senses are merely God's "lookouts."

PUPPETS OF GOD

In an essay entitled, "'Spiritual Paternity' and the 'Puppet Complex,'" Coomaraswamy explains the metaphysical ideas behind the symbolism of puppetry.

> Puppets seem to move of themselves, but are really activated and controlled from within by the thread from which they are superseded from above, and only move intelligently in obedience to this leash: and it is in this automatism, or appearance of free will and self-motion, that the puppet most of all resembles man.[19]

We are the puppets or toys of God, an image taken up by Plato in *Laws* where the Athenian explains true education.

> Let us suppose that each of us living creatures is an ingenious puppet of the gods, whether contrived by way of a toy of theirs or for some serious purpose—for as to what we know nothing; but this we do know, that these inward affections of ours, like sinews or cords, drag us along and, being opposed to each other, pull one against the other to opposite actions; and herein lies the dividing line between goodness and badness. For, as our argument declares, there is one of these pulling forces which every man should always follow and nohow leave hold of, counteracting thereby the pull of the other sinews: it is the leading-string, golden and holy of "calculation," entitled the [common law of the individual]; and whereas the other cords are hard and steely and of every possible shape and semblance, this one is flexible and uniform, since it is of gold. With that most excellent leading-string of the law we must needs cooperate always; for since calculation is excellent, but gentle rather

than forceful, its leading-string needs helpers to ensure that the golden kind within us may vanquish the other kinds.[20]

If we are the puppets of God then we ought to act accordingly, following His direction and not our own urgings. We should avoid the disorder created by our desires that pull us where they will and instead, hang onto this "golden cord."

Our powers of perception, expression, thought and action must be guided by Reason; not what we mean by reason—which Plato calls opinion and assigns a merely pragmatic value—but rather the Divinity within us. The Stoic Marcus Aurelius was of the same mind.

> Become conscious at last that thou hast in thyself something better and more god-like than that which causes the bodily passions and turns thee into a mere marionette. What is my mind now occupied with? Fear? Suspicion? Concupiscence? Some other thing?[21]

It is God who controls the central cord that guides the others.

> Bear in mind that what pulls the strings is the Hidden thing within us: *that* makes our speech, *that* our life, *that*, one may say, makes the man.[22]

Our goal is to identify with the true source of all perception and action and so become a witness to our own fate. This is accomplished through a kind of automatism, not of the mechanical kind, but through grace—both spiritual and physical — as in the case of the Balinese (Fig. 3.3). It is by means of this automatism that an intelligent and spontaneous life may be lived; an active life in the moment, in preference to a passive subjection to one's emotions. This is the same kind of automatism advocated in the Koran when it speaks of "submission to the will of Allah" or in the New Testament where we read, "Not what I will but what thou wilt" (Mark 14:36; cf. John 8:28).

The symbolism of the human puppet also appears in the odes of Rumi, the medieval Sufi poet.

> O ridiculous puppet, that leapest out of thy hole (box) as if to say 'I am the lord of the land,' how long wilt thou leap? Abase thyself, or they will bend thee like a bow.[23]

Fig. 3.3: Balinese girl dancing.

What will bend the puppet like a bow are his own emotions, which pull him this way and that.

The ancient Hebrews shared this basic conception of man and his relation to God as D. B. MacDonald tells us in *The Hebrew Philosophical Genius*.

> Some of them held that all the non-human creation existed for the sake of man and that man was, to some degree, a partaker of the divine nature. Others, however, held that all created things were on one level before Jehovah and existed for one purpose, to be a great animated toy with which Jehovah could occupy Himself and amuse Himself.[24]

India provides many examples of this motif. The Hindu god Vishnu in his role as Creator is referred to as the "Holder of every Thread." In the *Mahabharata* we find: "Human gestures are harnessed by another, as with a wooden doll strung on a thread";[25] and in the *Brhadaranyaka Upanishad*:

> Do you know that Thread, by which, and that Inner Controller by whom this world and the other and all beings are strung together and controlled from within, so that they move like a puppet, performing their respective functions?[26]

In Book VIII of the *Iliad*, Zeus seeks an end to the Trojan War and calls the gods to a conference. He warns them about interfering:

> But perhaps you gods would like to put me to the test and satisfy yourselves? Suspend a golden rope from heaven and lay hold of the end of it, all of you together. Try as you may, you will never drag Zeus the High Counsellor down from heaven to the ground. But if I cared to take a hand and pulled in earnest from my end, I could haul you up, earth, sea and all. Then I should make the rope fast to a pinnacle of Olympus, and leave everything to dangle in mid-air. By so much does my strength exceed the strength of gods and men.[27]

A different kind of tug-of-war is described by the medieval Hasidic writer Eleazer of Worms in *Sefer Hasidim* (Book of the Devout): "Man is a rope whose two ends are pulled by God and Satan; and in the end God proves stronger."[28]

The golden cord also appears in Orphic theogony where Zeus questions Nyx (Night).

> Having asked of Nyx how all things might be both one and divided, he was bidden to wrap *aither* round the world and tie up the bundle with the 'golden cord'.[29]

The Greek *aither* is not air, as it is sometimes translated, but the eternal, fiery, pneumatic power that holds the four material elements (earth, air, fire and water) together and animates them. The golden cord is itself ethereal and pervasive and holds all beings together until they die, come "unloosed," and return to their source.[30]

William Blake followed the same golden cord back to its source in his poem "Jerusalem":

> I give you the end of a golden string,
> Only wind it into a ball,
> It will lead you in at Heaven's Gate
> Built in Jerusalem's wall.[31]

Finally, far away from 18th century England, among the Negritos of the Malay Peninsula, a similar connection is established with the sky during a séance performed by the *hala* or shaman.

During his séance the *hala* of the Pehang Negritos holds threads made from palm leaves or, according to other accounts, very fine cords. These threads and cords reach to Bonsu, the celestial god who dwells above the seven levels of the sky. (He lives there with his brother, Teng; the other levels have no inhabitants.) As long as the séance continues, the *hala* is directly connected with the celestial god by these threads or cords, which the god sends down and, after the ceremony, draws back to himself.[32]

THINGS FALL APART

Just as the pins of a puppet hold its limbs together and allow movement, the human body is articulated by means of muscles and joints. We read in the *Maitri Upanishad*, "It is by 'the thread' that the parts are really co-ordinated and moved: as in man 'it is by the Breath that the joints are united….'"[33] This vital Breath is not our respiration but the thread-spirit that vivifies it. To use Aristotlian terminology, it is the First Cause of our being, rather than the mediate causes that govern the physical world.

Human beings depend on God to remain alive just as the puppet depends on the puppeteer to remain in motion. Death is the great devourer, the unstringer. When our life is "cut off," we are "undone," fall down, and our bones come apart. Life is a bond loosed at death. Sophocles wrote that Oedipus "blessedly loosed the bonds *(telos)* of life" much as Shakespeare has Hamlet say, "when we have shuffled off this mortal coil."[34]

What is true in the microcosm is true in the macrocosm. The thread-spirit holds the universe together. Dante understood this:

> In the order I speak of, all natures incline
> Either more near or less near to the source
> According as their diverse lots assign.
> To diverse harbours thus they move perforce
> O'er the great ocean of being, and each one
> With instinct given it to maintain its course.
> This bears the fiery element to the moon;
> This makes the heart of mortal things to move;
> This knits the earth together into one.[35]

The Renaissance humanist Marsilio Ficino agreed. In *De Lumine* he compares the light that connects heaven and earth with the Spirit: "And as in us the spirit is the bond [connecting link] of soul and body, so the light is the bond of the universe *(vinculum universi)*."[36]

The Old Testament story of Ezekiel in the Valley of the Bones (Ezek. 37) illustrates the same principle, only here the dead are reanimated. Isaiah is asked by God to "prophesy upon these bones, and say unto them, O ye dry bones, hear the word of the Lord."[37] He follows God's commandment and the bones come together with a great noise, and flesh and sinew grow upon them. Next he is commanded to summon the four winds to breathe upon the slain that they may live. Again he does as instructed and the Spirit enters the bones and a great army arises. The four winds are the breath of God (thread-spirit) that act as the animating and binding force in the world, holding the quarters together.

In the end, everything under the sun is subject to corruption and decay when the thread-spirit that supports it returns to its source. Clothing wears out, men die, buildings collapse, cities fall into ruin. In folklore, a yogi pulls a thread from his garment and a city collapses. In another tale, a man is given a test: thread the needle. If he succeeds, he is rewarded; if not, all of his belongings are confiscated.

ALL THE WORLD'S A STAGE

Puppets, marionettes and jointed dolls were once symbols of the drama of human existence, now reduced to child's play. Religious doctrine reminds us that the artisan, in fashioning his creations, acts in imitation of God, the Master Craftsman.[38]

Fig. 3.4: Eskimo mechanical doll.

We possess puppets and dolls from many cultures and time periods, some humble and commonplace toys (Fig. 3.4), some quite remarkable and clearly designed to create a sense of wonder and astonishment.

Excavations in Greece and Rome have uncovered dolls in a variety of media including wood, bone, terra cotta, ivory, marble, wax, linen and leather.[39] All are mature females, many with painted and modeled features including hair, earrings and inlaid eyes. Most are jointed, though the number of joints varies, and many have movable limbs, often attached by wires or cords (Fig. 3.5). In Greece, such dolls are found in the graves of children or in temple precincts. Greek girls dedicated their dolls to Artemis or to other goddesses before marriage. Egyptian specimens have been found in wood and pottery dating from the 3rd millennium.

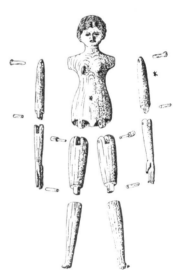

Fig. 3.5: Jointed Roman doll.

Dolls and marionettes are often associated with ancestors, which is why we find them in graves. On Bali, the *ukur-kepeng* is a doll fashioned to the size of the corpse and cremated with it (Fig. 3.6). It represents the skeleton, as indicated by its jointed composition. It is made of white yarn (the nerves) and "black" Chinese coins (the bones). The *ukur selaka* is used for the same purposes by the higher castes and is made of silver plaques strung on silver wires or of gold (*ukur-mas*). It is not cremated but kept as a family heirloom.[40]

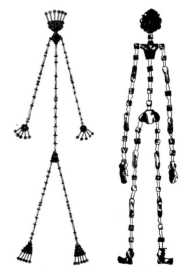

Fig. 3.6: Balinese *ukur-kepeng* and *ukur-mas*.

Indonesian *sigalegale*, giant mechanical puppets operated by strings, are even more spectacular (Figs. 3.7 and. 3.8).

> *Sigalegale*, some of the most complex puppets in the world, are made to propitiate the spirits of the dead who lack offspring to provide for them. Typically nearly life-sized, the puppets are capable of dancing, blinking, and even crying, and they appear to be self-animated because the puppeteer is at a distance behind the wooden box underneath. Formerly the puppet head was an overmodeled human skull or a wooden head covered with human skin....[41]

Fig. 3.7: Life-size mechanical doll (*sigalegale*).   Fig. 3.8: Head of *sigalegale,* Indonesia.

The symbolism of dolls and puppets reminds us that "all the world's a stage" with God the stage manager working behind the scenes. This conceit is best known to us from Shakespeare but is actually a rhetorical commonplace of ancient vintage.[42]

MAN AS A JOINTED BEING

It is worth noting again that the joints are of primary importance both in the operation of dolls and marionettes and in the composition and movement of the human body. Body joints make man a composite creature while sinews allow movement and hold the body members together. As Coomaraswamy noted, the sinews are the physical counterpart of the psychic "bonds of life."[43]

According to Bruno Snell, the archaic Greeks possessed no single word for the human body. Homer generally refers to limbs or to the skin but not to the entire body (Fig. 3.9).

> We find it difficult to conceive of a mentality which made no provision for the body as such. Among the early expressions designating what was later rendered as *soma* or 'body', only the plurals *guia* [limbs as moved by the joints], *melea* [limbs in their muscular strength],

Fig. 3.9: Ancient Greek representation of the human body.

70

etc. refer to the physical nature of the body; for *chros* is merely the limit of the body, and *demas* represents the frame, the structure, and occurs only in the accusative of specification. As it is, early Greek art actually corroborates our impression that the physical body of man was comprehended, not as a unit but as an aggregate.[44]

We find the same idea of "human puppets" and the same concern for body joints in Balinese culture. In a photographic study published in 1942, *Balinese Character*, Margaret Mead and Gregory Bateson remark on the strong kinesthetic basis of Balinese education (Fig. 3.10).

Fig. 3.10: Balinese teacher guiding student in dance.

Learning to walk, learning the first appropriate gestures of playing musical instruments, learning to eat, and to dance are all accomplished with the teacher behind the pupil, conveying directly by pressure, and almost always with a minimum of words, the gesture to be performed. Under such a system of learning, one can only learn if one is extremely relaxed and if will and consciousness as we understand those terms are almost in abeyance.[45]

Further, children are taught an economy of movement wherein they contract only those muscles required to perform a given activity.

Total involvement in any activity occurs in trance and in children's tantrums, but for the rest, an act is not performed by the whole body. The involved muscle does not draw all the others into a unified act, but smoothly and simply, a few small units are moved—the fingers alone, the hand and the forearm alone, or the eyes alone, as in the characteristic Balinese habit of slewing the eyes to one side without turning the head.[46]

The result of this training is an extraordinary grace of movement as regards the body as a whole, as well as an unusual capacity for controlling indi-

Fig. 3.11: Balinese dancer.

vidual body parts—seen most notably in the posturing and movement of the fingers while dancing (Fig. 3.11).

This kind of physical training both supports and is supported by two predominant ideas within the culture:

> These two habits, that of going waxy limp in the hands of a teacher and permitting the body to be manipulated from without, and that of moving only the minimum of muscles necessary to any act, find expression in the whole puppet complex on the one hand, and in the fear of decomposition on the other.[47]

This "puppet complex" takes a number of forms. Trance states are not uncommon among the Balinese especially during ritual and dance. In the *sangiang deling*, puppets, weighed with bells and representing *dedari* (angels) dance on a string that is tied at the ends to two sticks, each supported on a stand (Fig. 3.12). Each stick is held by a man who sits with his arm slightly flexed at the elbow. The tension of the string produces muscle contractions in the arms of the men, which shake the stick and move the puppets. Such clonic contractions appear involuntary (they are actually self-generated) adding to the feeling of possession.

Fig. 3.12: Balinese *sangiang deling* ritual.

Once the puppets are moving, two young girls come and sit beside the men. They grasp the lower end of the sticks. Older girls support them from behind. As the sticks move, one of the girls enters a trance. On-lookers begin singing and the girl sways sideways. Later she beats the sticks on the supporting stand to the sound of the music. When the song is finished the girl collapses into the arms of the older girls who are supporting her. She is then dressed in the appropriate garb and dances as a *dedari*.

The Balinese are also preoccupied with dismemberment and decay.

The Balinese cemetery is haunted not by whole ghosts but by the ghosts of separate limbs. Headless bodies, separate legs, and unattached arms that jump around and sometime a scrotum that crawls slowly over the ground—these are the boggles of Balinese fantasy. From this it is a small step to perceiving the body as a puppet or to imagining such supernaturals as *Bala Serijoet…*, the "Multiple Soldier" whose every joint—shoulders, elbows, knees, ankles, and so on—is separately animated and provided with an eye [Fig. 3.13].[48]

Coomaraswamy's comments on *Balinese Character* put the matter in a larger context.

> It is implied that these are especially Balinese peculiarities. Although the observation is unrelated to any governing first principle, and so not fully understood, it is excellent in itself: for it is realized that the dancer's puppet-like relaxation is that of an obedient pupil, who would be guided not by her own will, but by a teacher's. One cannot but recall the words of Christ: "I do nothing of myself," and "not what I will, but what thou wilt."[49]

THE FATES

Writing about the ancient Greek notion of fate, William Onians introduces another aspect of the sutratman doctrine.

> In Homer, one is struck by the fact that his heroes with all their magnificent vitality and activity feel themselves at every turn not free agents but passive instruments or victims of other powers. It is not merely that they and their foes 'lived dangerously' and life and fortune were precarious possessions. A man felt that he could not help his own actions. An idea, an impulse came to him; he acted and presently rejoiced or lamented. Some god had inspired or blinded him. He prospered, then was poor, perhaps enslaved; he wasted away with disease, or died in battle. It was divinely ordained (*theophaton*), his portion (*aisa, moira*) appointed long before.[50]

A man's fate was conceived as a thread bound around him at birth or as an allotment of wool from which his life was spun.[51] In referring to a hero's future, Homer uses the expression, "it lies on the knees of the gods," a reference to spinning, which was often done sitting down.[52] Throughout the *Iliad* and the *Odyssey* we read that the gods "spin" or "weave" the threads of a man's fate at birth and bind it upon him, and that death—the ultimate bond—hangs over each man like a thread. Fate is spun by Zeus or by an *aisa, moira,* or *daimon*.[53] The thread that binds a man is invisible to normal eyes and can be known only to those with "second sight."

In Hesiod, we find the more familiar spinners *(Klothes)*, the three daughters of Zeus and Themis in this version of the myth.[54] *Clotho* (spinner) spins the thread of life; *Atropos* (unturnable) severs the thread; and *Lachesis* (allotment) allots each man's portion. The Fates are depicted in classical Greek art holding their identifying symbols: a spindle, shears, and a globe and scroll, respectively (Fig. 3.14).

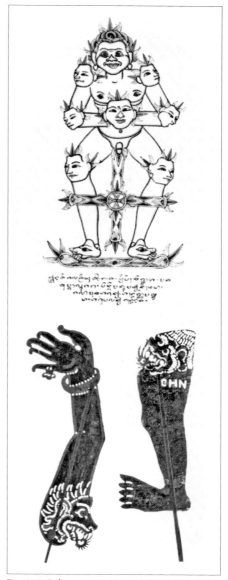

Fig. 3.13: Balinese protective spirit (Multiple Soldier) and shadow puppets of graveyard spirits.

Fig. 3.14: The Three Fates (Clotho. Atropos, Lachesis).

The Greek word *moirai* means those who apportion and is equivalent to the word *daimon*, which at root indicates something given, a gift. These terms are synonymous with the Christian Holy Spirit, God's gift of life. If Christian propagandists chose to emphasis the demonic at the expense of the *daimon* it was only to further their own cause. The gods of the old religion become the devils of the new.

In Norse mythology, the Norns both spin and weave. As *Disir* or "weird sisters" they weave the woof of war. Darrud in Caithness provides a gruesome vision of their work in the *Njals Saga*, which recounts the Battle of Clontarf (A.D. 1014) between the Norse and Irish:

> A loom has been set up, stretching afar and portending slaughter... and a rain of blood in pouring. Upon it has been stretched a warp of human beings—a warp grey with spears which the valkyries are filling with weft of crimson. The warp is formed of human entrails and is heavily weighted with human heads. Bloodstained javelins serve as heddles, the spool is shod with iron, the *hræll* is formed of arrows and it is with swords that we must sley this web of battle. Hildr is going to weave and Hjorbrimul, Sanngridr and Svipul with drawn swords...We are weaving, weaving the web of the spear. Young is the king who owned it in the past. Forth must we step and make our way into the battle where the arms of our friends are clashing.... We are weaving, weaving the web of the spear while the standard of the valiant warrior is advancing...I declare that death is ordained for a mighty prince. Even now the earl has been laid low by the spears. The Irish too will suffer a sorrow which will never be forgotten by men. Now the web is woven and the field dyed crimson.[55]

The Norns also supervise the birth of children as does their Greek and Roman counterpart, Eileithyia. Some are given easy lives, others hard.

In *Beowulf*, God grants Beowulf and his men "a weaving of war luck" and Hoc's daughter mourns "the web's short measure" when her son and brother are killed in battle.[56] Howell D. Chickering Jr. comments on the Anglo-Saxon concept of destiny:

> The Anglo-Saxons believed that life was a struggle against insuperable odds and that a man's *wyrd* or 'lot' would be what it would be.... Even in early pagan days, they do not seemed to have believed in a supernatural conception of Destiny. *Wyrd* originally meant simply "what happens" and later was used by King Alfred in his translation of Boethius as a term for "what comes to pass" under the ...'forethought' of God's Providence.[57]

Let us not forget that epic itself is a kind of weaving. The Greek word *rhapsodein* refers to the bard who "stitches together" new songs out of old and familiar material.

THE NEEDLE

The technology of sewing is central to the symbolism of the sutratman doctrine in which the Sun connects all things to Himself by means of a thread of spiritual light. This thread-spirit, seen in its progenitive aspect, holds the world together and all the beings in it.

> Primitive man already possessed his needle and thread of sinew, and just because his thread was of sinew could have felt in a designation of the act of kind as a sewing (cf. *Rg Veda* II.32.4 cited above, and *syuti* as both "sewing" and "offspring"), and in the expression "unstrung" applied to the body at death—and hence analogically to the cosmos at the end of the world—an image even more vivid than at a later time, when thread was of cotton.[58]

There are a number of reasons to regard creation as a kind of sewing. Carl Schuster believed that in Paleolithic times, human social identity was expressed through designs painted on or sewn into the skin as well as by clothing designs sewn from animal skins (Fig. 3.15). Tattoos and clothing transformed a spirit into a human being; that is, they provided people with a social identity without which they would be alive but not fully human. "Clothes make the man." Further, clothing acts as an extension of the skin, helping to keep us alive. Because the body is held together by sinews and falls apart upon death, it too appears to be sewn. The thread-spirit doctrine is not as esoteric as it might seem because most traditional symbolism is rooted in observation of the physical world.[59]

In practice, threading a needle is difficult and symbolically the eye of the needle serves as the narrow entrance into Heaven, excluding all but the worthy. Only our real Self can gain entrance when all of its disguises have been shed. The needle's "eye" is described alternately as the "Sundoor" or "Eye of the World" from which life emanates and returns.

Fig. 3.15 Samoyed woman making clothing.

Fig. 3.16: Double spiral fibula, Greek Geometric Period.

The process of emanation and return can be seen in the design of the double spiral fibula, another kind of needle or brooch (Fig. 3.16). Here, the paired spirals represent opposing forces such as day and night, inhalation and exhalation, and birth and death, which are inherent in the manifested world.

> The primary sense of "broach" (= brooch) is that of anything acute, such as a pin, awl or spear, that penetrates a material; the same implement, bent upon itself, fastens or sews things together, as if it were in fact a thread. French *fibule*, as a surgical term, is in fact suture. It is only when we substitute a soft thread for the stiff wire that a way must be made for it by a needle; and then the thread remaining in the material is the trace, evidence and "clew" to the passage of the needle; just as our own short life is the trace of the unbroken Life whence it originates.[60]

Drawn from a single piece of wire, the spiral fibula forms a continuous path ending where it begins, a trait common to a number of art forms including sand drawings and cat's cradles. In the New Testament, Jesus is described both as a "Door" and as the "Alpha and Omega." The same may be said for the spiral fibula.

This association is reflected equally well in the work of Claude Mellan (fl. 1598–1688), whose remarkable engraving of Christ is composed from a single spiraling line (Fig. 3.17). The Latin words underneath, *Formatur unicus una* (By one the One is formed"), refer both to Christ and to the technique used to construct the work.

The Sundoor or needle's eye can also be seen as death's noose, ready to snare the unworthy. In Pali, the eye of the needle is designated by the term *pasa*.

> This word is the same as the Sanskrit word *pasha* which originally had the meaning of 'knot' or 'loop'. This seems first of all to indicate, as Coomaraswamy observed, that in a very remote epic needles were not perforated as they were later, but simply bent over at one end so as to form a kind of loop through which the thread was passed…[61]

The lasso or running knot is used in many cultures to capture animals and it is one of the emblems of Mrityu or Yama as well as Varuna.[62] Réne Guénon explains this aspect of the symbolism:

> …the 'animals' that they take by means of this pasha are in reality all the living beings (*pashu*). Hence also the meaning of 'bond': the animal once it is taken, finds itself tied by the running knot which tightens around him; similarly, the living being is bound by the limiting conditions which hold it in its particular state of manifested existence. In order to come out of this state of *pashu* it is necessary that the being be set free from these conditions, that is to say, in symbolic terms, that he escape from the *pashu*, or that he pass through the running knot without its tightening around him.[63]

Fig. 3.17: Claude Mellan: Face of Christ on the Sudary (1649).

Like the knot in the rope, bondage is necessary for individuation. This "vital knot" holds together the different elements that make up each created being.[64] Elizabethan science supported this view.

> Man in his 'natural' life (that is mortal life, supported by the physiological processes described) is a fusion of corruptible, mortal, physical body and incorruptible, perfect, immortal, spiritual soul. The fusion is the result of the 'subtle' substance, at once body and soul, called spirit. 'Subtle and serious' is the description of spirit in a serious medical work; and 'that subtle knot' is John Donne's term for it in *The Extasy*, 'That subtle knot which makes us man.'[65]

Each human life is an opportunity, a chance to untie the knot before we die and return to the source of our being.

> On the other hand all determinations or knots are bonds from which one could wish to be freed rather than remain forever "all tied up in knots." One would be released from all these "knots (*granthi*) of the heart," which we should now call "complexes" and of which the ego-complex (*ahamkara, abhimana,* Philo's *oiesis*) is the tightest and hardest to be undone.[66]

Everything under the sun is in the grip of death as Ecclesiastes tells us, and the Sundoor is not only the way to the other world, but the very figure of Death the Devourer, sometimes figured as a lion, gorgon or *makara*.[67]

The upright needle forms an *axis mundi* through which the ethereal counter-currents flow to produce fire, light and life. This is how God creates the garments that adorn the world, like a tailor or embroiderer with an invisible thread. The phallic aspect of the needle expresses the vivifying and generative aspect of the Deity. Men enjoy a spiritual paternity which precedes and is the First Cause of sexual reproduction, a theme taken up by Coomaraswamy in "Spiritual Paternity and the Puppet Complex" where he quotes Matthew (23:9): "And call no man your father upon the earth: for one is your Father, which is in heaven."[68]

Needles are also related to fishing hooks. In the New Testament the fish are the souls of men. "And he saith unto them, follow me and I will make ye fishers of men" (Matthew 4:19) and "No man can come to me except the Father which hath sent me draw him" (John 6:44). Similarly, "And I, if I be lifted up from the earth, will draw all men unto me" (John 12:32). God is the supreme angler who sports with mankind with his solar, pneumatic fishing line.

There is also the matter of archery. The arrow is a kind of needle, used ritually to "sew the four quarters," while the "bull's eye" is the entrance to Heaven and the arrow the immanent Deity returning to itself.[69] For this reason Christ was sometimes referred to as the "Chosen Arrow" in early Christian writings.

WARP AND WEFT

Nowhere is the sutratman doctrine more carefully elaborated than in the symbolism connected with looms and weaving. Looms are generally categorized into two related types, the horizontal or ground loom and the vertical loom (Fig. 3.18).[70] Both kinds were known in Neolithic times and probably developed in the Middle East from whence they spread in opposite directions. Elizabeth Barber comments:

> What I find most fascinating about these two early looms is that neither is logically derivable from the other, but both are easily derived from a simple band loom. With a band loom, the weaver normally ties the near end of the warp in a single bunch to a post or her own waist and the far end to something else, like a tree or another post or her big toe. If the weaving is tied to the weaver, the tension of the warp that is necessary for weaving is provided by simply leaning back.[71]

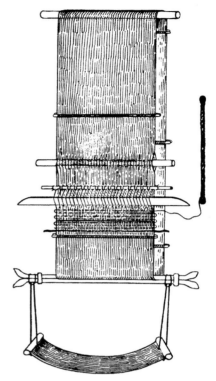

Fig. 3.19: Backstrap loom.

Fig. 3.18: Details of an Attic Greek vase (560 B.C.) showing vertical loom.

Such primitive looms, often called belt looms or backstrap looms, were used in many parts of the world including Asia, throughout the Pacific, and in the Americas in Pre-Columbian times (Fig. 3.19).[72] They are still in use today in some areas.

The development of vertical and horizontal looms from these earlier prototypes offered a definite technical advantage: a wider cloth could be woven once the weaver sat outside the work. These new looms were less portable which suggests that the change may have been related to a more sedentary lifestyle.

Coomaraswamy comments on the symbolism associated with primitive looms:

> In weaving, the warp threads are the "rays" of the Intelligible Sun (in many primitive looms they proceed from a single point), and the woof is the Primary Matter of the cosmic "tissue [Fig. 3.20]."[73]

The tree or pole to which the warp threads are attached is conceived as a Sun Pillar, Shaft of Light, World Tree, or Sacrificial Post, and serves as the *axis mundi* through which the ethereal counter-currents flow from Heaven to earth and back. It is only appropriate that these currents or rays—the source of all being— are physically attached to the weaver, whose work becomes an act of creation in the fullest sense.

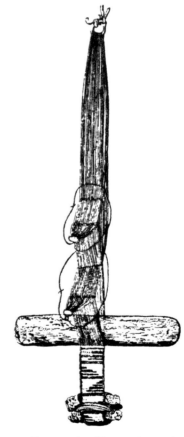

Fig. 3.20: Chirguano band loom with a single point of attachment.

Fig. 3.21: Horizontal ground loom.

Vertical and horizontal looms vary in design but their construction is equally symbolic. Horizontal looms are often pegged into the ground (Fig. 3.21) while vertical ones are sometimes hung from trees. Both kinds may employ one or more beams to provide the necessary tension for the woof threads. It is no coincidence that the word "beam" refers both to a shaft of light and to a piece of wood, with the attendant notion that the fire is immanent in the wood.[74]

René Guénon investigated the manifold but consistent symbolism of weaving in the Hindu, Islamic, Buddhist and Taoist traditions in an article entitled "The Symbolism of Weaving." He noted the close relationship between sacred books (texts) and cloth (textiles). The Indian sacred books are composed of *sutras* (threads) and the same may be said for the Koran where the Arabic word *sûrat* refers to the chapters. A book is formed of threads in the same way a cloth is. These ideas derive from a more ancient tradition in which knotted cords were used for mnemonic purposes.

Continuing the analogy, the Chinese associate the warp threads (*king*) with a fundamental text and the weft (*wei*) with the commentaries on it. In Hindu terminology the *shruti* or fruit of direct inspiration is associated with the warp and the *smriti*, the product of reflection and commentary on the text, is associated with the weft. More generally, the warp threads represent the divine, immutable element and the weft threads the human and contingent. It is the coming and going of the shuttle that makes possible the application of eternal principles to given conditions.

> [The symbolism of weaving] is also used to represent the world, or more precisely, the aggregate of all the worlds, that is, the indefinite multitude of the states or degrees that constitute universal Existence.[75]

What begins as an ideal pattern unextended in time and space, becomes fabric by the actions of the weaver, who creates a reflection of the divine prototype. Weaving, like all the traditional arts, has both a spiritual and material component and represents the re-creation of things as they were in the beginning.

The intersection of a warp thread with a woof thread forms a cross, representing the juncture of the Universal Spirit—which links all possible states of being—with a particular state of existence.[76] Each human existence results from the intersection of these two threads.

The warp thread also represents the active or masculine principle (*Purusha* in the Hindu tradition) while the weft represents the passive or feminine (*Prakriti*). Or astronomically, the warp threads may be conceived as solar (direct) light and the weft lunar (reflected) light. In either case, what is stressed is creation from complementary or contrary forces.

One interesting application of this symbolism is found in the field of number theory, formulated in ancient times and bequeathed to the Middle Ages through the quadrivium.

By definition the square is four equal straight lines joined at right angles. But a more important definition is that the square is the fact that any number [*sic*], when multiplied by itself, becomes a square. Multiplication is symbolized by a cross, and this graphic symbol itself is an accurate definition of multiplication. When we cross a vertical with a horizontal giving these line-movements equal units of length, say 4 for example, we say that this crossing generates a square surface: a tangible, measurable entity coming into existence as a result of crossing. The principle can be transferred symbolically to the crossing of any contraries such as the crossing of the male and female which gives birth to the individual being, or the crossing of a warp and weft which gives birth to a cloth surface, or the crossing of darkness and light which gives birth to tangible, visible form, or the crossing of matter and spirit which gives birth to life itself. So the crossing is an action-principle which the square perfectly represents.[77]

Carl Schuster was interested in crossed figures and collected examples from many cultures and time periods (Fig. 3.22).[78] He believed such figures represented the first Man and Woman of the tribe or group—like Adam and Eve—and their crossing signified the act of creation (Fig. 3.23).

The point of crossing was the center or navel of the world where creation began. In some traditions, a square or checkerboard was placed at this point and used for divination. These squares became gaming boards in later periods.[79]

If the intersection of each warp and weft thread represents a human existence then we need only recall the *Njals Saga* to understand the significance of loom weights, used to provide tension for warp threads in some vertical looms.

> A loom has been set up, stretching afar and portending slaughter… and a rain of blood in pouring. Upon it has been stretched a warp of human beings–a warp grey with spears which the valkyries are filling with weft of crimson. The warp is formed of human entrails and is heavily weighted with human heads.[80]

Here each warp thread represents an individual life and the loom weight the head. The fact that the loom weight hangs downward can be explained by the frequent association of inversion with the world of the dead (Fig. 3.24).[81] That is, these figures represent ancestors. Onians comments on this symbolism by noting the commonly repeated saying that a man's life hangs by a thread. He continues:

> A curious parallel to this exists among the Koryaks (N.E. Asia), who believe that the Supreme Being sends down from the sky the souls of departed ancestors to be reborn. He keeps a supply suspended from the cross-beams of the house; and as is the length of a soul's strap so will be the length of his life when he is reborn into the world.[82]

Fig. 3.22: Cast bronze plaque (Merovingian).

Fig. 3.23: Steatite sculpture, Neolithic Cyprus.

Fig. 3.24: Inverted figure on tombstone, Bella Coola, British Columbia.

A single loom weight is never assigned to each warp thread; rather, a cord called a thrum is used to connect several warp thread to a common weight. This brings us closer to the true intent of the symbolism. If each intersection of warp and weft is a life then an individual warp tread, *in toto*, represents a succession of generations from a single group, Several groups are linked to a common head which represents the original ancestor of all of the groups within this "tribe." Put another way, the entire weaving represents the "social fabric," hardly a fortuitous expression.

Each warp thread by itself can be conceived as a spinal column with the weft crossing representing a vertebrae and the loom weight the head. The spine belongs to a cosmic man (Adam, Manu, etc.) who comprises his descendants, one generation after another. This is the same model used for a mnemonic cord where names are associated with each knot. "From great-grandparents to great-grandchildren we are only knots in a string" say the Naskapi of Labrador.[83]

THE LOOM OF LIFE

The sutratman doctrine has managed to survive among a few remote peoples like the Kogi of the Sierra Nevada de Santa Marta in northern Columbia.[84] Weaving and spinning are spiritual activities and occupy a central role in the religious life of the Kogi. Men do the weaving, producing simple, course, cotton garments on an upright loom for themselves and their families (Fig. 3.25).

Fig. 3.25: Kogi Indian man weaving a cloth, Columbia.

> The Kogi are well aware of this technical simplicity and soberness of their dress. Almost all their material possessions, all the artifacts and utensils, are sturdy and devoid of ornamentation. The pottery, the few household goods, and even the houses themselves are bare and undifferentiated. And with an aloof expression their owners will say, "Yes, our things are simple, but they live."[85]

Despite this Shaker-like aesthetic, the objects of daily life are symbolically meaningful, acting as microcosmic models of the universe, the inner life, and the afterlife.

> …these objects or phenomena contain a mass of condensed information, a wealth of associations and meanings that make of each object a storehouse of detailed codes that are linked into interrelated concepts. These objects or phenomena, then, "speak" to the beholder; they can even answer his questions and guide his actions; they are his memory, his points of reference.[86]

The spindle, the loom and the act of weaving itself are central symbols to the Kogi and contain multiple meanings. This is in keeping with the nature of all traditional symbolism where, in the words of Réne Guénon, "the same symbol is always applicable to different levels in virtue of the correspondences that exist between them."[87] Among the Kogi, this symbolism is known to everyone but is understood in depth by only a few.[88] For this reason, a loom is kept in the temple and used for teaching purposes by Kogi priests. An examination of the symbolism of the spindle and loom reveals roots firmly within the ancient sutratman doctrine.

In the Kogi creation myth, it was the Great Mother who first taught men to weave. In the beginning she pushed an upright spindle into the newly created earth in the center of the Sierra Nevada Mountains. This formed the central post or *axis mundi*. Then, drawing a length of yarn from the spindle she drew a circle around the spindle whorl and said, "this shall be the land of my children."[89]

The spindle serves as a model of the cosmos; the flat whorl is the earth on which rests a cone-shaped body of white yarn wound around the world axis (Fig. 3.26). The yarn, described as the "thought of the sun," represents life, light and the masculine seminal element of fertility and growth. The white cone is divided horizontally into four ascending levels that form the Upper World. Underneath the disk rests an invisible, inverted cone of black yarn also divided into four levels that forms the corresponding Lower World.

Fig. 3.26: Kogi spindle.

> The sun, by spiraling around the world, spins the Thread of Life and twists it around the cosmic axis: during the day a left-spun white thread and during the night a right-spun black one.[90]

The Kogi loom consists of a strong rectangular frame reinforced by two cross-poles (Fig. 3.27). The structure forms a Saint Andrew's cross (or hourglass figure) within a four-sided square framework. A number of meanings are associated with this design.

Topographically, the loom is a map of certain features of the Sierra Nevada. The four corners of the square are the four Colombian cities in the region: Santa Marta, Riohacha, Fundación and Valledupar. The center of the square where the cross-poles meet represents the snow peaks. Other geographical landmarks such as rivers can then be located within this conceptual framework.

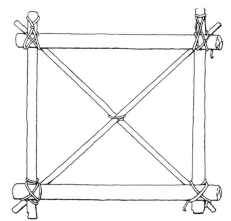

Fig. 3.27: Framework of a Kogi loom.

Anatomically the loom is a model of the human body from the shoulders to the hips. The five points where the wooden pieces are lashed together represent, from the top, the left and right shoulders, the heart in the center, and the left and right hips at the bottom. To represent a loom, a man crosses his arms over his chest with the outstretched fingers of his right hand touching his left shoulder and his left hand touching his right shoulder (Fig. 3.28). This is considered a ritual posture.

The five cross-points are also identified with the five main ceremonial centers of the Kogi founded by the five principal sons of the Mother Goddess. It is these "Lords of the World-Quarters" who rule over the five points of the loom and the human body.[91]

The progenitive power of the solar thread is reflected in the sexual symbolism associated with spinning and weaving. The spindle combines a "male" shaft that pierces a perforated "female" whorl. Further, the Kogi compare the act of weaving to copulation, with the warp thread conceived as the female element and the shuttle the male. Cosmically, Father Sun as Great Weaver uses a beam of impregnating light to weave on the cosmic loom or Mother.

Fig. 3.28: Kogi ritual posture of listening.

In an all-important cosmic vision, complementary to that of the spindle as world axis, the Kogi conceptualize the earth as an immense loom on which the sun weaves the Fabric of Life. This image is patterned after an empirical observation. The Indians are well aware of solstices and equinoxes; as a matter of fact these phenomena are the foundations of their agricultural and ritual calendars, and Kogi priests have considerable astronomical knowledge. The upper bar of the world loom is formed by the line traced between sunrise and sunset at the summer solstice, whereas the lower bar is drawn at the winter solstice. The equinoctial line is the central rod of the loom.[92]

This cosmic vision is enacted yearly within the temple, which serves as the womb of the Mother Goddess.

Fig. 3.29: The main Kogi temple at Takina.

Kogi temples are large, beehive-shaped structures about as tall as they are wide—seven to nine meters—made of wood and grass with a foundation formed of a circle of rough stone slabs (Fig. 3.29). There are two opposing doors generally placed on an east-to-west axis. Two main posts support each half of the building raised on both sides of the central axis. An open pathway runs from east to west. There are four corner posts, placed in the northeast, northwest, southeast and southwest of the temple and 40 to 50 smaller posts circling the walls. Four hearths are located on the radii running from the center of the temple to the main posts.

The temple is a universe in miniature and its construction is based on the same patterns exemplified by the spindle and loom. For example, the Kogi believe that the temple continues underground in an inverted form, in the same way as the spindle has a dark underside. Likewise:

> The four hearths correspond to the four lineages that were founded in the beginning of time by the Four Lords of the World-Quarters who are associated with the four corner posts of the circular periphery of the temple. The fifth lord is associated with the center and has his seat in the middle of the pathway between the two doors, exactly beneath the peak of the conical roof. The fifth lord represents the sun and is the Lord of Fire.[93]

There is a small hole at the top of temple roof normally kept covered with a potsherd. When the priests remove this sherd — generally on the days of the solstice or equinox—a beam of sunlight falls on the temple floor.

> …if this should be done on 21 June, a remarkable phenomenon will occur. At about 9 A.M. a thin ray of sunlight will fall into the dark interior of the temple, and a small brilliant spot will touch the hearth of the southwestern corner. In the course of the day the spot of sunlight will slowly wander across the floor, until, at about 3 P.M., it will have reached the hearth of the southeastern corner and will then disappear. If one were to leave the small orifice uncovered throughout the year, one would be able to watch the slow northward progress of the parallel lines traced by the spot of light until, at the equinox of 21 September, it has reached the equatorial line between the two doors. On 21 December the line will be drawn between the northwestern and northeastern hearths, and in this manner the sun will have delineated the sacred quincuncial space of the temple.[94]

In such a way, the sun weaves the Fabric of Life on the temple floor, which serves as the loom. The warp threads are conceived as part of the loom into which the solar ray puts a single weft thread each day, moving from left to right. As the sun moves through the sky from east to west, the beam moves widdershins, west to east. At the end of each day, the Kogi believe that the light, now referred to as the "black sun," enters the inverted temple beneath the earth where it weaves the underside of the garment, this time moving from right to left. One side of the textile that is produced symbolizes daylight and life, the other, darkness and death.

The sun weaves two such garments a year, one for himself and one for his wife, the moon. They are finished at the spring and fall equinoxes, in March and September.

On these dates the priests begin to dance at the eastern door of the temple and slowly proceed toward the western door, always dancing and gesturing as if they were drawing behind them a rope or a stick. This dance symbolizes the act of drawing out the rod located in the center of the loom. When the priest at last dances out of the western door, he completely draws out the rod; the fabric unfolds toward the north and the south, and the next day the sun begins to weave another piece of cloth, and life continues.[95]

This remarkable application of the sutratman doctrine does not exhaust the symbolic implications of the loom. There are eschatological considerations as well. The St. Andrew's cross formed by the cross-sticks of the loom represents the crossroads of eternity where departed souls await judgment. The soul remains at this juncture until a waft of incense from the Funeral Priest's hand points in the right direction.

> … the X-shaped cross is ever present among the Kogi. It stands for deliverance, for the fate of souls, for obedience to what the Kogi call "The Law of the Mother." It is found in nature and culture, in artifacts and gestures, in fleeting shapes, and in firmly traced lines.[96]

The ultimate goal is to return to the Mother Goddess, but many paths diverge from the crossroads. Souls can go up or descend into the maze-like underworld and lose their way. The soul's destination is determined by the kind of life a person has led. To find the right road in the afterlife a man must fulfill certain spiritual conditions during life, conditions which are not foreign to other religious traditions.

> In the first place, a person must turn *seivake* by becoming "like a boy," an innocent youth. He must be "whole," "complete," and "perfect" like a child. Second, the person must become *nakuiza*, that is, he must renounce all knowledge and must forget everything he has experienced in life. The third condition is that the person must "feel cold" (*sui seisi*), meaning that he must have mastered all emotions, he must be without passion, anger or sorrow.[97]

Lastly, the loom is a place of death, a sacrificial post or Holy Rood. "Crazy Brother (*Due Nugi*), the mythical adulterer, rapist, and incarnation of all vices, was tied to a loom in punishment."[98]

There is an even more ancient level of symbolism that forms the substructure of Kogi culture, centered on the hourglass or X-shaped figure of the Mother Goddess formed by the crosspieces of the loom. Carl Schuster identified such figures as generic ancestors.

AS THE WORLD TURNS

In many traditions the alternation of day and night and the turning of the seasons are symbolized as the working of a cosmic spindle or loom. The symbolism of the spindle is of particular interest since it shares a common form with other simple technologies like the wheel, the fire drill and the milk churn, which employ a similar rotary motion.[99]

The purpose of a spindle is to pull and twist fiber into thread (Fig. 3.30). A simple but ingenious device, it overcomes the problems inherent in producing thread by hand.

Fig. 3.30: Rucuyen woman spinning.

> Thread can be spun with no tools at all, simply by using the fingers to draw out and twist the fibers, perhaps on the thigh or leg as a handy working surface. The method has two disadvantages, however. The twisting process is tediously slow, since each movement of the fingers gives only a few twists to the strands. Moreover, there is a serious problem of keeping the finished part of the yarn from tangling, untwisting, or performing any of an amazing variety of nasty feats the moment you let go of any of it to make more; and let go you must when the yarn reaches arm's length. The thread has to stay constantly under tension until the twist has been permanently set, for example by wetting or plying.[100]

Most spindles consist of a shaft with an impaled flywheel, called a "spindle whorl." In some cultures a mere stick or rock suffices. As Elizabeth Barber points out, the shaft and whorl are really just a combination of these simpler forms.[101] Each part of the spindle serves a different function. The shaft is used to wind the completed thread while the whorl provides the tension and balanced spin that helps to draw and twist the fiber.

The act of spinning is associated with procreation in many cultures, as we saw with the Kogi. The shaft represents the male element and the whorl represents the female (Fig. 3.31). Cosmologically, the spindle also functions as an *axis mundi*, uniting the three worlds and acting as a conduit for the Spirit—solar in origin and often conceived as a ray of light—that endows the newborn with life. The thread may also be conceived as an umbilicus, connecting the child to the Great Mother, everywhere associated with the earth. The raw fiber used in spinning is the *prima materia*, which must be given form.[102] The act of spinning provides this, producing a life. Johannes Wilbert writes:

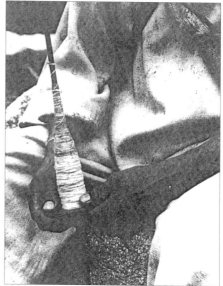

Fig. 3.31: Kogi spindle.

> The representations on Ecuadorian spindle whorls [Fig. 3.32], as well as the insight of Estrada and others that spindle whorls belong to a prehistoric "cult of fertility" in Ecuador, leave no doubt that the ancient artist who created the designs and the women who used them shared with many peoples, past and present, the symbolic meaning of the Magical Spinners, the Parcae, the Whirred Sisters, the Norns, and others. The dynamics of the ever-busy spindle, and its dualistic nature were no secret to them. Almost universally, the spindle-shaped mandorla…is perceived as the product of the conjunction of the sphere of matter (left) and the sphere of spirit (right).[103]

The rotation of the spindle symbolizes the passing of time, another reason for its association with the mysteries of birth and death. Many cultures use the metaphor of the spindle to describe the turning of the heavens around the *axis mundi*. Like the planets in their orbits or the rings of Saturn, the spindle was often thought to contain "whorls within the whorl." These multiple whorls were held accountable for the varying pace of day and night, the

Fig. 3.32: Spindle whorl, Ecuador.

seasons, and the world ages. In Plato's Myth of Er (*Republic*, X.613), the stars and planets are likened to nested bowls turning at different speeds and in different directions around a central shaft. The entire spindle-like device is turned by the Fates, who govern the destinies of souls awaiting rebirth.

The mill embodies the same cosmology in many traditions. The *Bhagavata Purana* relates how prince Dhruva, by virtue of his merit, ascended to the highest pole, "to the exalted seat of Vishnu, round which the starry spheres forever wander, like the upright axle of the corn mill circled without end by the laboring oxen."[104] Dhruva is associated with Polaris, the Pole Star.

> Just as oxen, fastened to a post fixed in the center of a threshing floor, leaving their own stations, go round at shorter, middle or longer distances, similarly fixed on the inside and outside of the circle of time, stars and planets exist, supporting themselves on Dhruva; and propelled by the wind, they range in every direction till the end of a *kalpa*.[105]

From the grinding of grain we move to the churning of liquid; specifically, the Vedic myth of the Churning of the Sea of Milk, a sort of cosmic tug-of-war orchestrated by Vishnu (Fig. 3.33).[106]

Fig. 3.33: Churning of the Sea of Milk, Ankor Wat, Cambodia.

A Cambodian bas-relief at Ankor Wat, represents the mythic theme of the Churning of the Sea of Milk. Here the churning pole pivots on the back of a turtle, twirled by gods & demi-gods pulling alternately on the body of Vasuki, King of Snakes. Two disks representing the sun & moon, identify the lotus stem as the axis of the universe, shown here with the God Vishnu in climbing posture, directing the twirling of the pole.[107]

According to tradition, two churning motions are involved, a slow churning brought on by the motion of the sun and causing the passage of time, and a fast churning centered within the churning stick (*axis mundi*) that produces Soma, the drink of immortality.[108] Since Soma is reserved for the gods, its creation does not occur within time and thus involves no physical motion. The center of the milk churn (or other rotary device) is conceived as immobile and immutable but the source of all motion and rest. All things revolve around it, but it does not participate in the motion, reflecting the basic distinction between time and eternity.[109] The center of the shaft is equivalent to Aristotle's "atomic now" (ατομοσ νυν) from which time flows, or more properly, appears to flow, much as the sun appears to move through the heavens because the world is in motion. In spiritual terms, those who are not "centered" cannot distinguish the manifested world from its unchanging source.

The central shaft is also conceived as the passageway to and from the other worlds. Once the device is set in motion, birth and death are possible. This is why the spindle is sometimes equated with the caduceus, with its upward and downward paths, symbolized by two snakes.

Yet another thought concerning the symbolic meaning of the spindle arises from the image of the accumulating thread coiling itself like a snake around the shaft. This symbol has been understood as one of mediation between earth and heaven. Hermes, the *psychopomp* of Greek mythology, carried it, as did the Roman god Mercury.[110]

The upward and downward paths of the caduceus have their astronomical counterparts in an ancient belief, articulated most clearly in Pythagoreanism and Hinduism, that the wheel of the heavens has two doors, the "gateway of men" and the "gateway of the gods." The gateway of men opens during the summer solstice in the sign of Cancer and facilitates the departure of souls to Heaven. The gate of the gods opens during the winter solstice in the sign of Capricorn and marks the incarnation of souls into bodies.[111]

Fig. 3.34: Large and small prayer-wheels, India.

These same pneumatic counter-currents can be activated when another rotary device, the prayer wheel, is set in motion (Fig. 3.34). Here the spinning carries prayers to heaven and brings back blessings. Often referred to as "Wheels of Time," "Wheels of Life," or "Wheels of Transmigration," prayer wheels are models of the Wheel of Law (*Dharma Chakra*) set in motion by Buddha when he delivered his initial teaching.[112]

Another rotary device reflects the same principles, the drill, used to generate fire—a sacred act—and to drill holes, often for divination purposes.[113] The earliest fire drills were probably simple sticks rotated between the palms. A thong of sinew twisted around the stick made the process easier by converting horizontal motion into rotary motion, the same technique used with the Indian milk churn. This reduced the amount of labor involved. It was then discovered that the ends of the thong could be attached to a bow to make the device even easier to operate. The result was the bow drill, used by Egyptians and Eskimos alike (Fig. 3.36). A last variation, the pump drill employs an up-and-down motion to turn the drill-head, but it seems to have been a later development used primarily for drilling holes (Fig. 3.35). Fire drills were used in Neolithic times, if not earlier, and are found in all parts of the world except Polynesia. (Fire, as every scout knows, can also be made through percussion or by sawing or "plowing" a block of wood.)

As with the spindle, the shaft of the fire drill is meant to represent the *axis mundi* that separates the three worlds and forms the channel through which the Spirit, in its manifestation as fire, is drawn down from Heaven. What is returned is smoke, an offering to the Deity, often associated with the sacrifice of animals or the cremation of human bodies. The needle-like point of the drill is a phallus and the drilling the act of creation.

In the Vedic rite of fire making, two sticks (*arani*) designated male (*uttarani*) and female (*adharani*) are employed. The vertical male stick is inserted into a notch on the horizontal female stick and rotated to produce fire.[114] The ancient Greeks had a similar practice involving sacred fire sticks and attributed the invention of fire making to Hermes, the messenger god.

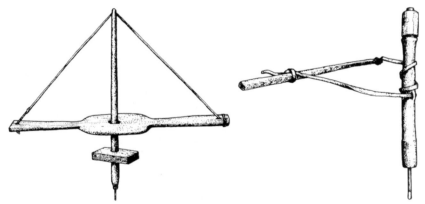

Fig. 3.35: Pump and bow drills.

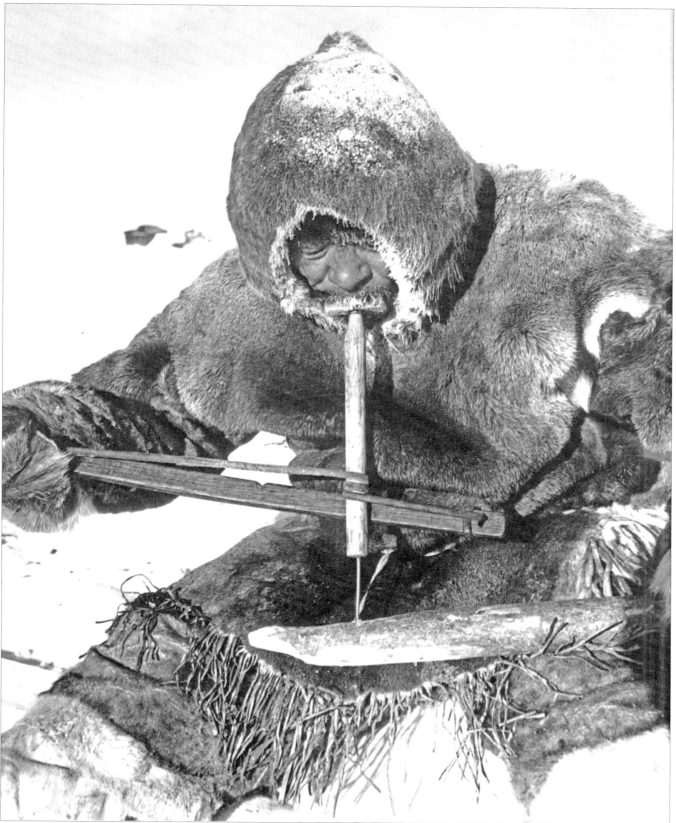

Fig. 3.36: Eskimo with bow drill.

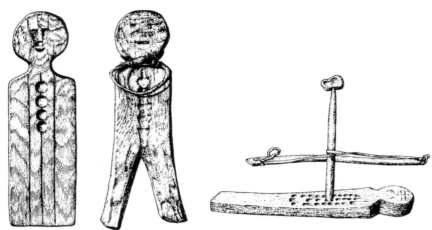

Fig. 3.37: Maritime Koryak fire boards and drill.

The Chukchee and Koryak of Siberia drilled into a board carved in the likeness of the First Ancestor (Fig. 3.37).[115] They believed the creation of the world and the tribe had its origin in a sexual act performed at the base of the *axis mundi*, the center or navel of the world.

Fireboards were also drilled for divination purposes, as were turtle shells in ancient China.[116] We should remember that the turtle also served as the support for the *axis mundi* during the Churning of the Sea of Milk.

The cosmic and procreative symbolism of spindles is also reflected in the designs carved on spindle whorls. Not all whorls are decorated, but those that are often feature designs found on other disk-shaped objects like coins, gambling chips and buzzers (Fig. 3.38).

Fig. 3.38: Hopi Indian buzzer.

Johannes Wilbert's study of designs on spindle whorls from prehistoric Central America revealed a common motif.

Fig. 3.39: Spindle whorl with hockers, Ecuador.

A frequent representation in spindle-whorl iconography is a figure shown with knees apart of the type sometimes described as the "hocker" motif [Fig. 3.39]. Similar figures can be found in the Manteno Culture, carved in low relief and on stone slabs where "the upper end of one surface is dominated by a human or animal figure with the legs and arms bent to one side. The head often fits into a niche in an ornamental frieze with a repetitive geometric pattern. A pair of birds, disks, or monkeys often accompanies the principal figure." (Meggers 1966: 126)[117]

The hocker, as Wibert notes, is often identified with the so-called "heraldic woman" or "shameless woman" motif found widely in Oceanic art and elsewhere, so named because the figure appears to be giving birth or *in coitus* (Fig. 3.40). Such figures appear both in human and animal form.

Fig. 3.40: Painted wooden house gable with hocker, Palau.

In Mexico, the Earth Mother as monstrous toad (Tlalecuhtli), is depicted in the same "hocker" position, emphasizing her creative, birth-giving function just as her claws and fangs symbolize the other side of her dualistic life-death nature. That the "hocker" or squatting position, is in fact symbolic of birth—i.e., creation—is overwhelmingly clear from the depiction of the goddess Tlazolteotl in the *Codex Borbonicus*, where she is shown in the act of giving birth to the young maize god Centéotl.[118]

It fell to Carl Schuster to identify the hocker more precisely as an ancestor figure excerpted from a repeating pattern, and to demonstrate its prehistoric roots. While the squatting position may have come to be associated with birth or coitus this was not its original significance. These meanings are not mutually exclusive, however, in that they both involve generation.

The Tlingit of Alaska sometimes place a large hocker in the center of a wall-screen: its open vagina serves as a threshold to an inner chamber behind the screen. On Salish spindle-whorls, a hocker's vagina or navel often marks the point where the *axis mundi* penetrates This World, linking it to the World Above and the World Below: again, the cosmic threshold [Fig. 3.41]. This symbolism goes on & on, supporting, elaborating beliefs wholly congenial to genealogical iconography.[119]

Fig. 3.41: Salish Indian spindle whorl.

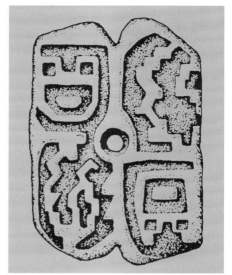

Fig. 3.42: Wooden spindle whorl, Argentina.

Fig. 3.43: Illustration of ofannim from the Winchester Bible.

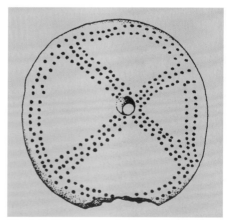

Fig. 3.44: Neolithic perforated and drilled amber disk.

Again we should note that the act of spinning sets these hocker figures in motion, surely a significant element in the design. Carl Schuster found another specimen, a wooden spindle whorl from the San Juan province of Argentina attributed to the Barreales culture (fl. A.D. 500), which reinforces this idea (Fig. 3.42).

Inscribed on this object, which was apparently intended to be rotated around its central hole, are two human-headed mazes in inverse relation to each other. The twirling of the disk (which was evidently a spindle-whorl, perhaps made in imitation of a ritual object) would then have had the effect of facilitating the passage of the soul into the Afterworld.[120]

The two heads represent the point of departure from this world and of arrival in the other. Schuster also linked these human-headed mazes to continuous-line drawings and to the labyrinth motif. These mazes were conceived as ancestors through whom one could pass to enter the World Beyond, if properly prepared. The question of qualification is paramount because the spinning of any rotary device was also seen as a barrier. The two opposing heads of San Juan spindle whorl also act as the clashing rocks, monstrous jaws, or automatic jambs of folklore, which seek to prevent the hero from entering the Other World.[121]

The footless Bhauvana defends the Active Door, and this is described as a revolving razor-edged sun-bright wheel, an engine (*yantra*) "fitly devised by the Gods for the cutting to pieces of Soma-thieves."[122]

In this case, the hawk is swift enough to fly through the spokes in the wheel and eventually obtain the Water of Life that he "twirls" or "grinds" from the rock.[123]

Similarly, in the Kabalistic tradition, the fiery chariot-throne (*Merkabah*) of the Creator is guarded by various hosts of angels including the *ofannim* (wheels) as described in the visions of Ezekiel in the Old Testament (Fig. 3.43).[124]

Louis Raymond, who made a more exhaustive study of the designs carved, incised, or painted on spindle whorls—mostly in the Americas but with some older European examples—found the majority of them to be geometric. Noting that the earliest known spindle whorls date from about 7500 B.C. he suggested that the origins of these designs lay in the more distant past. A Neolithic example from Germany is typical of those found in graves near the south coast of the Baltic Sea (Fig. 3.44).

A review of decorative art found on Paleolithic artifacts such as bone, antlers, ivory and on cave walls show the earliest use of most of the simple, primary geometric motifs found on spindle whorls, even though a time gap exists before the first recorded use of spindle whorls.[125]

These geometric designs include dots, circles, chevrons, zigzags, diamonds, straight and undulating lines, and a variety of other simple forms. A study of Bronze Age spindle whorls from Cyprus revealed many of the same patterns (Fig. 3.45).[126] In keeping with the circular nature of the whorl, designs were often disposed in sections. Human or animals figures were arranged as mirror images, one in each half or quarter of the whorl. Artists also took advantage of the movement of the whirl to create illusionistic effects; lines and dots that transform into human figures or colors that blend to the surprise of the viewer. Children's toys like tops and yo-yos preserve these techniques.[127] In some cases, designs might be hidden from view on the underside of the spindle, meant for the spirits alone, like petroglyphs carved in inaccessible locations.

It was Carl Schuster's belief that these "geometric patterns" were the remnants of an ancient system of linked human-like figures, intended to represent ancestors.[128] He also felt that the halving and quartering of the disks and other circular objects reflected basic social divisions that had an analogous cosmological significance (Fig. 3.46). The spinning facilitated the rebirth of the Spirit (personified in some cultures as an original ancestor), while the figures on the whorl represented the enduring continuity of the group made possible by procreation.

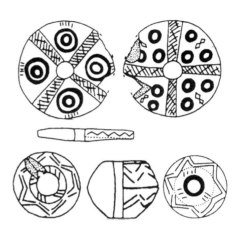

Fig. 3.45: Spindle whorl designs, Bronze Age Cyprus.

Fig. 3.46: Araucanian shamans with drums.

Fig. 3.47: Silk spiders (male and female).

THE SOLAR SPIDER

The spider is an important figure in mythology and folklore. At once a creature of the ground and the air, the spider acts as an intermediary between earth and heaven. In many parts of West and Central Africa the spider plays a major role in the myth of creation, forming the earth and the human race, bringing fire to men and spinning a thread that provides a bridge to heaven. More significantly, the sun itself is described as a spider whose rays form the web of creation.

In Ghana, the ancestor spider is Anansi, who is both messenger and trickster, crafty and malevolent by turns. God as trickster, juggler or stranger is a common theme in folklore and signifies the multiple forms the Deity assumes in the world. As both messenger and trickster Anansi corresponds to the Greek Hermes.

The solar spider also appears in North America. M.E. Opler recounts a birth rite of the Jicarilla Apache in which "a cord of umblemished buckskin, called in the rite a 'spider's rope,' is stretched from the umbilicus of the child towards the sun."[129] Here the progenitive power of the Deity is emphasized as it is in the Hindu and Christian traditions.

> This [the Jicarilla rite] combines the Indian symbolism of the Sun as a spider...whose threads are rays (*sutratman doctrine*), with the concept of the Sun equated with the vivifying Spirit, at the same time that it corresponds exactly to the Orthodox Christian conception of the Nativity, where (as at Palermo and in many Russian ikons) the Madonna is evidently the Earth Goddess, and a (seventh) ray of light extends directly from the (otherwise six-rayed) Sun to the Bambino.[130]

The solar spider represents a variant form of weaving symbolism inasmuch as the web is formed from his own substance just as the universe and all being is an extension of God (Fig. 3.47). The circular form of the web produces a spherical cosmos with the solar spider sitting in the center, like the sun. Further:

> The remarkable perfection of the "spider" symbolism extends to the fact that the radii (warp threads) of the web are not sticky, while the spiral (woof) is adhesive; the spider himself walks only on the radii while the flies are caught on the sticky thread.[131]

In Buddhist and Hindu contexts sense perception depends on contact and he who touches may be caught. This is the "stickfast" motif of folklore found in such diverse writings as the Buddhist *Jatakas* and the Uncle Remus stories, in the figure of the Tar-Baby (Fig. 3.48).[132]

> "All fruitions are contact-born" (*Bhagavad Gita* V.21) Perception is a "grasping," "handling," or "taking hold of" (*grahanam*) of objects, the sense organs themselves are referred to as "graspers" (*graha*), but in their turn are "grasped" (*grhita*) by their objects as "over-graspers," and all these experiences "are the food of Death" (Brhadaranyaka Up. III.1.-10).[133]

Fig. 3.48: Tar-Baby and Brer Rabbit from Uncle Remus.

Our sense life is a thread or ray from God. Its proper object lies not in the pleasures of perception but in the recollection of its source. Like the fly stuck in the spider's web, attachment to the physical world is an entanglement that results in death. Liberty is attained through nonattachment. In the *Maitri Upanishad* the exaltation of the contemplative is compared to the ascent of a spider on his thread.[134] He who would be a "mover-at-will" must untie the bond of individuality and follow the thread back to it's source. "Come into my parlor," said the spider to the fly.

THE CONTINUOUS LINE

Just as the solar spider spins a web from a single unbroken thread, the use of a single line to construct a work of art has a long history and examples can be found in a wide variety of media from sand drawings, to metalwork, to engraving.

> It is of little importance, in the different forms that the symbolism takes, whether it be a thread in the literal sense, a cord, a chain, or a drawn line such as those already mentioned, or a path made by architectural means as in the case of the labyrinth, a path along which the being has to go from one end to the other in order to reach his goal. What is essential in every case is that the line should be unbroken.[135]

Coomaraswamy took up the matter of the continuous line in "The Iconography of Durer's 'Knots' and Leonardo's 'Concatenation'"[136] where he discussed the symbolic meaning of certain knot-work designs found in the engravings of Albrecht Dürer and the works of Leonardo da Vinci.

He began with a wood engraving of Albrecht Dürer's taken from a series, *Sechs Knoten* (Fig. 3.49). In each of the six engravings, the central design is constructed from a single white line on a black ground. Four smaller knot designs, all of them identical, occupy the corners. In each case, a single white line forms an extremely complex series of knot designs that resemble lace work or embroidery patterns. The function of this artistic tour de force is uncertain, but the designs may be patterns intended for use in other media.

In the opinion of many scholars, Dürer's knot designs are variations on a copper engraving attributed to Leonardo Da Vinci that bears the words, "Academia Leonardi Vinci" within the central medallion (Fig. 3.50). In the words of Vasari:

> He [Leonardo] spent much time in making a regular design of a series of knots so that the cord may be traced from one end to the other, the whole filling a round space.[137]

Coomaraswamy noted the similarity between Leonardo's *Concatenation*, as it is called, and the cosmic diagram known as a *mandala*.

> The significance of Leonardo's "decorative puzzle"—which from an Oriental viewpoint must be called a *mandala*—will only be realized if it is regarded as the plane projection of a construction upon which we are looking down from above.[138]

Fig. 3.49: One of Durer's "Sechs Knoten".

Fig. 3.50: Leonardo's "Concatenation".

The dark ground represents the earth, which is associated metaphysically with the substantial, potential aspects of manifestation. The white line is the Spirit, the essential, active aspect of manifestation whose source is the summit or center (Heaven). The four corner ornaments are the cardinal directions and reflect the seasons (time), and the older conception of a quartered universe held together by the Spirit.[139] The whole construction is summarized best in the words of Dante (*Paradiso* XXIX.31-6) to whom the meaning of these esoteric symbols was familiar.

> Co-created was order and inwrought with the substances; and those were the summit in the universe wherein pure act was produced: Pure potentiality held the lowest place; and in the midst potentiality with act strung such a withy as shall never be unwound.[140]

Did Leonardo understand the symbolic meaning of his own work or was he merely copying an older design?

> Leonardo's Concatenation is a geometrical realization of this "universal form." He must have known Dante, and could have taken from him the suggestion for this cryptogram. But there is every reason to believe that Leonardo, like so many other Renaissance scholars, was versed in the Neo-Platonic esoteric tradition, and that he may have been an initiate, familiar with the "mysteries" of the crafts. It is much more likely, then, that Dante and Leonardo both are making use of the old and traditional symbolism of weaving and embroidery.[141]

Fig. 3.51: Coin with labyrinth, Crete.

Coomaraswamy also explored the connection between these knot-work designs and the labyrinth (Fig. 3.51). Several points are of interest. If the continuous line represents the Spirit that connects us to God, then it must be followed back to the center, summit, or door. The labyrinth was trod in much the same spirit by pilgrims who entered these constructions, whether of stone, turf, or traced on a cathedral floor, and paced off the journey to the center. In considering the continuous line as a path, we may also remember that the story of Theseus and the Minotaur includes a thread that served as the means of escape.

Coomaraswamy felt it was significant that both Dürer and Leonardo had inscribed their names in the center of their engravings and noted that the center of the labyrinth at Amiens Cathedral contained an effigy of the architect, in imitation of the mythical Daedalus. This comparison drew fire from the art historian Erwin Panofsky who noted a number of errors including the fact that Amiens Cathedral has no such figure and that Dürer's name does not appear anywhere in the *Sechs Knoten*.[142]

Fig. 3.52: Labyrinth with city towers.

These minor matters aside, the comparison is not without validity. Many labyrinths do have drawings in the center, often of cities (Jericho, Jerusalem, or Troy, for example) (Fig. 3.52) or of mythical monsters like the Minotaur who devour those who reach the center. The point is that the center is the goal and represents the way to other worlds, both above and below.

A second issue is why the lines of the labyrinth never cross each other as the lines in these knot-work designs do. Coomaraswamy answered this question by pointing out that the designs "represent a translation of the idea of a maze into three-dimensional and textile terms.[143] While it is true that these kinds of design move easily from one medium to another, the labyrinth is not a true continuous-line drawing as we shall see, but simply a clever variant of this ancient technique. Deeper connections are revealed by the methods used to construct these complex figures.

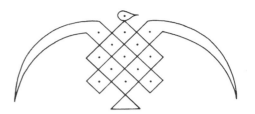

Fig. 3.53: Sand drawing of bird, Angola.

Carl Schuster was interested in continuous-line drawing and collected examples from many cultures (Fig. 3.53). To construct such a drawing, an artist usually begins with a framework of dots and draws an unbroken line through or around them to form a figure or pattern. The essential element, as we noted, is the unbroken nature of the line.

Many continuous-line drawings are created to the accompaniment of chanting or drumming as befits their ritual character (Fig. 3.54). The continuity of the line imparts a sense of motion, a fact that did not go unnoticed by artists like Miro, Klee and Picasso, who borrowed this technique in their own works.[144]

Fig. 3.54: Exorcism of snakes using a serpentine diagram, South India.

Fig. 3.55: Celtic knot-work design.

Fig. 3.56: Sand drawing of a turtle, New Hebrides.

Perhaps the most familiar continuous-line drawings are the knot-work designs of Celtic art (Fig. 3.55) that were used to decorate metalwork, stone monuments, and manuscripts like the famous *Book of Kells*. George Bain, who unraveled the methods used in constructing these complex designs, found their astonishing complexity to be based on a few simple geometrical principles.

> Referring to a page of the "Book of Armagh," Professor J. O. West-wood wrote, "In a space of about a quarter of an inch superficial, I counted with a magnifying glass no less than one hundred and fifty-eight interlacements of a slender ribbon pattern formed of white lines edged with black ones upon a black ground. No wonder that tradition should allege that these unerring lines should have been traced by angels." One of the aims of this book is to show that there is nothing marvellous in a design having not a single irregular interlacement. Indeed, a wrong interlacement would be an impossibility to a designer conversant with the methods. One might as well marvel at a piece of knitting that had not a mistake in its looping.[145]

Another remarkable set of continuous-line drawings was collected in the early part of this century from the New Hebrides, a Melanesian archipelago, by the anthropologists John Layard, Bernard Deacon, and Raymond Firth.[146] A missionary, Ms. M. Hardacre, added several more examples. The drawings were both religious and secular and depicted a variety of subjects including birds, animals, fish, and plants (Fig. 3.56). They were generally drawn for amusement and in some cases, stories were related as the figures were drawn. On the Island of Raga, two sides took turns drawing, each trying to outdo the other.

> …knowledge of the art is entirely limited to men; women, of course, may see the designs. The whole point of the art is to execute the designs perfectly, smoothly, and continuously; to halt in the middle is regarded as an imperfection.[147]

The techniques used to draw these complex figures are handed down from generation to generation and each design is practiced assiduously to ensure mastery. Once learned, the skill remains in the body of the practitioner, like dancing or jumping rope.

The methods of construction used in the New Hebrides are common to the tradition wherever it is found. First a patch of sand or earth is made level and smooth, or an area with volcanic dust may be used. Sometimes ashes are spread on the earth to provide a clean drawing surface. Next, the artist draws a framework consisting of lines set at right angles and crossing one another, or a series of small circles arranged in a regular pattern. This preliminary layout serves as a guide for constructing the drawing. The artist then smoothly traces the curves, circles, and ellipses around or through the guides until the figure is completed.

> In theory, the whole should be done in a single, continuous line which ends where it began; the finger should never be lifted from

the ground, nor should any part of the line be traversed twice. In a very great many of the drawings, this is actually achieved.[148]

In some drawings lines must be retraced to avoid lifting the finger. In others, small details are added to complete the drawing, like a tail feather or eyes. More complex designs may involve several interconnected line drawings.

Of particular interest are those New Hebridean designs that are the property of the secret societies and relate to initiation and the mysteries of life after death. In Vanuatu on Malekula, the second largest island in the group, and elsewhere in the New Hebrides, the home of the dead is reached by an arduous journey.

> Ghosts of the dead…pass along a 'road' to Wies, the land of the dead. At a certain point on their way, they come to a rock…lying in the sea…but formerly it stood upright. The land of the dead is situated vaguely in the wooded open ground behind the rock and is surrounded by a high fence. Always sitting by the rock is a female [guardian] ghost [called] Temes Savsap, and on the ground in front of her is drawn the completed geometrical figure known as *Nahal* [Fig. 3.57], 'The Path'. The path which the ghost must traverse lies between the two halves of this figure. As each ghost comes along the road the guardian ghost hurriedly rubs out half the figure. The ghost now comes up but loses his track and cannot find it. He wanders about searching for a way to get past the guardian ghost of the rock, but in vain. Only a knowledge of the completed geometric figure can release him from the impasse. If he knows this figure, he at once completes the half which Temes Savsap rubbed out; and passes down the track through the middle of the figure. If, however, he does not know the figure, the guardian ghost, seeing he will never find the road, eats him, and he never reaches the abode of the dead.[149]

Among the northern peoples of the New Hebrides, the Lambumbu, Legalag, and Laravat, similar ideas prevail only here the land of the dead is called *Iambi* or *Hambi* and the geometrical figure, 'The Stone of Iambi' (Figure 3.58). Further, no test is required of the traveling soul. Variants of the story are told in Mewn and among the Big Nambas tribe, where the ghost is known as Lisevsep.

Initiates in the secret ghost societies such as those on Ambrim are taught these designs so they may enter the Afterworld when they die. They are also part of a larger cycle of rites.

> A key dance in the Malekulan cycle of ceremonies represents, simultaneously, a sacred marriage, an initiation rite and, most important of all, the Journey of the Dead. At one point, participants enact a swimming movement to represent the crossing of the channel to the land of the dead. In the final movement, Maki-men form in two rows: then members of the introducing 'line', already fully initiated, thread their way between these ranks. This progression of initiates corresponds with the path followed by the dead man through the maze-like design *Nahal*.[150]

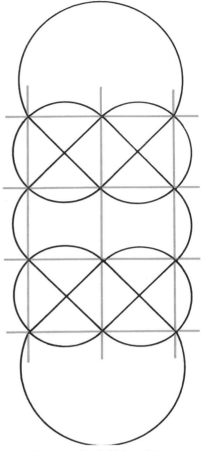

Fig. 3.57: Drawing of *Nahal* (The Path), New Hebrides.

Fig. 3.58: Geometric figure called the "Stone of Iambi," New Hebrides.

101

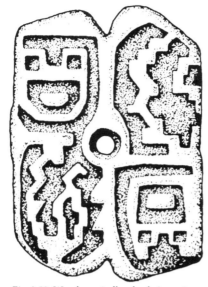

Fig. 3.59: Wooden spindle whorl, Argentina.

It was the anthropologist John Layard who first noticed the link between the Malekulan drawings and dances and the classical labyrinth.[151] Like the Malekulan examples, the labyrinth was both drawn on the ground and walked or danced in. It was also constructed in a manner similar to the Malekulan figures, as we shall see later.

The Malekulan figures also appear to have two heads, linking them to the San Juan spindle whorl, with its two human-headed mazes (Fig. 3.59). All of these images are related to death and rebirth, characterized by the passage from one world to the next.

Continuous-line drawings are also common in the southeastern part of India where they still drawn today (Fig. 3.60). The Tamils refer to such drawings as *kolams* and they are drawn in front of dwellings, normally before sunrise. The woman of the house will smear a bit of ground with cow dung or sweep the threshold and sprinkle it with water to prepare her canvas. In the past, rice powder was run between the fingers to form the design. Quartz powder is used today. Dots or crossed lines are used as a framework and the *kolam* is formed from a single, uninterrupted line. Traditional designs are strictly geometrical though more naturalistic forms have developed in modern times. Similar designs are also found as tattoos and on mortuary pottery.

Fig. 3.61: *Rangoli* of bird, India.

Fig. 3.60: Woman drawing threshold design, South India.

In Northern India, figures called *rangoli* or *rangavalli* are drawn in courtyards, on the walls of buildings, and at places of worship (Fig. 3.61). *Rangoli* designs tend to be more elaborate than *kolams* and are often multicolored. Elaborate floral or animal designs are drawn using the fingers or brushes. Many of the older designs are geometric, however, and bear the telltale dots and guide lines.

In Africa we find numerous examples among the Bantu speaking tribes of Angola, Zaire, and Zambia. Paulus Gerdes has documented these drawings, called *sona* by the Tchokwe, and analyzed the tradition as a whole, both in Africa and elsewhere (Fig. 3.62).[152]

The continuous line also survived in Scotland, where M. M. Banks documented it in 1935.[153] In some rural areas, housewives traced such patterns in pipe clay on thresholds, the floors of houses, and in dairies and byres. The designs, not all of which were continuous line drawings, were refreshed each morning and were thought to keep away ghosts or evil spirits. One elderly woman in Galloway said that her grandmother had explained the tradition with a couplet:

> Tangled threid and rowan seed
> Gar the witches lose (or lowse) their speed

The technique was also known in ancient Mesopotamia as evidenced by a number of serpent designs engraved on argillite cylinder seals from the 3rd millennium (Fig. 3.63). While the serpent is not constructed from a continuous line, its shape indicates that the artist was familiar with the dot-and-line method common to the tradition.

Another interesting example from ancient Babylonia is made of clay and appears to be constructed from a single coil.

> One popular method of divining the future was to examine the entrails of a sacrificial animal. This Babylonian baked clay plaque from Sippar, dating to about 700 BC, illustrates one such examination and on the other side the interpretation of the omen is recorded. The face is identified as belonging to the demon Humbaba, who was slain by the epic hero Gilgamesh.[154]

Here we find the familiar equation of the intestines, human or animal, with the underworld and by extension with the labyrinth, due to their convoluted but unicursal form.

This Greek vase provide further proof of the ubiquity of this ancient art form (Fig. 3.64).

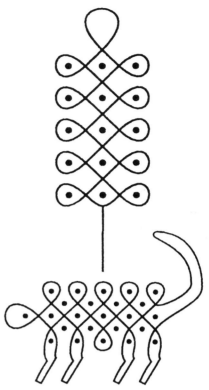

Fig. 3.62: Animal drawings, Angola.

Fig. 3.63: Drawing of snake, Mesopotamia.

Fig. 3.64: Greek vase, 8th century B.C.

STRING FIGURES

String figures are known on every inhabited continent and show evidence of the greatest antiquity. Americans are most familiar with the game called cat's cradle in which a string is looped in a cradle-like pattern on the fingers of one person's hands and transferred to the hands of another to form a new pattern. In fact, cat's cradle is but one variant of an art that while simple in principle, is far more complex in practice.

To create a string figure, a loop of string, fiber, hair, sinew, bark, or other pliable material is manipulated to form patterns using the hands, feet, mouth, knees and even teeth (Figs. 3.65 and 3.66). The art is practiced alone or by several people. In the hands of a skilled practitioner, the loop of fiber can be manipulated to create complex figures that transform to illustrate a story or song or to prepare the viewer for a sudden denouement. Completed patterns may represent objects in the natural environment like plants and animals, activities such as hunting or fishing, or geometric patterns such as diamonds or zigzags. There are also tricks in which the completed pattern resolves suddenly into a continuous loop, or "catches," in which a figure tightens suddenly around the finger of an unsuspecting participant.

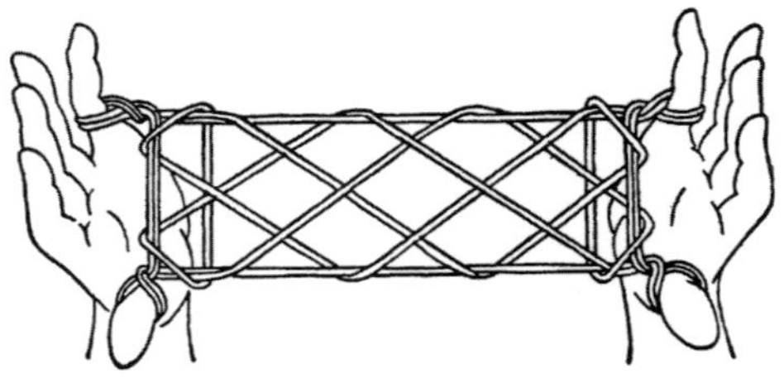

Though the name assigned to a given string figure may vary, certain patterns are nearly universal; others are restricted to a given place or culture. Like music, there are standard openings and progressions fundamental to the art and variations on these patterns. The same string figure can be made in different ways.

Though many practice the art, male and female, young and old, a master of the form must combine the legerdemain of the professional magician with the singing and story-telling art of the bard or shaman. String figures are at once an amusement, a lesson to help the young remember, a means to illustrate stories and myths, and a doorway for initiates into the mysteries of death and rebirth.

Our historical knowledge of string figures dates roughly from the middle of the 19th century when anthropologists began to take an interest in the practices and pastimes of non-western cultures. An extensive literature has developed on the subject.[155] Both scholars and practitioners of the art have identified and classified a large number of figures, their methods of construction and geographical distribution. They have also sought to determine what meaning they have, beyond mere amusement, for the people who make them.

Starting with the assumption that the string represents the Spirit, the artist in string is in a position to re-create the world in microcosm. Like Proteus or the other shape-shifters of mythology, the string can be transformed from one figure into another. It is the drama of human existence that is on display. When the game is over, everything returns to the endless loop so the play may begin anew.

String figures are closely related to continuous-line drawings. The loop of string is the three-dimensional equivalent of the continuous line, used to

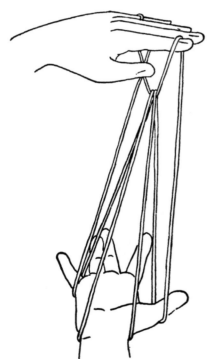

Fig. 3.65: Method of constructing a string figure.

Fig. 3.66: String figure called "Teepee" or "Tent".

create a pattern in the sand. In some cultures, completed string figures are actually removed from the hands and placed on the ground, emphasizing this connection. Both forms are used for storytelling and both once had deeper meanings centered on death and rebirth.

Among the Cahuilla Indians, the string figure played the same role as the sand drawing did among the Malekulans.

> Moon also taught the people to play what we call Cats' Cradle — a string figure game and a predictive technique necessary to know in order for the soul, it was said, to get into Telmekish, the land of the dead (Hooper 1920: 360). They had to know many figures because as the soul traveled to the land of the dead they had to tell Montak-wet, the shaman-person who guarded the entrance to Telmekish, what they meant. If they couldn't tell him, they would not be admitted. The same game, a favorite recreation for Cahuilla women, could predict the sex of a child.[156]

A similar story is related concerning the residents of the Gilbert Islands.

> Prayers and incantations accompanied the making of string figures in the Gilbert Islands, as in other cultures. In Gilbertese mythology two notables were associated with string figures, *Na Ubwebwe* and *Na Areau* the Trickster (Maude & Maude 1958:9). Not only did *Na Ubwebwe* use sympathetic magic in the assistance of creation, but he also smoothed the way for the dead.

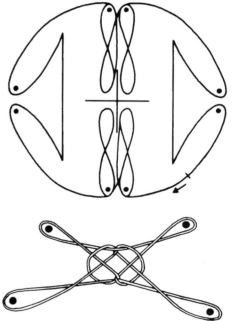

Fig. 3.67: Framework for constructing continuous-line drawings and string figures.

> At the ceremony known as *tabe atu* (the lifting of the head) an individual described as the "straightener of the path" performed a series of string figures beside the corpse. The figures included *Tangi ni Wenei* (The Wailing Over the Dead), (Maude & Maude 1958:25). On the way to the land of the departed ancestors the spirit meets a woman with the beak of a bird, *Nei Karamakuna*. Unless the spirit has been tattooed, in which case the tattoo marks are pecked out, the eyes will be pecked out instead. Naturally most Gilbertese take the precaution of being tattooed. Soon after meeting *Nei Karamaku-na* the spirit meets *Na Ubwebwe* who makes a series of string figures with him or her. The spirit must make the series without a mistake until the first figure, called *Na Ubwebwe*, appears again. Only then can the spirit "pass on." The authors conclude that whether the sequence for one player used at the raising of the heavens, or the series performed by two persons during the *tabe atu* ceremony, "the figure *of Na Ubwebwe* is made as a rites de passage connected with death." (Maude & Maude 1958:10).[157]

String figures also resemble continuous-line drawings in their manner of construction (Fig. 3.67). Instead of guiding dots drawn on the ground, the finger joints (or other body parts) serve as the guides around which the string passes. The essential point is that the guiding dots used to construct continuous-line drawings were also once understood as body joints. Joint marks are the link between the various versions of the sutratman. The line is the Spirit connecting the joints and reanimating the being.

Fig. 3.68: Shang Dynasty inscription, China.

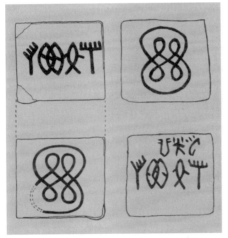

Fig. 3.69: Copper plates from Mohenjo-Daro, Pakistan.

Fig. 3.70 Theseus killing the Minotaur.

Carl Schuster was particularly interested in a continuous-line drawing that appears in a Shang Dynasty inscription from the 13th century B.C. (Fig. 3.68). According to Carl Henzte, it represents an archaic form of the Chinese character, *hsi*, "to bind" which comprises two elements: a simplified hand (shown at the top) and a skein of silk thread.[158] There is also a two-handed version of the inscription that developed into the Chinese character *luan*, "to bring into order," by adding another element that means "speech". A similar development led to the modern Chinese character, *tzu*, meaning "concept, speech, expression, written composition." It would seem that the ancient Chinese associated the idea of spoken and written communication with the endlessly looped cord. Hendtz explains:

> Therefore, something must have been spoken while the skein of silk was brought into order; or else the putting into order of the skein was in itself an action somehow equivalent to a sign-language or the expression of a concept. This reminds us inevitably of the thread-games ['string figures' or 'cats' cradles'], known to us especially from Polynesia.... Indeed, the function of the thread-game is in a sense mnemonic, in so far as the production of each figure was accompanied by the recital of a specific chant or mythological story, which was then acted out. Today the thread-game is unknown in China. But was it unknown in ancient times? ... The *I-Ching* (Book of Changes) mentions a kind of knot writing.[159]

Was the development of writing derived from the use of mnemonic devices like continuous-line drawings and string figures? Schuster found some evidence to support this contention among the Bataks of Indonesia and more significantly in the writing or proto-writing found at Mohenjo-Daro (Fig. 3.69). A similar design appears on seals used in Egypt between 1800 and 1600 B.C. and even earlier as a pictograph.[160]

MAZES AND LABYRINTHS

Although the origins of the labyrinth are unknown, mythology and archeology both connect it to the Minoan-Mycenaean culture of ancient Greece. The story of Theseus, Ariadne and the labyrinth of King Minos has many versions, and forms part of a cycle of stories centered around Theseus, the hero of Athens.[161] It is best known to modern readers from Plutarch's (A.D. 46–120) *Parallel Lives of the Greeks and Romans* where it is included in a life of Theseus. The story, or at least certain episodes within it, dates from an earlier time and is mentioned in one form or another in Homer, Hesiod, and Sappho, among others. Artistic representations of the events in the story are also numerous and date from as early as the Archaic period (8th century B.C.) (Fig. 3.70).

In its general form, the story fits a pattern that is found in many myths involving the descent of the hero into the Other World and his adventures there.

> In the *Odyssey* Odysseus goes among the ghosts to meet his mother and Teireseas. In most Greek myths the hero descends to recover a goddess of life, Persephone, Helen, or Ariadne. But in the epic of *Gilgamesh* it is an ancestor whom Gilgamesh seeks, to gain immortal secrets from him.[162]

Fig. 3.71: Grotto of the Sibyl.

What these stories have in common is an underlying motif of death and rebirth. While the labyrinth does not figure in all of these tales, it does play a role in a number of them. In his *Cumaen Gates*, W. Jackson Knight relates an episode from the *Aeneid* (VI, 9-44) where Aeneas visits the Temple of Apollo at Cumae to gain entrance to the underworld so that he may visit his dead father, Anchises. On the gate outside the temple is a picture of the Cretan labyrinth. Beyond is the cave of the Cumaen Sibyl, who guards the entrance to the land of the dead (Fig. 3.71). Knight notes the similarities to the practices of the Malekulans (Fig. 3.72).

> The Malekulans and Vergil have these elements in common. To reach the land of the dead, a cave near the sea shore, guarded by a female guardian, is entered. Clearly the sibyl corresponds with Temes Savsap. Near the entrance is a maze or labyrinth which delays the journey. Only those who are qualified may enter and qualifications depend on ritual, wholly or partly.[163]

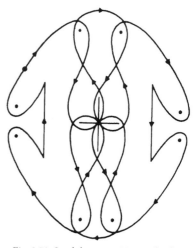

Fig. 3.72: Sand drawings, New Hebrides.

René Guénon, in his review of *Cumaen Gates*, clarifies the relation between the funerary and initiatic aspects of the cave, which is partly misunderstood by Knight.

> In fact, strictly speaking, there is only a preparation for initiation in death to the profane world, followed by a 'descent into Hell,' which is, of course, the same thing as the journey in the subterranean world to which the cave gives access; as for initiation itself, far from being considered a death, it is on the contrary like a 'second birth,' as well as like a passage from darkness to light.[164]

There is more to the underworld than a place of death and burial. The journey underground is normally followed by a trip in the open air, which many cultures, including the Malekulan, represented as a navigation. This would correspond, in our case, to the trip taken by Theseus and Ariadne by ship after their escape from the labyrinth. In some traditions, the stages of this voyage are equated with spiritual progress.

> This would indeed be inconceivable if it were only a question of a vivid description of a ritual inhumation; but it becomes perfectly comprehensible when we know that it is in reality a question of the various phases passed through by the being in the course of a navigation that is truly 'beyond the grave,' and which in no way concerns the body which it has left behind in quitting terrestrial life.[165]

The initiatic use of caves may date from Paleolithic times. Caves are conceived as places of birth and death, both wombs and tombs, and many traditional peoples relate how their ancestors arose from a hole in the ground. If the earth is our mother then the analogy of caves and wombs is a natural one. Creation begins in darkness and initiates must return to the place of their birth to be reborn. From this perspective, Ariadne's thread is an umbilical cord.[166] The same ideas are found in North America.

> Hopi Indians call the labyrinth, *tapu'at*, 'Mother and Child'. They say its path leads to rebirth and they liken its form to the enfoldment of the unborn child by its mother. A parallel is provided by their *kiva*, a sacred underground chamber sometimes referred to as 'Earth Mother'. A small hole in its floor represents the womb, or Place of Emergence from the preceding world; and a ladder leading out through its roof represents, as the Hopi say, the umbilical cord to the succeeding world which the soul follows to achieve another Emergence. Enactment of the Emergence is given during the *Wu-wuchin* ritual, when initiates undergo spiritual rebirth.[167]

Like the sacred *omphalos* at Delphi, the umbilicus also marks the center of the world, the point at which the labyrinth is located. Ariadne's thread is comparable to Blake's golden cord that leads the elect into the door built in Jerusalem's wall. The labyrinth is often depicted as a city and associated by name with sacred centers such as Jerusalem, Troy, and Knossos (Fig. 3.73). The placement of the labyrinth on medieval church floors has the same significance; it allows the devout to simulate a pilgrimage to the Holy Land by treading its path.

Fig. 3.73: *Rangoli* of labyrinth with castle in center.

Fig. 3.74: Labyrinth drawing, India.

Before any serious discussion of the labyrinth is possible it is first necessary to distinguish it from a maze. A labyrinth is unicursal; it is impossible to get lost in one since its path, despite its wanderings, leads inexorably to the center (Fig. 3.74).

A maze is full of twists, turns, and dead ends. It is specifically designed to confuse the poor souls caught within it and prevent them from finding their way out. The Labyrinth of Minos was really a maze or Theseus would have had no need of Ariadne's thread to find his way.

> Today the word 'labyrinth', at least in common speech, is used in-
> terchangeably with 'maze', though they differ in all significant ways.
> In any true labyrinth, participants must cover the entire ground by
> one pathway, and one pathway only. That pathway must include,
> just before the center, a sudden switch back, caused by the upper
> part of the cross. Nothing should block that path, nor should any
> openings appear in its 'walls', as do occur in both mazes and gapped
> circles. The mystique (or perhaps just involvement) of the labyrinth
> depends upon a sense of drawing nearer & nearer to the center, yet
> each time being forced away. Even when you approach the center,
> you are unaware how close it is, for a 'wall' theoretically hides it from
> view. You must go on & on, drawing closer, turning back, then sud-
> denly you make a small, quick turn—and you are there![168]

The word "labyrinth" is of unknown origin but the root word *la* may denote "stone," as in the Greek *laos* and the Latin *lapis*.[169] A labyrinth may have referred originally to a large stone monument or building, but we cannot be certain.[170] By classical times the word had come to have a fairly general significance and was used by Pliny to denote any formal, winding path.

> It had long been used in a metaphorical sense, even as we find Plato,
> over four centuries earlier, employing it to describe an elaborate argu-
> ment. We also find it applied by extension to other objects, such as
> traps for fish, to judge by a certain passage in the works of Theocritus.[171]

How the labyrinth and maze became conflated is not entirely clear but the confusion is an old one. Speaking about the Labyrinth of Crete, Pliny wrote:

> We must not compare this to what we see traced upon our mosaic pavements or to the mazes formed in the fields for the entertainment of children, and thus suppose it to be a narrow path along which we may walk for many miles together, but we must picture to ourselves an edifice with many doors and galleys which mislead the visitor…[172]

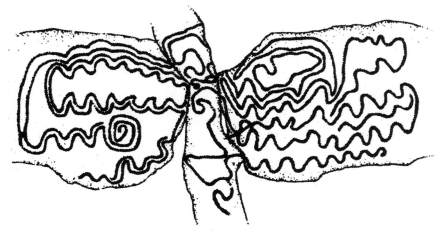

Fig. 3.75: Maze engraved on a tomb lintel, Ireland.

The maze is clearly the older of the two forms. Maze-like patterns have been found on cave walls from prehistoric times (Fig. 3.75).[173] The subterranean world with all its sinuous passages and dead ends is the original model for the maze. Until Arthur Evans discovered the Palace of Knossos at the turn of the century, most people—including the local Cretans—believed that the real Labyrinth of Minos was located in the cave of Gortyna.

> As early as 1632, Sandys, in his notes on Ovid, already quoted, records that although Pliny says that no trace of the Labyrinth survived, 'yet at this day the inhabitants undertake to show it to strangers. For between the ruins of Gortina and Grossius, at the foot of Mt. Ida, are many Meanders, hewn out of the rock underground, in so much as not to be entered without a conductor. I have heard a merchant say, who had seen it, that it was so intricate and vast, that a guide who for twenty years together had shown it to others there lost himself and was never more heard of.'[174]

Crete is full of caves many of which were used as burial chambers in ancient times. The geologist George Wunderlich makes a convincing case that Evan's Palace of Minos was really a necropolis, a kind of man-made cave serving both as a place of burial for the nobility and a shrine to their memories.[175] Similar burial practices prevailed both in Egypt and Etruria where they were also associated with megalithic structures.

A number of ancient writers describe a famous Egyptian labyrinth at Lake Moeris, which according to Herodotus, served as a meeting place for the twelve kings of Egypt who reigned after the death of Sethos.

It has twelve covered courts—six in a row facing north, six south—the gates of the one range exactly fronting the gates of the other, with a continuous wall around the outside of the whole. Inside, the building is of two storeys and contains three thousand rooms, of which half are underground, and the other half directly above them. I was taken through the rooms in the upper storey, so what I shall say of them is from my own observation, but the underground ones I can speak of only from report, because the Egyptians in charge refused to let me see them, as they contain the tombs of the kings who built the labyrinth, and also the tombs of the sacred crocodiles.[176]

Flinders Petrie discovered the actual site in 1888 at the ancient town of Arsinoë and attributed its construction to King Amenemhat III (fl. 2300 B.C.). We can assume that it was the maze-like character of the rooms and its association with the dead that caused the building to be characterized as a labyrinth. The fact that crocodiles where buried there is also of some significance since the labyrinth often features some kind of devouring creature in the center.

Pliny mentions a number of other maze-like structures including one built on the island of Samos by Theodorus and another on Lemnos built after an Egyptian model by Smilis of Aegina.[177]

The Etruscans were also familiar with the form as we know from Pliny's description—borrowed from Varro—of the tomb of the famous Etruscan general Lars Porsena, at Clusium. It was a large, square monument of dressed stones that covered some kind of mazed burial chamber.

We also have the famous Etruscan wine jar, found at Tragliatella, incised with a traditional labyrinth design from which mounted horsemen emerge, apparently engaged in the *Lusus Troiae* (Game of Troy) described in Book 5 of the *Aeneid* (Fig. 3.76). This equestrian maneuver was performed by the patrician youths of Rome after a funeral. Virgil describes their movement on horseback as resembling the windings of the Cretan labyrinth. The anthropologist Edmund Carpenter, following the work of Petrikovits, suggests that the riders followed the pattern of a labyrinth drawn on the earth beforehand (Fig. 3.77).

Fig. 3.76: Tragliatella vase with detail of horseman.

Fig. 3.77: Hypothetical reconstruction of *Lusus Troiae* based on one method of drawing the labyrinth.

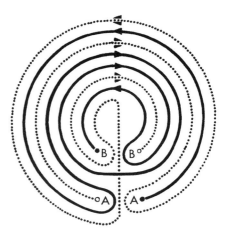

Petrikovits argues that the plan of the *Lusus Troiae* was the plan of the labyrinth as it appears in the Tragiatella vase, and that the course followed by the two groups of riders in this military exercise was that described by the lines of the design, not by the spaces between the lines. The two teams of riders begin at the two points marked A, and end at the two points marked B. Since the distances traveled are unequal, presumably the group that traveled the shorter distance advanced more slowly, while the other quickened its pace, so that both arrived at the end points simultaneously, for a dramatic finale.[178]

Seneca referred to the *Lusus Troiae* as an annual rite of purification that needed to be performed so that the dead did not return.[179] This is interesting in light of what is known about mazes, but it does not describe the function of the labyrinth.

Similar military equestrian maneuvers based on formal diagrams were also practiced in 14th century Mamluk Egypt and in India where they are described in the *Mahabharata*.[180]

In a related vein, Jackson Knight suggested that the maze form itself was used as a means of defense or protection at the entrance of ancient cities like Troy, and equally to defend forts and tombs.[181] Perhaps the intention was military or merely to keep looters away from the tombs. In either case, the practical application developed from the underlying spiritual principle as René Guénon noted.

> …we have simply to remember that this 'labyrinthine' mode of defense was used not only against human enemies, but also against hostile psychic influences, which clearly indicates that it must have had in itself a ritual value.[182]

The purpose of a maze—in contrast to a labyrinth—was to keep the dead from coming back to bother the living. Claude Lévi-Strauss relates a relevant story in *Tristes Tropiques*:

> As we drew nearer to the trees, we reached the object of our visit—a gravel pit where peasants had recently discovered fragments of pottery. I felt the thick earthenware, which was unmistakably of Tupi origin, because of the white outer coating edged with red and the delicate black tracery, representing, so it is said, a maze intended to confuse the evil spirits looking for the human remains which used to be preserved in these urns.[183]

In many Meso-American cultures it was thought that the wicked could be mazed in the underworld so their souls would not return. The Aztecs, like the Mayas, believed that while the celestial house—of which their own houses were models—was woven in a straight, orderly, and measured way, the "evil knotted earth" was a twisted and tangled web in which one could become ensnared.

The Chilam Balam of Tizimin refers to the "many roads that lead to death" during the times of injustice, and contrasts the obviously straight and vertical "good roads" by which the dead can ascend quickly to heaven, with the "evil roads" that descend, spreading out on the earth. Ultimately, the latter led to the land of the dead in the thick of the underworld, a place described by Sahagún as having "no outlets and no openings."[184]

In general, the Meso-American deities or monsters of the underworld were depicted with nets and snares useful for catching evil-doers or other persons unworthy of reaching heaven.

Sometimes, the undulant forms that describe the underworld are aquatic plants; in other instances, the material cannot be identified. What seems to have mattered was not the substance, but its unruly condition. The Popol Vuh describes the jaguars of hell, for example, as "all tangled up"…squeezed together in a rage," while one Aztec god was named Acolnahuácatl "The One From the Twisted Region," according to Caso.[185]

The twisted underworld was also associated with the human intestines, an idea that is not as strange as it might seem. If the underworld is conceived as the body of a god, or a god in animal form, and death is a kind of devouring, then the dead must pass through the intestines of this primordial creature. The analogy is also based on the coiled and snake-like appearance of the human intestines and on the purifying role they play within the body. The Aztec goddess of lust and sexual perversity, *Tlazolteotl*, was called "the eater of ordure." Those who confessed to her had their sins transformed by her digestive system into fertilizer.[186] We are also told that the Aztec underworld was a kind of digestive system located deep within the "bowels of the earth" (an expression we still use) where dwelled monstrous crocodiles not unlike those found in Egyptian or Sumerian mythology.

Another aspect of the same complex of ideas can be found in the use of animal or human entrails for telling the future. Generally it was the liver and intestines that were used. The Etruscan and Roman *haruspices* are the best-known examples but the practice was once common worldwide.

The Babylonians divined in this manner and recorded the results on the back of baked clay tablets (Fig. 3.78). A number of these have survived from about 1000 B.C. They depict maze-like patterns on the front; one is inscribed *ekal tirani*, "palace of the intestines."[187] In ancient Egypt, the dead king was eviscerated and his entrails put into Canopic jars. According to W. Jackson Knight, the bearers of the Canopic jars within the pyramids performed evolutions symbolizing the twisting path of the intestines they were carrying.[188]

Fig. 3.78: Babylonian tablets showing entrail divination.

The intestines also play a role in both Eskimo and Tibetan mythology. *Totanguak*, the Spirit of String Figures, creates string figures using his own intestines. (String figures were sometimes used for divination.) The Tibetan sorcerer and saint Boktè disembowels himself in front of a crowd of priests and pilgrims and uses his own entrails to answer questions and foretell the future.[189]

The origins of the labyrinth are lost to us. It may have begun as an esoteric symbol whose meaning and method of construction were restricted to initiates. If this is the case, it probably existed for millennia before it appeared in a public setting. The earliest dateable labyrinth is from Pylos, Greece (c. 1200 B.C.), a product of the Minoan-Mycenaean culture (Fig. 3.79). It was found on the back of a clay tablet the front of which was inscribed with Linear B writing. Despite the legend of Theseus and the association of the labyrinth with Crete, there are no other Mycenaean examples.

Fig. 3.80: Coins with labyrinth design, Crete.

Fig. 3.79: Labyrinth on a Linear B tablet with detail, Greece.

It is not until classical times that we find the symbol reappearing on Greek soil. The coins issued by the city of Knossos provide the best examples, in both square and round form, dating from 400 B.C. to 67 B.C. (Fig. 3.80).

Examples from the Camonica Valley in the Italian Alps may be older than those in Greece but they cannot be dated (Fig. 3.81). Many are really spirals or debased forms, but a number show a human or demonic figure in the center, an important element in the tradition.

> In certain cases a demon is represented in abstract and stylized manner, as a labyrinth whose twistings end at the center of the image in two dots standing for eyes; a third dot sometimes marks the mouth or the nose. These are probably monsters comparable to those of ancient Greece; the legend of the Minotaur doubtless draws its origins from this kind of concept. Sometimes the monster is pictured within the labyrinth; sometimes he seems to be one with it, to be himself the labyrinth. These figures are very common in the rock carvings of Scandinavia, and they constitute one of the principle subjects of the Atlantic megalithic art which stretches from Galicia in Spain to Brittany and Ireland.[190]

Fig. 3.81: Petroglyph from the Camonica Valley, Italy.

Carl Schuster found a suggestive example jabbed on a ladle excavated in Southern Denmark and dated from the early 3rd millennium

(Fig. 3.82). Not a true labyrinth, it is close enough to suggest that its creator was familiar with the design but didn't have the skill to re-create it. This is thoroughly in keeping with the history of the motif.

> The procedure is simple—literally child's play in many parts of the world. Still, relatively few persons, seeing the design drawn according to this scheme for the first time, are able to reproduce it accurately. The blunders which most people make today are precisely the blunders that have been made for thousands of years, in many parts of the world. In fact, this motif has been more often bungled than made correctly—and those blunders are themselves illuminating.[191]

A variety of simplified forms exist, closer to mazes or gapped circles (Fig. 3.83). The most common mistake is the enlargement of the entrance, significant in itself, for many labyrinths were constructed to be entered.

The labyrinth motif is widely distributed and is found in Europe, India, Southeast Asia, parts of Oceania (often in a debased form), North America, Mexico, and perhaps South America—though definitive proof is lacking. Labyrinths constructed of rocks or boulders were once common, particularly in Scandinavia. Many are large enough to enter and were probably used for rituals or games in which the participants walked or danced along the path between the boulders.[192] Labyrinths, mazes, and other cosmic diagrams cut from turf were used in the same way. Shakespeare writes in *A Midsummer Night's Dream* (2:1):

> The nine men's morris is filled up with mud
> And the quaint [cunning] mazes in the wanton green
> For lack of tread are indistinguishable

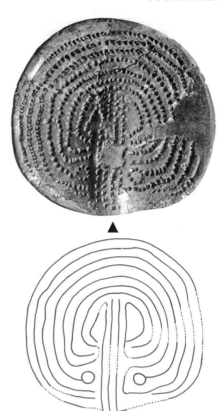

Fig. 3.82: Ladle with jabbed decoration with detail, Denmark.

Fig. 3.83: Labyrinth carved on a bed-board, Iceland.

115

Fig. 3.84: Boulder labyrinth, England.

Fig. 3.85: Sandstone carving of labyrinth, Arizona.

Fig. 3.86: Church fresco, Finland.

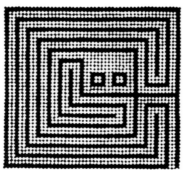

Fig. 3.87: Detail of a woven grass mat, Sri Lanka.

Many examples survived in the British Isles (Fig. 3.84); referred to by the local inhabitants under a variety of names including Troy Towns, Julian's Bower, Mizmaze, and Shepherd's Race. We cannot be sure what kinds of games were played there as no precise descriptions have survived. It is likely that they were threaded as part of seasonal festivals, or used for dancing or other merrymaking.

Examples from North America, such as those found among the Yaqui Indians of Sonora, Mexico, and the Pima of Arizona differ in no significant way from European examples (Fig. 3.85). Some are incised on rocks while other larger examples are constructed of rocks or boulders. In more recent times, the Pima, Hopi, and Papago used the design on trays and baskets. We don't know how old the motif is in North America because rock carvings cannot be dated but Carl Schuster believed that the design was part of the cultural heritage of these peoples and not learned from Europeans.

The labyrinth, like the maze, is associated with the underworld and the afterlife. In many traditions, it is the home of some kind of monster or primordial ancestor who acts as a gatekeeper, restricting access to the Other World.

People who make the labyrinth often describe it as the refuge of some legendary rogue. The Finns have such a story [Fig. 3.86]. So do the Pima of Arizona. In India, the labyrinth is known as the domain of the demon Ravana, while the Bataks of Sumatra explain their version of this design as the refuge of the trickster Djonaha. In the Caucasus, the labyrinth is known as the dwelling of Syrdon, a *nart* or legendary ancestral hero. And in Crete, it served as the lair of the Minotaur, that monster—half-bull, half-human—who was given an annual tribute of seven youths and seven maidens.[193]

As we have seen, what is clear from the idea of a tangled and intestine-like underworld is that the monster does not so much live inside the labyrinth, as it *is* the labyrinth (Fig. 3.87). That is to say, passage through its body is required to effect rebirth. A few examples will suffice.

The Seneca Indians described *Kaistoanea*, a two-headed serpent (shown here with one head) and denizen of the underworld who devoured the inhabitants of a hilltop village, except for one warrior and his sister (Fig. 3.88). They killed him and he vomited forth his victims alive.[194] A related story from the Kwakiutl of Cape Scott tells of a sea monster that swallowed tribesmen when they were out canoeing. One day, a chief walking near the seashore meets Kosa, a young girl, and asks her to fetch water for him to drink. She is afraid of the sea monster but agrees.

> As soon as she agreed to obey, she put her *Sisiutl* belt on, and the vampire instantly killed her. The chief, a wizard, sang an incantation which caused the beast to burst open and disgorge all the people it had devoured. Coming back to life, they limped forward or tripped sideways; their bones were all mixed up. But the chief soon sorted them out, and they became the present Koskimo tribe.[195]

Fig. 3.88: Drawing titled "Seneca Legend of Bare Hill".

Fig. 3.89: Vessel depicting T'ao-tieh, China.

The mixed-up bones of the tribesmen are an important element in the story as we will see shortly.

T'ao-tieh (Glutton), a mythic bear or tiger according to the ancient Chinese, vomited forth "the whole of humanity from the abyss of Chaos (Fig. 3.89)."[196]

In Australia, the Walbiri describe the mythic serpent Warombi, which travels underground and is the source of life (Fig. 3.90). He swallows initiates and returns them as men.[197]

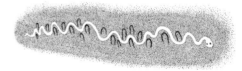

Fig. 3.90: Pictograph of Warombi, Australia.

And in the Judeo-Christian tradition Jonah is reborn from the belly of the whale crying, "Salvation is of the Lord."

The challenge is to pass through this primordial creature without being destroyed.[198] Rites of initiation prepare the young for the ordeal and ensure a safe passage to the Other World upon death. This generally involves the learning of some kind of esoteric information of which the labyrinth design seems to be a remnant. The relationship of the labyrinth to continuous-line drawings, cat's cradles, and other sacred diagrams is revealed most clearly in its method of construction.

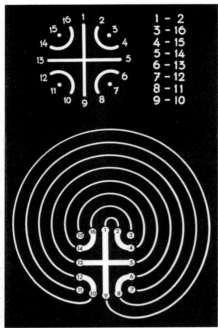

Fig. 3.91: Drawing the labyrinth using a framework.

Fig. 3.92: Hollywood Stone, Ireland.

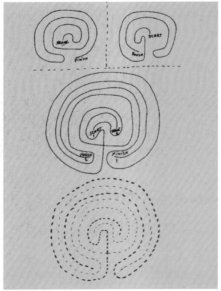

Fig. 3.93: Letter from William Denton with diagrams.

CONSTRUCTING THE LABYRINTH

It was the American scholar Carl Schuster who first understood that the key to the labyrinth lay in its method of construction. His extensive research revealed several strategies for drawing the design. The most common employs a preliminary framework built from a cross, four arcs, and four dots within each arc. Once the framework is in place, the rest is simple (Fig. 3.91):

> Connect any of the four ends of the cross with the nearest end of an arc, either on the right or on the left; and thereafter connect the following dot with the next position on the other side of the diagram, and so on in orderly progression until the design is completed.[199]

There is a satisfying rhythm to the process as the hand completes successive movements from one side of the diagram to the other. The method is easy to learn and execute, which accounts for its widespread diffusion and survival.

> The design is drawn in precisely this way by school children in Finland, Sweden & Ireland; housewives in southern India; Batak sorcerers in Sumatra; and American Indians in southwestern United States, Mexico & Brazil. There is good reason to believe it has been drawn in this way, though not exclusively this way, wherever the motif is known.[200]

Despite its ubiquity, Schuster was not convinced that this was the original method for drawing the labyrinth, feeling that the arcs and dots were really just guidelines for novices who were learning to make the figure. Ever resourceful, he had a friend place an article in the *Irish Press* (January 9, 1952) asking readers if they knew how to draw the labyrinth depicted on the famous Hollywood Stone, in County Wicklow (Fig. 3.92).

He received twenty responses; all but one used the cross-arc-dots method, but the lone exception proved to be of some importance. A man named William Denton wrote and recalled that as a boy, an elderly Dubliner who knew all kinds of tricks and puzzles had shown him and his friends how to draw the figure using just two lines (Fig. 3.93). He included a drawing illustrating the method. Schuster was intrigued and recalled a prior discussion with John Layard.

> The old Dubliner's method was the method suggested to Schuster by John Layard, when Carl showed him the four-dot method, common in so many parts of the world. ...Layard pointed out that one essential feature of all such designs is that they be drawn by means of continuous lines, without raising the hand.[201]

While the Old Dubliner's method is not a true continuous-line drawing, it is closer in spirit than the cross-arc-dots method. Further, the two points of departure and arrival formed by the two lines are consistent with the two paths taken by the horsemen in the Game of Troy and with the two human-headed mazes found on the San Juan spindle whorl. Schuster wrote to a friend, "To me the Dublin story rings true. It's disturbing, of course, that we seem to have only one person as a carrier of this tradition, but I still believe it is a bona fide survival of one ancient method of drawing the labyrinth."[202]

Fig. 3.94: Four-line method for drawing the labyrinth.

Schuyler Cammann, Professor of East Asian Studies at the University of Pennsylvania and an old friend of Schuster's, also felt that the dots and arcs were not part of the original design. He pointed out that the labyrinth could be constructed without the arcs, by using a cross and four dots and drawing four lines (Fig. 3.94).

This would help to explain the familiar Bronze Age motif of the cross with four dots, often found on personal rings and protective amulets in the Near East and Central Asia (Fig. 3.95). The same designs also appear as rock carvings in Shipaulovi, Arizona, in the same vicinity as labyrinth designs. Cammann thought this might be an abbreviated form of the labyrinth, understood only by those who shared the secret of its construction.

A last method for drawing the labyrinth starts with a cross but includes twelve dots, three within each quarter (Fig. 3.96). Four lines are needed to complete the figure, one from each end of the cross.

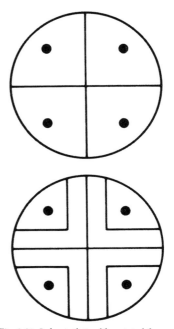

Fig. 3.95: Labyrinth in abbreviated form.

Fig. 3.96: Twelve-dot method for drawing the labyrinth.

Fig. 3.97: Joint-marked ancestor figures.

The twelve dots represent the primary joints that make up the human body. In keeping with the sutratman doctrine, the connection of these joints by means of a Spirit-line amounts to a re-animation or "re-membering" of an ancestor figure in whatever form it is conceived (human, reptilian, or avian) (Fig. 3.97).

It was Carl Schuster's contention that joint marks—often in the form of faces or eyes—represented the souls of primary ancestors. To achieve re-union with one's ancestors and thereby qualify for rebirth, all the joints must be connected with a continuous line to form an image of the First One or Original Ancestor.

> Thus a genealogical diagram, in the form of a human image, serves as a path to be followed into the Afterworld, by tracing one's origins, as it were, through the pattern of one's ancestors, commonly shown as joint marks.[203]

The notion of a dismembered First Ancestor or other religious figure from whom all beings are descended is among the oldest and most widespread of human beliefs. Commenting on the task of the Masonic Masters to "diffuse the light and to gather that which is scattered," Réne Guénon makes reference to the Hindu tradition.

> 'what has been scattered' is the dismembered body of the primordial Purusha who was divided at the first sacrifice accomplished by the Devas at the beginning, and from whom, by this very division, were born all manifested beings....The Purusha is identical with Prajapati, 'the lord of beings brought forth', all of whom have issued forth from him and are thus considered in a certain sense his progeny.[204]

The same story is told of Osiris and Dionysius whose reintegration forms the basis of their respective religious traditions. One need only remember that cannibalism lies at the root of the Vedic and Christian rituals of communion.

> By devouring, or as we may phrase it in the present connection, drinking Makha-Soma, Indra appropriates the fallen hero's desirable qualities by an incorporation that is at the same time sacrificial and Eucharistic, cf. John VI.56, "He that eateth my flesh and drinketh my blood, dwelleth in me, and I in him." [205]

In earlier times, the "host" was treated as an honored guest, later to be sacrificed and eaten. The Latin word *hostis* (enemy) is related to *hospes* (guest), expressing this ambiguity. More directly, the related Sanskrit root *ghas* means to eat, consume, or destroy.

> And what is the essential in the Sacrifice? In the first place, to divide, and in the second to reunite. He being One, becomes or is made into Many, and being Many becomes again or is put together again as One. The breaking of bread is a division of Christ's body made in order that we may be "all builded together in him."[206]

The Hebrew Kabalists preserve the tradition in a slightly different but recognizable form.

> ...though here it is no longer really a question of either sacrifice or of murder, but rather of a kind of 'disintegration', the consequences of which are, moreover, the same—it was from the fragmentation of the body of Adam Kadmon that the Universe was formed with all the beings that it contains, so that these are like particles of this body, their reintegration into unity corresponding to the reconstitution of Adam Kadmon, who is 'Universal Man'...[207]

The re-membering of an ancestor figure is at once an act of personal, social, and cosmic reintegration, as well as a preparation for the life beyond. As a ritual, it found expression in a wide variety of forms.

> Joint-marks varied in number, twelve being a complete set (shoulders, elbows, wrists, hips, knees, ankles). Generally fewer were shown. Ideally all were reached in clockwise order. When the last joint was reached, and image was turned and the ritual repeated; or, if the image was a ground drawing, the performer turned, as in hopscotch. The first sequence 're-membered' the Guardian of the Lower World; the second 're-membered' the Guardian of the Upper World.[208]

In terms of social organization, division by twelve was quite common in antiquity. In the Old Testament (Exodus 24:4), Moses erects an altar surrounded by twelve pillars, representing the twelve tribes of Israel. A similar story is repeated in the Book of Joshua (4:1-24) where twelve stones are erected at Gilgal in memory of the crossing of the Jordon on dry land. The Hebrew word *gilgal* comes from a root word meaning "rolling" or "turning" so that the stones might be considered as spokes in a wheel. There are actually a number of cities so named in the Old Testament and one, north of Bethel, was the scene of Elijah's departure to heaven in a fiery chariot (2 Kings 2:1-11).

In Kabalistic thought, each Hebrew tribe is associated with a zodiacal sign. The idea of a nation comprising twelve tribes was known to a wide variety of peoples including the Greeks and Celts, and Christ had twelve disciples, adumbrated by the twelve fruits of the Tree of Jesse.[209]

Astronomical and calendrical preoccupations were superimposed on this older idea of dismemberment starting in the 4th millennium. Birth and death mark the passage of time and body joints arranged in a circular fashion became both clocks and calendars.

Fig. 3.98: Wooden peg-calendar, Yakut, Siberia.

The Christian Yakut of Siberia created peg-calendars within the framework of a two-headed bird (Fig. 3.98). A peg was moved from hole to hole, clockwise, to mark the passage of the week. The circular form was meant to represent the sun, placed in the chest of the solar bird that guards the sundoor or entrance to Heaven. The two heads represent darkness and light, night and day, death and life. Clocks were given the same form. The division of

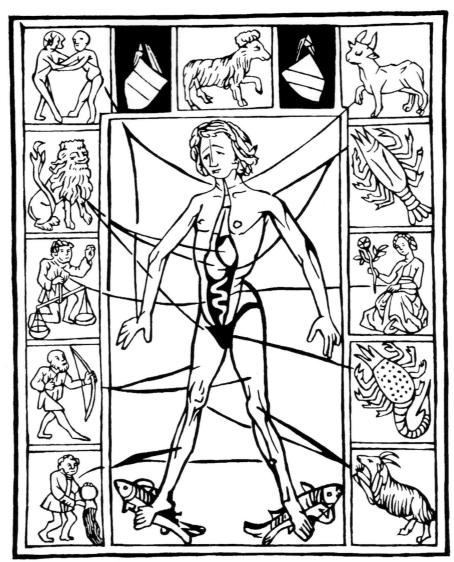

Fig. 3.99: Woodcut of zodiac-man.

the equinoctial day into twelve hours of light and twelve hours of darkness is attributed to the Egyptians but the roots are clearly much older.

The same pattern was reflected astronomically as evidenced in the once common belief that the constellations represent a dismembered ancestor, whose body was strewn across the sky. The twelve signs of the zodiac were conceived as body joints that the sun touched in turn to complete a yearly cycle. The cycle was personified as the World Man or World Year in some traditions.

> Prajapati is, of course, the Year (*samvatsara*, passim); as such, his partition is the distinction of times from the principle of Time; his "joints (*parvani*)" are the junctions of day and night, of the two halves of the month, and of the seasons ....In the same way Ahi-Vr-tra, whom Indra cuts up into "joints (*parvani*, RV iv.19.3, viii.6.13, viii.7.23, etc.)" was originally "jointless" or "inarticulate (*aparvah*, RV iv.19.3)," i.e., "endless (*anantah*)."[210]

We find an echo of these ancient ideas in the words of Shakespeare's Hamlet (Act 1, Scene 5):

> The time is out of joint, O cursed spite,
> That ever I was born to set it right.

A medieval astrological chart shows the same underlying pattern (Fig. 3.99).

> ...a cosmic figure marked with twelve zodiacal signs divided into four categories according to Season & Direction. Each sign, representing a 'temperament' from its category, marked a location corresponding to a primary joint. Such signs were also conceived as constellations, scattered across the heavens. Re-membering this dis-membered figure meant reassembly of its members: the tribal body made One; reembodiment of God and Cosmos.[211]

Initiates must know how to complete the labyrinth design—or a related diagram, string figure, or other exercise—in order to ensure a safe passage into the Afterworld and a successful rebirth. This initiation is itself conceived as a kind of death and rebirth for which the participant must be prepared. The figure to be drawn is at once a mythical ancestor, a devouring creature, and the path to the Other World. The monster *is* the labyrinth in the most basic sense; death the devourer who swallows and regurgitates initiates. To pass through the beast one moves from joint to joint much as one completes the diagram. Many Chinese dragons are joint-marked in this way.[212]

Mircea Eliade describes a Koryak tale "in which a girl lets a cannibal monster eat her so that she can quickly descend to the underworld and return to earth, with all the rest of the cannibal's victims, before the 'road of the dead' closes." He goes on to note that:

> this tale preserves, with astonishing consistency, several initiatory motifs: passage to the underworld by the stomach of a monster; search for innocent victims and their rescue; the road to the beyond that opens and shuts in a few seconds.[213]

KNOTS, JOINTS AND ANCESTORS

We have looked at a lot of evidence and it points to certain inescapable conclusions that may be summarized as follows: knots are equivalent to joints; joints are equivalent to ancestors. Thus, *knots equal ancestors*. A brief recapitulation will help clarify the matter. It will also prepare us for the work of Carl Schuster, which provides a broader context for this remarkable bit of cultural history.

• Knotted cords are used to remember ancestors. In keeping with the sutratman doctrine, each knot represents a unique individual who is an incarnation of the Spirit of the First Ancestor, represented by the cord itself. The same symbolism applies to weaving where the warp threads represent the eternal and the woof threads the phenomenal. Each intersection forms a life. In either case, a cord or thread can represent a given tribe or group, or the society as a whole. In the major religions, the thread-spirit is an extension of God.

- Counting systems have their origin in the touching of body parts (fingers, toes, joints) in a fixed order. The use of terms like the Latin *articulus*, and the suffixes *konta, ginta, kosi, ginti* connect the use of knots and joints as counting devices.

- Knotted cords and body joints are also used as mnemonic devices for teaching music, surveying, and other skills.

- Binding and kinship are closely related as is evident from many marriage ceremonies. The Sanskrit *bandhu-h* is a "kinsman."

- String figures are constructed by connecting body joints with a cord, meant to represent the Spirit. Continuous-line drawings use a framework of holes punched in the ground, meant to represent body joints. The object is to connect the joints and re-member the First Ancestor.

- Puppets and dolls are jointed in imitation of the human body. Many cultures once believed that humans were the animated puppets of God. Man is held together by a thread-spirit and death is an unstringing, causing the body to come apart at the joints (the "knots" of the body).

- The creation of the manifested world is seen as the dismemberment of a mythic figure or "World Man" in many traditions. Similarly, a dismembered First Ancestor, thrown into the sky, forms the underlying structure of the zodiac, with its twelve signs. Each sign represents a joint through which the sun passes to complete the yearly cycle.

- In some traditions creation begins with a "jointless" snake that is cut or chopped into sections to create the form and measure that characterizes the physical world. This "articulation" is reflected in the measures of music, dance, and song.

There is also evidence in language, that great repository of ancient ideas. The reconstructed Indo-European root *ar*, to "fit together," contains many of the meanings we have been discussing, including "art," *articulus* (Lat. joint), and *aristos* (Gk. best, most fitting), as well as the Greek *arthron* (joint), which provides the English "harmony" and "arithmetic." In summary, the notion of an ordered presentation or arrangement refers ultimately to the articulated nature of the human body. "Man is the measure of all things."

ENDNOTES

1. In A. K. Coomaraswamy's "The Iconography of Durer's 'Knots' and Leonardo's 'Concatenation,'" p. 115.

2. René Guénon, *Fundamental Symbols*, p. 278.

3. A. K. Coomaraswamy, *Time and Eternity*, p. 77.

4. Ibid., p. 76.

5. René Guénon discusses the related motif of double-edged weapons including the Lance of Achilles, which both causes and heals wounds. *Fundamental Symbols*, pp. 124-128.

6. Ibid., p. 423.

7. Ibid., p. 408, ft. 1.

8. Mircea Eliade, "The God who Binds and the Symbolism of Knots," *Images and Symbols*, pp. 92-124.

9. Coomaraswamy, *Collected Works*, I, pp. 296-297.

10. Ibid., p. 467.

11. Coomaraswamy, *The Bugbear of Literacy*, p. 108, nt. 7.

12. Coomaraswamy, *Collected Works*, I, p. 467.

13. Plotinus, *The Enneads*, p. 590.

14. *Jaiminiya Upanishad Brahmana* (ii.9.10) and *Maitri Upanishad* (vi.26).

15. Diogenes Laertius, VIII.28, quoted from Coomaraswamy, *The Bugbear of Literacy*, p. 109, ft. 18.

16. See Coomaraswamy, "Spiritual Paternity and the Puppet Complex," in *The Bugbear of Literacy*.

17. In the *Sarabhanga Jataka,* the act is performed by the Bodhisattva Jotipala ("Keeper of the Light"), where it is referred to as the "threading of the circle." See Coomaraswamy, *Collected Works*, I, pp. 442-443 and "The Symbolism of Archery" in *What is Civilization?* For other versions, see Stith Thompson, *Motif-Index of Folk-Literature.*

18. There is a connection here to the central candle on the Jewish menorah that is used to light the other candles.

19. Coomaraswamy, *The Bugbear of Literacy*, pp. 99-100.

20. Plato, *Laws*, bk. 1, 644D, LCL, translated by R.G. Bury. Coomaraswamy emends the translation as indicated in brackets. The original reads "the public law of the State." See *Collected Works*, II, p. 368, n. 110 for an explanation.

21. *Marcus Aurelius*, XII.19, LCL, translated by C.R. Haines.

22. Ibid., X.38. Cf. III.16, VI.16, VII.3, and VII.29.

23. Rumi, *Divan*, Ode XXXVI. Quoted from Coomaraswamy, *Collected Works*, II, p. 149, ft. 3.

24. D. B. MacDonald, *The Hebrew Philosophical Genius*, pp. 133-134.

25. *Mahabharata, Udyoga Parvan* 32:12; quoted from Coomaraswamy, *The Bugbear of Literacy*, p. 111, ft. 40.

26. *Brhadaranyaka Upanishad* III:7.1; quoted from Coomaraswamy, *The Bugbear of Literacy*, p. 111, ft. 41.

27. *Iliad*, VIII.18 ff. Translation by E.V. Rieu. Plato comments on this passage in *Theaetetus* (153): "And shall I add to this the all-compelling and crowning argument that Homer by 'the golden chain' refers to nothing else than the sun, and means that so long as the heavens and the sun go round everything exists and is preserved among both gods and men, but if the motion should stop, as if bound fast, everything would be destroyed and would, as the saying is, be turned upside down."

28. Gershom Scholem, *Major Trends in Jewish Mysticism*, p. 92.

29. A. B. Cook, *Zeus*, vol. II, p. 1029.

30. Ether is considered the substance and abode of the Supreme Deity in many traditions including the Greek, Hebrew and Vedic. It is equated with

the Logos or Word of God, which unites the contraries and holds the world in its embrace. See Réne Guénon, "The Ether in the Heart," in *Fundamental Symbols* and Coomaraswamy, *Guardians of the Sundoor*, "The Concept of 'Ether' in Greek and Indian Cosmology."

31. *Complete Poetry and Prose of William Blake*, Jerusalem 3: "To the Christians," p. 231.

32. Mircea Eliade, *Shamanism*, pp. 338-339.

33. *Maitri Upanishad* 1:4; quoted from Coomaraswamy, *The Bugbear of Literacy*, p. 111, ft. 38.

34. Sophocles, *Oedipus at Colonus*, 1720; Shakespeare, *Hamlet*, III, I, 64. See R.B. Onians, op. cit., p. 436 and passim.

35. Dante, *Paradiso*, Canto 1, lines 109-117. Translation by Laurence Binyon. The Italian reads: "Questi nei cor mortali e permotore, Questi la terra in se stringe."

36. Paul Oskar Kristeller, *The Philosophy of Marsilio Ficino*, translated by Virginia Conant, p. 116.

37. The dryness of the bones is emphasized because life is everywhere associated with water or other liquids (sap, tears, semen, oil, fat, marrow) while aging and death are associated with dryness. See Onians, op. cit., pp. 261-263. More specifically, these ideas are part of an ancient water cosmology explained by Coomaraswamy in *Yaksas* (p. 110): "...from the primeval Waters arose the Plants, from Plants all other beings, in particular the gods, men, and cattle. *Rasa*, as an essence of the Waters, or as sap in trees, is variously identified with soma, *amrta*, semen, milk, rain, honey, mead (*madhu*) and liquor (*sura*). There is a cycle in which the vital energy passes from heaven through the waters, plants, cattle and other typically virile or productive animals and man, thence ultimately returning to the waters."

The same conception is found in Porphyry's *De Antro Nympharum* where the Naiades, water nymphs, are associated with generation and birth and where souls are described as attracted to moisture in the same way as plants depend on moisture for survival.

38. The Creator, as Divine Artificer, may be represented in a variety of ways. Symbolically, the material world is a "wood" in which we may or may not be lost as Dante noted, and that Jesus was not coincidentally, a carpenter. He is also depicted as an architect. The traditional doctrine of art is discussed by Coomaraswamy in a number of works including *The Christian and Oriental Philosophy of Art* and *The Transformation of Nature in Art*.

39. See Kate Elderkin, "Jointed Dolls in Antiquity". For a general review of the literary evidence for dolls and marionettes in ancient Egypt, Greece, and Rome, see Charles Magnin, *Histoire des marionnettes en Europe*.

40. See Miguel Covarrubias, *Island Bali*, pp. 366-367 and Paul Wirz, *Der Totenkult auf Bali*.

41. Jerome Feldman, *Arc of the Ancestors*, p. 29.

42. See Ernst Robert Curtius, *European Literature and the Latin Middle Ages*, pp. 138-139, for examples including Plato, Seneca, Horace, Clement of Alexandria and St. Augustine.

43. Coomaraswamy, *The Bugbear of Literacy*, p. 111, ft. 38.

44. Bruno Snell, *The Discovery of the Mind*, pp. 5-7.

45. Gregory Bateson and Margaret Mead, *Balinese Character*, p. 15.

46. Ibid., p. 17.

47. Ibid., p. 17.

48. Gregory Bateson, *A Sacred Unity* (1991), p. 86. Perhaps we find echoes of these ideas in the fragments of Empedocles, where he describes the

genesis of humans by the aggregation of isolated organs. See John Burnett, *Early Greek Philosophy*, fragments 58-63.

The reason for the placement of an eye at each joint of the Multiple Soldier will become clear when we discuss the work of Carl Schuster.

49. Coomaraswamy, *The Bugbear of Literacy*, p. 97.

50. R. B. Onians, op. cit., p. 303.

51. These are not mere figures of speech as Onians points out "but allusions to one of the images under which a whole people interpreted life and saw the workings of fate, the action of the gods in things human...." Coomaraswamy called them "figures of thought" and demonstrated that they constituted a symbolic 'language' that was everywhere consistent and could be understood. René Guénon and Carl Schuster shared these basic assumptions.

52. See R. B. Onians, "On the Knees of the Gods," *Classical Review*, Feb., 1924.

53. The gods act providentially and atemporally, a point that confuses Onians, who tries to assign a temporal sequence to their actions. There is no predestination here. In the more fully articulated Hindu, Buddhist and Christian doctrines of fate and Providence, fate is described as residing in created causes themselves, which Aristotle and the Scholastic philosophers termed "mediate causes." Men have free will but are subject to the cause and effect relations governing the material world. God is only involved providentially, as First Cause. We tend to think of a man's fate as his end but as Coomaraswamy notes, the word is plural in Latin (*fata*), which suggests *all the things that happen to him*. In Greek mythology, the Fates are conceived as powers of Zeus over whom he has no direct control. "But it is essential to the conception that the allotment once made be respected. There is a moral sanction intrin-

sic in it. *Aisa* is the expression of an ordered world, 'measure' that should be observed…. Thus it is that Zeus is restrained. He cannot play 'fast and loose'." *Origins of European Thought*, p. 390. Similarly, in the Bible we are told that the world was made according to form and measure.

54. Pindar makes them bridal attendants of Themis during her marriage to Zeus while a third version describes them as the children of Erebus (Hades) and Nyx (Night).

55. R. B. Onians, op. cit., pp. 355-356.

56. *Beowulf*, lines 698, 1077.

57. Ibid., p. 269.

58. Coomaraswamy, *Collected Works*, I, p. 484. Coomaraswamy adds a footnote (nt. 95): "More vivid, too, inasmuch as 'in Indian vehicles the different parts are held together by cords' (Eggeling on SB XIII.2.7.8), and *ratha* as the typical 'vehicle' is employed throughout the Indian tradition as a valid symbol of the bodily 'vehicle' of the Spirit."

59. In *De Antro Nympharum* Porphyry provides a Neo-Platonic interpretation of a passage from Homer where Odysseus describes the Cave of the Nymphs in Ithaca. Within the cave—meant to represent the world—the nymphs weave purple cloth upon looms of stone, which Porphyry likens to the act of generation. The purple cloth is flesh and blood, while the stone looms are the bones of men.

60. Coomaraswamy, "The Iconography of Durer's 'Knots' and Leonardo's 'Concatenation,'" op. cit., p. 120.

61. Réne Guénon, *Fundamental Symbols*, p. 231.

62. See also, Mircea Eliade, "The 'God Who Binds' and the Symbolism of Knots" in *Images and Symbols*, pp. 92-124. It is believed in many cultures that the dead may be netted, snared, tangled, or mazed in the underworld and never reach Heaven.

63. Réne Guénon, op. cit., p, 232.

64. For an explanation of the "vital knot," which plays a role in the guild system and in sacred architecture, see Réne Guénon, *Fundamental Symbols*, p, 232.

65. B. L. Joseph, *Shakespeare's Eden*, p. 254.

66. Coomaraswamy, "The Iconography of Durer's 'Knots' and Leonardo's 'Concatenation,'" op. cit., p. 117.

67. Lions' heads often appear on doorknockers. The ring hanging from the lion's mouth is the entrance to heaven. The snakes surrounding the gorgon's head are solar rays.

68. Coomaraswamy, *The Bugbear of Literacy*, p. 95.

69. See Coomaraswamy, "The Symbolism of Archery," pp. 105-119. Similarly, the shuttle of the loom is an arrow and the *kairos* the entrance to heaven.

70. See E. Barber, *Prehistoric Textiles* and Marta Hoffman, *The Warp Weighted Loom* for a history of weaving and looms. Vertical looms are generally subdivided into two classes: tapestry looms and warp-weighted looms. The tapestry loom has two beams; the weaver sits and beats the weft threads down. The warp-weighted loom has one beam; the weaver walks about and beats the weft threads upward.

71. Ibid., p. 81.

72. See H. Ling Roth, "Ancient Egyptian and Greek Looms" and Otis Tufton Mason, *Aboriginal Indian Basketry*.

73. Coomaraswamy, *Collected Works*, II, p. 415, ft. 13.

74. Compare the burning bush of the Old Testament (Exodus 3:1). See Edmund Carpenter, *Social Symbolism in Ancient & Tribal Art*, vol. 2, bk. 1, pp. 93c-95. Note also the traditional etymology connecting the Latin *ignis* (fire) and *lignis* (wood). The ancients were fond of rooting out these hidden connections between words. Such etymologies would hardly satisfy a modern linguist, but they are significant from the perspective of traditional symbolism.

75. René Guénon, *Symbolism of the Cross*, p. 67.

76. The cross is the proper setting for the crucifixion of Jesus in that the vertical and the horizontal beams represent respectively his Divine and human natures.

77. Robert Lawlor, *Sacred Geometry*, p. 24. In the same regard, 'In the Sumerian number sequence, "one" and "two" have the meaning "man" and "woman," respectively.' Menninger, *Number Words and Number Symbols*, p. 13.

78. Edmund Carpenter, op. cit., vol. 1, bk. 1, pp. 239-251.

79. George Santillana associated these crossed figures with the Babylonian constellation *I-Iku* (the Pegasus Square) with its flanking fishes (*Hamlet's Mill*, Appendix 39). The *I-Iku* was the standard field measure of the Sumerians, which makes the association quite reasonable. His assertions that myth has its origins in astronomy are not convincing. These myths predate astronomy by thousands of years and the fact that they become incorporated into astronomy should not be allowed to confuse the issue. Traditional symbolism has its roots in the observation of the physical world but this does not make it science.

80. R. B. Onians, op. cit., pp. 355-356.

81. See Edmund Carpenter, op. cit., vol. 3, bk. 3, for a discussion of inversion; in particular, the use of inverted human figurines to represent ancestors.

82. R. B. Onians, op. cit., pp. 349,

ft. 5. For similar examples, see Geza Róheim, *Fire in the Dragon*, p. 92. Some vertical looms are hung from roof beams.

83. Frank Speck, *Naskapi*, p. 236.

84. The material on the Kogi is summarized from G. Reichel-Dolmatoff, "The Loom of Life: A Kogi Principle of Integration," *Journal of Latin American Lore*, vol. 4:1, (1978), pp. 5-27 and G. Reichel-Dolmatoff, *The Sacred Mountain of Columbia's Kogi Indians*.

85. G. Reichel-Dolmatoff, "The Loom of Life," p. 8.

86. Ibid., pp. 9-10.

87. René Guénon, *Fundamental Symbols*, p. 206.

88. Such was the case with the Dogon of Mali, where the underlying metaphysic governing the culture was known in full only by a selected group of elders. See Marcel Griaule, *Conversations With Ogotemmêli*.

89. G. Reichel-Dolmatoff, "The Loom of Life", op. cit., p. 13.

90. Ibid., p. 14.

91. The correspondences outlined here are sketchy at best and do not represent the full texture of all the associations derived from the loom. Each ceremonial center has associated priests, lords, mythological beings, plants and animals. The symbols help to maintain a larger body of oral lore and tradition. The shape of the loom is also incorporated into architectural construction where the square frame and cross-poles playing a role in reinforcing the walls of the houses and temples.

92. G. Reichel-Dolmatoff, op. cit., p. 15.

93. Ibid., p. 17.

94. Ibid., p. 18.

95. Ibid., p. 19.

96. Ibid., pp. 21-22.

97. Ibid., p. 21.

98. Ibid., p. 23.

99. Under the heading of rotary devices we include chariot wheels, potter's wheels, prayer wheels, and millstones. We add such natural phenomena as whirlpools and whirlwinds that play a role in many mythologies. In regard to the whirlwind, so prominent in the Old Testament, the Hebrew word *chul* signifies both "to turn about," "twist," and "whirl," as well as "to bear," "bring forth," "create" or "form". It also has the meaning, "to dance," bringing to mind the whirling dervishes of Sufism. Lastly, the symbolism associated with rotation is embodied in children's toys like tops, yo-yos and buzzers. As a point of clarification, the Indian milk churn, which forms the cosmic axis in the Vedic myth of the "Churning of the Sea of Milk," was not operated with a pumping motion. Instead, a stick with a rope twisted around it stood upright in the milk and was pulled alternately from opposite ends. Some ancient drills were operated in the same manner.

100. Elizabeth Barber, *Prehistoric Textiles*, p. 42.

101. Ibid., p. 42.

102. Jason's search for the Golden Fleece is relevant here. Gold is a symbol of light, life, and immortality, and is to be equated with the Sun, the source of all life. The fleece is akin to Soma, the tree, plant, food, or water of life. The Fleece, Soma, and the Holy Grail are equivalent formulations for the vivifying principle that gives life to all things.

103. Johannes Wilbert, op. cit., p. 31.

104. De Santillana and Von Duchend, *Hamlet's Mill*, p. 138. The authors provide a great deal of evidence for the antiquity of this motif which is related to that of the whirlpool, seen as a kind of undersea mill that provides a conduit to the lower world. The attempt to connect the symbolism of the mill to the precession of the equinoxes and the related idea that myth is encoded science rest on less solid ground.

105. Ibid., ft. 2. We are also told that Dhruva earned his exalted seat by standing on one foot for a month. Carl Schuster identified this particular custom—still practiced in some parts of the world both in rituals of state and as a resting posture—as an arrested step. It represents the act of climbing the *axis mundi*, much as shamans do when ascending a ritual pole or ladder to reach the heavens. This is the posture in which Vishnu is depicted during the Churning of the Sea of Milk. See Edmund Carpenter, op. cit., vol. 3, bk. 1, Ch. 8, "Climbing to Heaven."

106. Aristotle compares the formation of the fetus to the curdling of milk (*De Generatione Animalium*, bk. I, 729a, 7-14 and bk. II, 739b, 22-31), an idea shared by the Basque people in modern times. See Sandra Ott, "Aristotle Among the Basques: 'The Cheese Analogy' of Conception." She finds evidence for the same belief in India and the Old Testament. Cf. Carlo Ginzburg, *The Cheese and the Worms*, which documents the survival of similar beliefs in Renaissance Italy.

107. Edmund Carpenter, op. cit., vol. 3, bk 1, p. 75. Also, Ananda Coomaraswamy and Sister Nivedita, *Myths of the Hindus and Buddhists*, pp. 314-316.

108. See Jean Canteins, *Les Barrateurs Divins*, p. 82.

109. The failure to distinguish time from eternity makes it difficult to understand many ancient doctrines such as Creationism and Transmigration, which are not historical. The *in principia* (Gr. εν αρχη) of Genesis is not so much a beginning as a principle. Modern languages lack the timeless tenses necessary to explain these ideas

effectively. See Coomaraswamy, *Time and Eternity*.

110. Johannes Wilbert, op. cit., p. 32.

111. See Réne Guénon, "The Symbolism of the Zodiac Among the Pythagoreans," *Fundamental Symbols*, pp. 162-166.

112. See William Simpson, *The Buddhist Praying Wheel*. Some prayer wheels were even designed as revolving bookshelves, meant to hold religious scripture, giving new meaning to the term "circulating library". For a discussion of the symbolism of wheels, see A. K. Coomaraswamy, *Collected Works*, vols. 1 and 2, passim.

113. For a history of fire drills, see Charles Singer, *A History of Technology*, vol. 1, pp. 189-228.

114. It is of some interest that the Hindus used percussion to produce fire at home and reserved fire sticks for ritual occasions. The same division took place with pottery making. Both men and women make pottery by hand but pottery wheels, at least until recent times, were reserved for men, due to their ritual nature. See Jean Canteins, *Les Baratteurs Divins*, p. 18, for a more complete discussion of these issues.

115. Edmund Carpenter, op. cit., vol. 3, bk. 1, pp. 70-75.

116. The turtle as a creature of the earth supports the *axis mundi* in many traditions and is widely used for divination. It is believed to be asexual or bisexual which makes it suitable as a totemic First Ancestor. See Edmund Carpenter, ibid., pp. 76-79.

117. Johannes Wilbert, op. cit., p. 98.

118. Ibid., p.98.

119. Edmund Carpenter, op. cit., vol. 1, bk. 1, p.. 233.

120. Carl Schuster, "Genealogical Patterns in the Old and New Worlds," p. 54. Schuster adds an interesting footnote relevant to the subject at hand: "Since the purpose of the San Juan disk thus appears to be similar to that of the Tibetan prayer-wheel, could there be an historical connection between the two devices? What is the relation between such ritual uses of the 'wheel' and its practical use as a bearing for vehicle, which developed in the Old World but hardly in the New? Did ritual carts precede secular conveyances?"

121. See Coomaraswamy, "The Symplegades," *Collected Works*, I, pp. 521-544.

122. Coomaraswamy, "The Early Iconography of Sagittarius," in *Guardians of the Sundoor*, p. 12.

123. See Coomaraswamy, "Angel and Titan," pp. 373-377.

124. See Gershom Scholem, *Major Trends in Jewish Mysticism*, p. 67. Cf., Ezek., ch. 1.

125. Louis Raymond, *Spindle Whorls in Archaeology*, p. 80.

126. Lindy Crewe, *Spindle Whorls*. For numerous examples of Chinese spindle whorls, see Needham, *Science and Civilization in China*, vol. 5, part 9, section 31.

127. Some of the techniques involved are on display in the movie "Tops," by Ray and Charles Eames. *The Films of Ray and Charles Eames*, vol. 5.

128. In the same regard, Johannes Wilbert wrote, "The same reservation regarding the meaning of 'representational' vs. 'abstract' or 'geometric' designs applies here as in the case of the Manabi whorls. Iconographic and symbolic studies of contemporary Indians and other non-Western art show that designs which to us look abstract or geometric may be no less 'representational' to the native observer than those we would call 'realistic.' "The Thread of Life," p. 29.

129. M. E. Opler, *Myths and Tales of the Jicarilla Apache Indians*, p. 19.
130. Coomaraswamy, *Collected Works*, I, p. 530, ft. 22.

131. Coomaraswamy, "The Iconography of Durer's 'Knots' and Leonardo's 'Concatenation,'" op. cit., ft. 9.

132. See Coomaraswamy, "A Note on the Stickfast Motif," pp. 128-131.

133. Ibid., p. 129.

134. See Coomaraswamy, *Collected Works*, I, p. 326.

135. René Guénon, *Fundamental Symbols*, p. 277.

136. A.K. Coomaraswamy, "The Iconography of Durer's 'Knots' and 'Leonardo's 'Concatenation,'" op. cit., pp. 109-128.

137. Coomaraswamy, ibid., p. 109.

138. Ibid., p. 113. See also, René Guénon, *The Esoterism of Dante*.

139. The Taoist symbolism of Earth, Man and Heaven, which is reflected here, with parallels in other traditions, is the subject of René Guénon's *The Great Triad*. Coomaraswamy provides an Indian example of the same cosmology, op. cit., p. 114.

140. Ibid., p. 114. The metaphor of the "withy," is taken from wickerwork and basketry, a connection to the name "Da Vinci." For the esoteric underpinnings of the *Divine Comedy*, see René Guénon, *The Esoterism of Dante*.

141. Ibid., p. 114. An older embroidered Chinese cosmic diagram is discussed by Carl Schuster in "An Archaic Form of Chess in Chinese Peasant Embroidery," p. 148.

142. Erwin Panofsky, *Albrecht Dürer*, 3rd edition, vol. II, p. 165.

143. Coomaraswamy, "The Iconography of Durer's 'Knots' and Leonardo's 'Concatenation,'" op. cit., p. 113. It should be noted that Coomaraswamy here confuses a maze and a labyrinth, as many scholars continue to do. A true

labyrinth is unicursal; a traveler can only arrive at the center. A maze is full of blind alleys; a sort of flypaper for unclean souls.

144. For an interesting discussion of the renewed interest in this ancient art form in the early part of the 20th century, see Siegfried Giedion, *Mechanization Takes Command*, pp. 101-113.

145. Bain, *Celtic Art*, p. 21.

146. For the requisite background, see John Layard, *Stone Men of Malekula*, Arthur Bernard Deacon, *Malekula: A Vanishing People in the New Hebrides*, and Tom Harrisson, *Savage Civilization*.

147. Deacon, "Geometrical Designs from Malekula and other Islands of the New Hebrides," p. 129.

148. Ibid., p. 133.

149. John Layard, "Maze-Dances and the Ritual of the Labyrinth in Malekula," pp. 126-27.

150. Edmund Carpenter, *Patterns That Connect*, p. 303.

151. John Layard, *Stone Men of Malekula*, ch. 25.

152. Paulus Gerdes, *Une Tradition Géométrique En Afrique. Les Dessins Sur Le Sable*.

153. M. M. Banks, "Tangled Thread Mazes," p. 78.

154. Michael Roaf, *Cultural Atlas of Mesopotamia*, p. 76.

155. The International String Figure Association (ISFA) (P.O. Box 5134, Pasadena, California, 91117) publishes a number of works on the subject including the *String Figure Bibliography*, which lists hundreds of books and articles. The ISFA also issues a number of newsletters, bulletins and magazines of interest to both scholars and enthusiasts.

156. Ray A. Williamson and Claire R. Farrer, eds. *Earth & Sky. Visions of the Cosmos in Native American Folklore*. "Menil (Moon): Symbolic Representation of Cahuilla Woman" by Lowell John Bean, p. 169. Cf., Lucille Hooper, *The Cahuilla Indians*.

157. Audrey Small, "Selected String Figures, Myths and Mythmakers," p. 15. The original research can be found in H.E. Maude and H.C. Maude, "String Figures from the Gilbert Islands."

158. See Carl Schuster's introduction to P. Voorhoeve, *Catalogue of Indonesian Manuscripts*, pp. 39-85. Hentze's comments are discussed on pp. 65-66.

159. Ibid., p. 66.

160. Ibid. See also, Paulus Gerdes, *Une Tradition Géométrique En Afrique. Les Dessins Sur Le Sable*, vol 3, passim.

161. For a more thorough analysis of the myth see Jean Canteins' *Dédale et Ses Oeuvres*. The diverse literary and artistic sources for the story are provided by Timothy Ganz, *Early Greek Myth*, ch. 8.

162. W. Jackson Knight, *Cumaen Gates*, p. 174.

163. Ibid., pp. 17-18.

164. René Guénon, *Fundamental Symbols*, p. 140.

165. Ibid., p.140.

166, Some cultures preserve the umbilicus after birth and use it as an amulet, believing that it possesses special powers to heal. Gypsies in Hungary once referred to it as "God's chain" or "God's rope," stressing its spiritual function in connecting the living with the Other World. See Geza Roheim, *Fire in the Dragon*, pp. 88-101. I wonder if the removal of the umbilicus is not equated with the loss of primordial wisdom that is believed to occur at birth in many cultures. The fact that the umbilicus is attached at the center of the body makes it a physical representation of the seventh ray that connects us to the Deity. See Réne Guénon, *The Lord of the World*, for a discussion of the symbolism of geographical/spiritual centers. The sacred *omphalos* at Delphi is but one example.

167. Edmund Carpenter, *Social Symbolism in Ancient & Tribal Art*, vol. 3, bk. 2, p. 421.

168. Edmund Carpenter, ibid., p. 344.

169. In opposition to this theory, it has been argued that the suffix *-inth* (as in Corinth, hyacinth, plinth) is non-Indo-European.

170. René Guénon takes up the connection between stones and ancestors in *Fundamental Symbols*. Stones are equated with the bones of ancestors and pebbles colored with red ocher—meant to represent blood—were cached in prehistoric times. John Layard's study of the megalithic culture of the New Hebrides, *Stone Men of Malekula*, explores some of these themes.

171. W. H. Matthews, *Mazes and Labyrinths*, p. 41.

172. Quoted from W.H. Matthews, ibid., p. 41.

173. Carpenter, op. cit., vol. 3, bk. 2, pp. 424-425.

174. Anne G. Ward, *The Quest for Theseus*, p. 225.

175. Hans George Wunderlich, *The Secret of Crete*.

176. Herodotus, *The Histories*, bk. 2, 147-150.

177. Matthews, op. cit., p. 37.

178. Edmund Carpenter, *Social Symbolism in Ancient & Tribal Art*, vol. 3, bk. 2, p. 377.

179. W. Jackson Knight, op. cit., p. 83.

180. Ibid., pp. 390-391.

181. W. Jackson Knight, op. cit., chapter IV, "Abydos."

182. René Guénon, *Fundamental Symbols*, p. 143. Knight notes that the Chinese built 'spirit walls' at the entrance to their cities to keep out ghosts.
.

183. Lévi-Strauss, *Tristes Tropiques*, p. 84.

184. Cecelia Klein, "Woven Heaven, Tangled Earth," p. 7.

185. Ibid., p. 9. Egyptian mythology also includes a netted underworld. See Mead, *Thrice Greatest Hermes*, pp. 40-44.

186. Cecelia Klein, "Snares and Entrails: Mesoamerican Symbols of Sin and Punishment." *Res*, vol. 19/20, p. 82. A similar description is provided in the Egyptian Book of the Dead. See E. A. Wallis Budge, *Osiris and the Egyptian Resurrection*, vol. 2, p. 146.

187. W. Jackson Knight, op. cit., pp. 115-117.

188. Ibid., p. 129. Martin Bernal adds the following point: "The god Hpy was the Guardian of the Canopic jar containing the small intestine, and in The Book of the Dead one of his major functions in protecting the dead was to kill demons in the shape of serpents. Apollo was generally equated with Hpy's father, Horus." *Black Athena*, vol. 1, p. 93.

189. Audrey Small, "Selected String Figures, Myths and Myth-makers," pp. 14-15.

190. Emmanuel Anati, *Camonica Valley*, pp. 217-218.

191. Edmund Carpenter, *Social Symbolism in Ancient & Tribal Art*, vol. 3, bk. 2, p. 265. For a fuller description of the errors involved, see chapter 12, "Bungled Labyrinths & Gapped Circles."

192. This method would differ from that used with a labyrinth drawn on the earth, such as the suggested diagram for the Game of Troy, in which the participants rode on the lines, and not between them. For a discussion of this issue see Edmund Carpenter, ibid., pp. 378-381.

193. Edmund Carpenter, *Social Symbolism in Ancient & Tribal Art*, vol. 3, bk. 2, p. 411.

194. Ibid., p. 419.

195. Marius Barbeau, "The Old-World Dragon in America," p. 120.

196. Ibid., p. 414.

197. Ibid., p. 420.

198. These are the original "jaws of death" that find expression in folklore as the clashing rocks, revolving doors, double-edged swords or other guardian pairs protecting the entrance to Heaven. See Coomaraswamy, "Symplegades," *Collected Works*, II, pp. 521-44, and *Guardians of the Sundoor*.

199. Carpenter, op cit., p. 265.

200. Ibid., p. 265.

201. Ibid., p. 382.

202. Ibid., p. 383.

203. Carpenter, ibid., p. 406.

204. René Guénon, *Fundamental Symbols*, pp. 204-205.

205. A. K. Coomaraswamy, "Angel and Titan: An Essay in Vedic Ontology," p. 379, ft. 7.

206. A. K. Coomaraswamy, *Collected Works*, II, p. 145.

207. René Guénon, ibid., p. 206.

208. Carpenter, op. cit., vol. 3, bk. 2, p. 406.

209. See John Michell and Christine Rhone, *Twelve-Tribe Nations and the Science of Enchanting the Landscape*.

210. A. K. Coomaraswamy, op. cit., pp. 145-146.

211. Carpenter, op. cit., vol. 3, bk. 1, p. 150.

212. See Carl Schuster, "A Survival of the Eurasiatic Animal Style in Modern Alaskan Eskimo Art," pp. 35-45. Also, "Joint Marks: A Possible Index of Cultural Contact Between America, Oceania, and the Far East."

213. Mircea Eliade, *Shamanism*, pp. 251-252. Eliade also documents the role of ritual dismemberment in many shamanic practices around the world. The shaman's body must be replaced with a new one to enable entry to the other world and subsequent return to this one.

Compare the famous rope trick of the Indian fakirs in which the illusion is created that a rope has been thrown into the sky. A young boy climbs the rope and shortly thereafter, his bloody limbs fall to the ground one by one. He later reappears intact. The whole performance is highly convincing if we can judge from the testimony of those who have seen it over the centuries. See Eliade, p. 428. For the history of the rope trick, see Siegel, *Net of Magic*, pp. 197-221.

   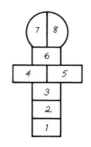  

Fig. 4.1: Carl Schuster collecting embroideries in West China, 1935.

THE WORK OF CARL SCHUSTER

It is equally surprising that so many scholars, meeting with some universal doctrine in a given context, so often think of it as a local peculiarity.

Ananda K. Coomaraswamy

The writings of Carl Schuster (1904-1969) represent the single most important body of work ever assembled on traditional art and symbolism yet they remain unknown to the general public. Schuster's life work resembles a detective story, spanning thirty years and five continents; its protagonist a shy and retiring scholar, skilled in cryptography and languages, whose life of collecting, correspondence, and research ultimately revealed a system of genealogical iconography fully 30,000 to 40,000 years old.

Carl Schuster was born in Milwaukee, Wisconsin, in 1904, to a prominent Jewish family. His gift for languages was evident from an early age along with an interest in puzzles, codes, and ciphers. These skills would later help him both as a scholar and as a cryptanalyst for the Navy during the Second World War. Schuster received a B.A. (1927) and an M.A. (1930) from Harvard where he studied art history and sinology. A growing interest in traditional symbolism led him to Peking (1931-1933) where he spent three years studying with Baron von Stael-Holstein, a Baltic refugee and scholar. It was during this period that he began collecting textile fragments and ventured on the first of his many field trips in search of specimens. His travels eventually took him to some of the most remote parts of the world, photographing rock carvings, visiting small museums or private collections, and talking to missionaries, scholars, or anyone else who might have information he was seeking. Schuster returned to Europe to study at the University of Vienna with the noted art historian, Josef Strzygowski, and received his doctorate in 1934. He worked briefly as the Curator of Chinese Art at the Philadelphia Art Museum but was soon back in China (1935-38) pursuing his researches and traveling until the Japanese invaded (Fig. 4.1). After World War II, he lived in Woodstock, New York, where he began to develop his ideas, publishing well-illustrated monographs with titles like "Human Figures with Spiral Limbs in Tropical America" and "Skin and Fur Mosaics from Early Prehistoric Times to Modern Survivals." Harvard University was on the verge of publishing a book, *The Sun Bird*, but he withdrew it at the last moment because it contained errors. He continued to travel, attending conferences and doing fieldwork, and to correspond with others who shared his interests.

Scattered around the world, often in remote or unlikely places, were hundreds of self-trained scholars, who in response to some personal passion, sought to preserve the last remnants of fading, local traditions. They were primary sources: rigorously trained in other disciplines, self-taught in their special interests, totally dedicated in their researches. Many were far better scholars than the professionals who ignored them. Most had no one to talk to until Carl arrived. They welcomed him; opened their records to him; corresponded with him. Long after his death, letter from isolated places continued to arrive, filled with data, drawings, photographs. His archives contain incalculable riches from a world now forgotten.[1]

Schuster's ability to gather and evaluate data was extraordinary. In an age before the copier and the personal computer, he accumulated an archive comprising some 200,000 photographs, 800 rubbings (mostly of petroglyphs), 18,000 pages of correspondence in multiple languages, and a bibliography of 5670 titles filed by alphabet (Chinese, Cyrillic, Latin)—all meticulously cross-referenced. Nor was he afraid to share his insights with others.

He also served as an important link in international scholarship, not only through his personal contacts during his research trips, but also because from his home-base in Woodstock, N.Y., he conducted a free information bureau for the exchange of questions and ideas among scholars and specialists in different fields, between whom he was the only direct link.…When he could not answer a question from his own vast knowledge, or from his files, he would introduce the inquirer, by letter, to some specialist, thus widening the chain of international communication among scholars in many fields.[2]

Like Ananda Coomaraswamy, whom he greatly admired, Schuster believed that traditional symbolism constituted a definite form of language that communicated the beliefs of ancient peoples from the earliest times.[3] A practitioner of the comparative method, he learned to look for cross-relations between the arts, following the evidence where it led, across time periods and boundaries, both geographic and academic. He expressed some of his feelings about these matters in a letter to Heiner Meinhard in 1967.

First in the natural sciences, and then to some extent in the humanities (eg in linguistics), empirical observations by individuals over decades established certain facts permitting certain conclusions. But in the study of the traditional arts, we are still in a pre-scientific age. Nobody seems to have any idea even how to go about learning what the world of traditional culture actually is: this can only be learned by the painstaking tracing of traditional forms on the widest possible comparative basis, empirically, without any arbitrary limits set by academic preconceptions and compartmentation.[4]

Schuster did not live to see his work completed. He died in Woodstock, New York on July 3rd, 1969. The daunting task of assembling, editing, and publishing his findings fell to a friend, the anthropologist Dr. Edmund Carpenter. The result of fifteen years of labor was *Social Symbolism in Ancient and Tribal Art*, published privately in three volumes (1986-88) and distrib-

Fig. 4:2: Schuster archives in Basel.

uted free of charge to scholars and libraries throughout the world. *Patterns That Connect*, published by Abrams Press in 1996, is an abridgment of the larger work. Schuster's archives, which contain a lot more unpublished material, reside in the Museum der Kulturen in Basel, Switzerland (Fig. 4.2).

PATTERNS THAT CONNECT
Schuster's initial publications centered on traditional design motifs that he found preserved on textile fragments he had collected in western China during the 1930s. These textiles were homemade items of white cotton, embroidered in blue thread with a simple cross-stitch, generally household linens that had been passed down from one generation to the next (Fig. 4.3).

Fig. 4:3: Detail of a bed valence, Pachow, China.

Created by both townspeople and country folk, they dated no earlier than the 19th century. This "folk art," as Schuster termed it, was of little interest to art collectors and museums and was already dying out when Schuster began collecting it, having been displaced by cheap, machine-made textiles. Once a source of great pride, these objects were viewed by their owners with some embarrassment and were often cut up to patch children's clothes (Fig. 4.4). Schuster first noticed these designs adorning the "soiled and tattered jackets of little children playing in the streets of Hanchung in Shensi."[5] He was struck initially by the wide variety of motifs that ornamented these simple valences, bed-sheet borders, and apparel, and impressed with the imagination and creativity of the women who had embroidered them. But as his collection grew, his thinking began to change.

Fig. 4:4: Child's dress, China.

Fig. 4:5: The Triumphant Scholar, China.

Fig. 4:6: Scene from Sassanian cliff sculpture.

It is only gradually, as one begins to find repetitions of motives, and of whole motive groups or complexes, with only minute variations, sometimes from the same district, sometimes from places separated by hundreds of miles, that one begins to realize that in spite of the freshness and vigor of the designs, they have really only been copied again and again—that they are merely types.[6]

While the textiles themselves were not very old, the designs were, having been preserved by endless imitation. Even where the motifs seemed specifically Chinese, like the return of the triumphant scholar (*chuang yüan*) on horseback (Fig. 4.5), the oldest known prototypes were found in distant times and places. In the case of this particular motif, which Schuster termed the "triumphant equestrian," related examples were found in Sassanian Persia (Fig. 4.6). These appeared to be the most direct ancestors given the contact between the two cultures during the T'ang period (A.D. 618-907). But there were earlier examples as well, from classical Greece and imperial Rome, and certain elements within the design were spread throughout India and Siam. The triumphant horseman even reached Sweden in A.D. 1000, perhaps by way of south Russia.[7]

Schuster tried, where possible, to provide historical evidence for the movement of these ideas and images but this proved increasingly difficult as the trail moved backward in time. Writing later about the difficulty of providing historical support for the idea of cultural contact between Asia and the Americas in prehistoric times, he defended his methodology.

> However convincing some of these arguments for relationships appear to be, it is inevitable that they remain inconclusive in the absence of any historical documentation. It is the writer's belief, nevertheless, that attempts at the comparative study of traditions, more especially artistic traditions, of the Old and New Worlds should not be abandoned because of the obvious difficulties of historical documentation, but should, on the contrary, be systematically pursued, on a frankly tentative or hypothetical basis, in an effort to assess the true extent and significance of existing similarities.[8]

His intention was not to explain an historical problem—how people or artistic motifs got from one area to another—but to demonstrate morphological similarities not possible by chance. This is the model used in linguistics where a comparative study of vocabulary and grammar can reveal that different languages, sometimes geographically remote, have a common ancestor.

To further complicate matters, designs often moved from one medium to another, depending on the culture; from clothing, to ivory and wood, to pottery, to metal and back to clothing. It was Schuster's wide knowledge of artistic styles and his uncanny ability to identify design motifs, often hidden beneath popular styles or religious or political propaganda, that enabled him to detect relationships between art forms that others had missed.

> When Carl reported his findings in very thorough articles or in profusely illustrated reports at the congresses, he often evoked op-

position from specialists in particular fields, who were annoyed to see their areas of research opened up—or linked to others—by chains of facts and ideas that they themselves had failed to discover. But, in time, many of these opponents came to see the validity of his thinking, and they profited from his suggestions to learn more themselves.[9]

It was only through such a scrupulous and wide-ranging comparative study that these motifs revealed their ancestry. In the end, the distribution and antiquity of some of these designs would surprise even Schuster himself.

JOINT MARKS

In September 1949, Schuster delivered a paper titled "A Significant Correspondence between Old and New World Design" before the 29th International Congress of Americanists in New York. The goal of the conference, sponsored by the American Museum of Natural History, was to determine the influence of the ancient civilizations of the Far East on the cultures of the Pacific and the Americas.[10] An expanded version of the paper was printed two years later with the more explicit title, "Joint Marks: A Possible Index of Cultural Contact Between America, Oceania, and the Far East."

The paper began with a number of illustrations of a puzzling design motif found extensively in both the Pacific and the Americas, a squatting human figure (hocker) with a disk between each flexed elbow and knee (Fig. 4.7). Schuster believed that these disks were not decorative but once had significance. They were clearly related to a similar motif found in the same areas, figures with markings on the elbows and knees themselves, and often on the other body joints as well.

> Though the relationship between these two types of designs—those with disks between the elbows and knees, and those with disks on the joints themselves—cannot be demonstrated as clearly as we might wish by means of transitional forms, still there is enough circumstantial evidence for such a development to warrant an inquiry into the later motive as a possible explanation for the former. Hence, it will be our object, in the first place, to investigate the character and trace the distribution of the motive of the joint-mark, as it occurs in the decorative arts, and sometimes on the living human body, in both parts of the world.[11]

This exercise was to take him well beyond the confines of the paper. In fact, he had been gathering examples of joint marks for many years, not only from Asia, the Pacific, and the Americas, but from Europe and Africa as well.

Many ceramic examples from South American had single or double rings stamped on the joints (shoulders, wrists, knees), probably made with a hollowed reed pressed into the wet clay (Fig. 4.8). These same joint marks were also applied to various animal figures such as frogs and lizards just as they were in areas of the western Pacific.[12] Schuster believed that these nucleated circles were meant to represent eyes because in many areas, human faces, rather than disks or circles, were placed on the joints.

Fig. 4:7: Carved paddle, Borneo.

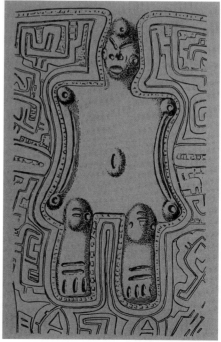

Fig. 4:8: Bowl with joint-marked frogs, Venezuela.

Fig. 4:9: Haida house-screen with detail.

As we found in the New World, so also here in the Pacific the use of eyes as joint-marks is associated with the similar use of complete human faces from which the eyes are presumably derived, and of which they probably represent a rudimentary survival.[13]

Both forms commonly appear in the art of the Pacific Northwest Coast. A painted design on a Haida house-front shows each shoulder and hand marked with a ring (Fig. 4.9). The added triangles of the shoulders are meant to represent the canthus of the eye. Another Haida house painting from the same area shows complete faces at the joints as does a Tlingit house-screen (Fig. 4.10). Franz Boas had come to the same conclusion at the turn of the century.

Fig. 4:10: Detail of a Tlingit house-screen.

An examination…will show that in most cases, it [the eye] is used to indicate a joint. Shoulder, elbow, hand, hips, knees, feet, the points of attachment of fins, tails, and so forth, are always indicated by eyes.[14]

Additional support was provided in 1896 by Rudolph Virchow who reported that the Bella Coola believed that the wrinkled skin over the knuckles of men were rudimentary eyes that had survived from earlier times when each part of the body had terminated in an eye.[15]

If eyes were used to represent faces this would help to explain the circle-and-dot motif common in Eskimo art and tattooing. Simple dot tattoos, placed on body joints, were known among the Eskimo of St. Lawrence Island in the Bering Sea and among the maritime Chuckchee of northeastern Siberia. These practices were reinforced by spiritual beliefs.

In this connection, an observation of Thalbitzer seems of special significance. "According to Eskimo notions," he says, "…in every part of the human body (particularly in every joint, as for instance, in every finger joint) there resides a little soul…."[16]

Schuster would later dedicate a separate paper to the survival of joint marks in the art of the far north, "A Survival of the Eurasiatic Animal Style in Modern Alaskan Eskimo Art." An earlier paper by Helge Larsen and Froelich Rainey had suggested that the art of the prehistoric Eskimo culture, referred to as Ipiutak, was derived from the Bronze Age and Iron Age "Animal Style" art of the Eurasiatic steppes.[17] Schuster agreed but took the matter a good deal further. One of the similarities between Ipiutak ivory carvings and Animal Style metal work was the presence of nucleated circles and pear-shaped bosses placed on the bodies of animals (Fig. 4.11). Schuster believed these were displaced joint marks that had lost their significance and become surface decoration. In fact, joint marks were present in the art of early civilizations of the Mediterranean and Near East, from at least the 2nd millennium, and certainly long before the appearance of the Animal Style. It was changing fashion that had helped to reduce this once meaningful form to mere ornament.

Fig. 4:11: Decoration on a bronze vessel, China.

> The underlying symbolic quality of the joint mark—what we may call its indispensability to the theme of animal representation (or perhaps even its magic significance)—has been obscured throughout its history by the rationalizing tendency of an art under the more or less direct domination by early urban civilizations of the Ancient East—an art forever bent upon naturalistic representation.[18]

The use of joint marks had survived from archaic times as a living tradition only in more remote and peripheral areas like the Far North (Fig. 4.12). Connections were hard to trace because examples created in perishable materials like wood had not survived. Only an indirect link existed in metal.

Fig. 4:12: Scythian gold plaque, Siberia.

Fig. 4:13: Design on interior of wooden bowl, Eskimo.

Fig. 4:15: Cast metal plaque, Siberia.

Another connecting link between Eskimo and Animal Style art was the coiled animal motif. A modern Eskimo example from the area between the lower Yukon valley and the Alaskan coast is a six-legged monster "regarded by the natives as an extinct beast of prey with habits like those of a crocodile (Fig. 4.13)."[19] This type of design was painted on the inside of dishes, befitting its coiled form. A straightened version, much larger in size, was painted on sea-going boats (*umiaks*) (Fig. 4.14). Designs of similar conception executed in metal are found in most of the areas where Animal Style art flourished, typically coiled animals with their snouts touching or almost touching their tails. In many cases joint marks are present (Fig. 4.15).

Fig. 4:14: Sea monster painted on umiak, Eskimo.

The Eskimo example is of particular interest because it combines a number of related motifs. The three circles are clearly joint marks though the wing-like appendages and the horned head are not typical of Animal Style art. Schuster felt that they might be Chinese in origin. Horned serpents do occur in the mythology and art of a number of North American Indian groups.[20] According to George MacDonald, former Director of the National Museum of Canada, among the Woodlands Indians of Canada (Ojibwa and Cree), horned serpents appear as rock-images where they are associated "with the abodes of supernatural underwater beings. Such beings may manifest themselves in human or animal form or as composite beings with human heads and animal or fish bodies."[21]

If the circles of the Eskimo design represent faces then the beast comprises several creatures like itself. A similar design incised on a pottery vessel from Argentina dating from the Barreales period (circa A.D. 500) makes this more explicit by placing jaws at each joint (face) (Fig. 4.16). This arrangement suggests another familiar motif found on Northwest Coast spindle whorls.

Fig. 4:16: Dragon design on a pottery vessel, Argentina.

There are many variations on the theme of serpents devouring their tails on Salish spindle whorls in which pairs of dragons devour each other's tails and thunderbirds alternate with dragons in this same cosmic devouring sequence. I am particularly interested in spindle whorls as cosmic models and as representations of whirlpools, by which creatures are pumped out of the underworld and into rivers by the action of weavers.[22]

The spinning action of the whirlpool, like that of spindle whorl itself, facilitates the movement of souls from one world to the next. If the home of the fish lies far beneath the waters in the underworld, as many Northwest Coast tribes believed, the whirlpool is the door to that world. It is also a door like those found in many mythologies, and serves to draw new souls—in the form of fish in this case— into the world.

Another motif is suggested by the placement of jaws on the joints of the Barreales figure.

Fig. 4:17: Design on an ivory tobacco pipe, Eskimo.

> That the coiled-animal motif of Alaskan Eskimos came directly from Asia seems wholly reasonable. But Argentina? That would require the transmission of bronze age forms through Asian ports to South America. Or was it independently invented in Argentina? Or—and this is what I favor—do these and certain other American examples derive ultimately from an ancient tradition of a Primordial Reptile that swallows neophytes and passes them through its joint-marked body?[23]

We discussed the theme of death the devourer earlier in relation both to knots and to the labyrinth, where death was personified as a female creature whose jointed-marked body was itself the path to the other world. Another Eskimo example supports this view. It shows human body parts within each of the monster's joints (Fig. 4.17). The Aztec earth goddess is also depicted as joint marked, as is a related Aztec image from the Central Mexican plateau, the earth-toad (Fig. 4.18).

> In both types of representations eyes are placed at the wrists and ankles in such a way as to suggest that the hands and feet are faces, whose jaws are formed by the fingers and toes in the likeness of fangs. These faces, which look like snakes, are repeated at the elbows and knees.[24]

Fig. 4:18: Aztec earth-goddess.

Writers from the early period of European contact provide further confirmation.

> Mendieta reports: "They regarded the earth as a goddess and represented her as a ferocious frog, with bloody jaws at all the joints, saying that thus she devoured and swallowed everything." And in a 16th century French manuscript we read: "…the goddess of the earth, Tlaltecuhtli…had eyes and mouths at every joint, with which she snapped like a savage beast (Fig. 4.19)."[25]

Fig. 4:19: Tlaltecuhtli, Aztec earth-goddess.

Fig. 4:20: Maori shell-inlaid board, New Zealand.

Fig. 4:22: Tattooed Marquesan Islander.

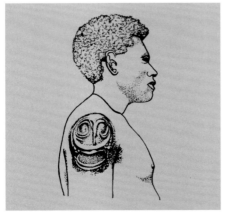

Fig. 4:23: Scarified male, New Guinea

Fig. 4:21: Carved wooden bowls connected by joint-marked human figure, Hawaii.

A Maori shell-inlaid board from New Zealand also features jaws at the joints though they may not be apparent at first glance (Fig. 4.20). Conventionalized eye-like figures called *manaia*-heads occur in pairs, the juncture of each pair forming an open jaw. The use of shell or other inlay to emphasize the joints is quite common wherever joint marks are found. A beautiful carved double-bowl from Hawaii has similar shell-inlaid eyes at the joints (Fig. 4.21).

Joint marks may first have been applied to the human body via tattooing and scarification. In addition to the Eskimo example discussed earlier, eye-like designs and human faces were once placed on joints in other cultures. A tattooed Marquesan Islander has human faces on his shoulders and knees (Fig. 4.22) while another man from the Sepik River has a face scarified on his shoulder (Fig. 4.23).

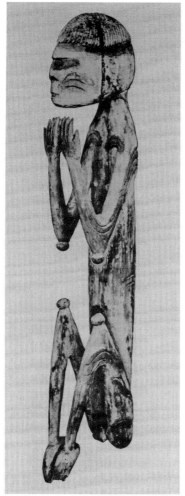

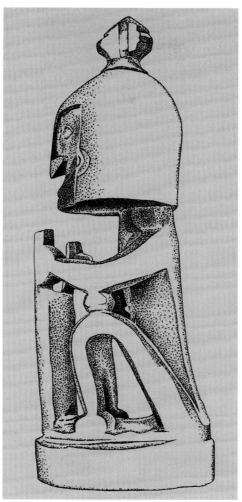

Fig. 4:26: Chief's chair, Cameroon.

Fig. 4:24: Wooden figure, Irian Jaya.

Fig. 4:25: Human figure of wood, Irian Jaya.

Joint marks also occur on three-dimensional sculpture where they appear as interarthral balls or props, looking strangely out of place. Of the many examples collected by Schuster, two from New Guinea and one from Cameroon will suffice (Figs. 4.24. 4.25, and 4.26).

A complete face appears on the leg of a Classical Greek statue of Ares (Fig. 4.27).

As the evidence mounted, Schuster became convinced that the tradition of joint marking was very old. The distribution was interesting in itself. Joint marks were present in Asia, North and South American, Europe, and throughout the Pacific, though less common in Africa and unknown in Southern Australia. Clearly the tradition is related to the use of body joints for counting ancestors.

> Australian aborigines who reckon genealogy on their finger-joints may preserve man's earliest method. Perhaps in neolithic times, conceivably first in Asia, genealogical reckoning by joints was transferred to the body as a whole. This might explain the absence of joint-marks in Southern Australia and their rarity in Africa.[26]

Fig. 4:27: Stone leg with greave from a statue of Ares.

145

Whatever the historical sequence, the equation of ancestors with joints and by extension, with knots, is not in doubt. Neither is the connection between counting systems and body parts, as we have already seen.

GENEALOGICAL ICONOGRAPHY

Writing to an old friend in Taiwan in 1957 Schuster expressed a growing excitement:

> I have been undergoing a "change of life," in this sense: my work has suddenly branched out and is growing so rapidly and luxuriantly that it is simply becoming impossible to keep up with it and with everything else too. It is extremely exciting: I have at last begun excavating a vein of incalculable richness. To try to get down to earth: I have the clue, at last, to one of the central symbols of *all* human cultural history, which explains the survival of traditions from at least upper paleolithic times through all subsequent cultures.[27]

His study of joint marks had gradually revealed an underlying system of genealogical iconography that appeared to have its origins in Paleolithic times. He published his initial findings in Brazil in 1956 under the title, "Genealogical Patterns in the Old and New Worlds."[28] Its goals seemed modest enough for a work of such importance.

> The purpose of this paper is to call attention to a type of design which occurs among various peoples in both hemispheres, and to offer an explanation of its form, which may at the same time account for its surprisingly wide distribution. Designs of this type are made up of a series of human bodies joined by their arms and legs in such a way as to form an endlessly repeating "all-over pattern" (*Muster ohne Ende*).[29]

The anthropologist Edmund Carpenter has illustrated the basics of this iconography in schematic form in his three-volume presentation of Schuster's findings, *Social Symbolism in Ancient and Tribal Art*. His treatment has greatly simplified the problems involved in reading the symbolism, which can be quite puzzling at first sight. I will use Dr. Carpenter's examples to summarize the system. Much will be omitted. Readers interested in a more thorough analysis should consult the original work or the abbreviated treatment in *Patterns That Connect*.

Schuster believed that Paleolithic peoples developed a system for illustrating their ideas about genealogy. Not a kinship system—which depicts actual relations—but an idealized system linked to certain cosmological ideas. The resulting designs were used to decorate their bodies, clothing, and tools. The function of these images was to clothe the individual in his/her tribal ancestry.

> For thousands of years, this iconography served as a single system, everywhere obedient to the same rules, everywhere addressing itself to the same ideas. It was never a true 'language', but its glyphs were simple, its rules clear. With ease & clarity, one could illustrate a symmetry of silent assumptions underlying tribal genealogies.

These assumptions, along with their special iconography, fell into disfavor with the rise of city-states and the invention of writing. But neither wholly disappeared. Both survive as living traditions among isolated tribesmen and as deep metaphors in urban cultures.[30]

DESCENT AND RELATIONSHIP

The basic units of the system are conventionalized human figures, meant to represent ancestors (Fig. 4.28). The figures are linked together to illustrate descent and relationship.

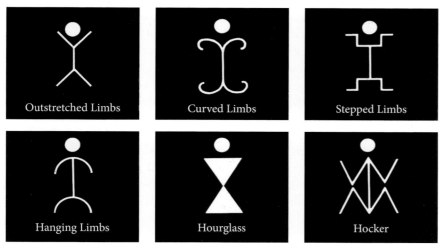

Fig. 4:28: Basic "bricks" used in constructing genealogical patterns

To depict descent, the leg of one human figure is linked to the arm of a lower, adjacent one. Figures can also be linked leg to leg if the adjacent figure is inverted. The linkage serves to fuse the limbs to create an overall pattern (Fig. 4.29).

Fig. 4:29: Genetic descent.

Figures can also be linked horizontally, arm to arm and leg to leg, to depict relationships within a single generation (Fig. 4.30).

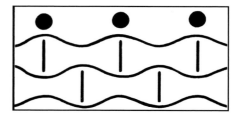

Fig. 4:30: Relationship within a single generation.

147

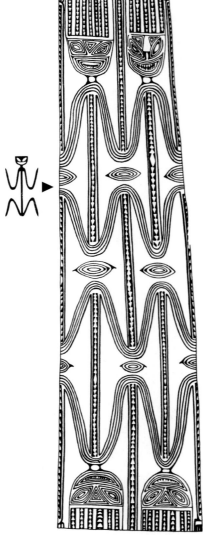

Fig. 4:31: Design incised on a club, New Ireland.

A design incised on a club from Melanesia illustrates both descent and relationship (Fig. 4.31). A series of humanlike figures are connected both arm to arm and leg to arm to form an overall pattern. The heads at the top and bottom are meant to represent skulls while intermediate figures have "eyes" for heads (now recognizable as joint marks). Notice how the eyes/heads appear between the knees and elbows of each figure. This accounts for the residual presence of such markings on the artworks we saw earlier. The individual jointed-marked figures were once conceived as part of an overall pattern from which they were excerpted long ago. The joint marks are all that remains of the continuous pattern. The presence of joint marks above the knees of each human figure helps to account for the widespread myth of children born from the knees of an ancestral figure. This is logical given the fact that the leg-to-arm linkages depict descent. The lower figures are descendants of the upper.

The picture-puzzle nature of this design can be read equally from the top down or from the bottom up. The vertebrae of the spinal columns are oriented in opposite directions around a central point (navel) to help produce this effect.

An Indonesian *ikat* from the Celebes reveals a similar genealogical pattern only here the leg of each quasi-human figure is linked to the arm of the one below it by a Z-shaped turn. In this way, the sides of each body form a continuously extending line linking with those diagonally above and below (Fig. 4.32). Some figures have enlarged heads with distended ear lobes, and prominent spines and navels. Figures in intermediate columns are simplified. The significance of the overall pattern reflects the genetic theories of certain Indonesian peoples, theories shared by a wide variety of other cultures.

> According to these beliefs, the body of each person is composed of two halves, derived respectively from the corresponding halves of each parent. When viewed in terms of this idea, the figures to the right & left immediately above each individual represent the father & mother, each of whom contributes one half to his formation. The figures to the right & left immediately below the same individual represent his children, or rather his share in their creation by virtue of marriage [Fig. 4.33].[31]

It is clear that such an arrangement was not meant to represent actual kinship relations; it is not specific enough for that. But the design is a perfect illustration of the endless repetition of the genetic process itself—from parents to children to grandchildren and on down the generations. The Indonesian *ikat* represents the "social fabric" and surely merits the designation "genealogical pattern."

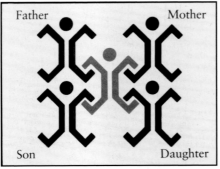

Fig. 4:33: Halved body with parents and children.

Fig. 4:32: Cotton ikat, Celebes.

The connectedness of these adjacent figures is an instantiation of the sutrat-man doctrine, similar to the use of cords and knots to bind the bride and groom during a marriage ceremony. Two families become one by being interlinked. In a similar manner, each row created on a loom can be said to represent a generation, even where human figures are lacking. This can be more easily understood when we remove the heads from these ancestor figures. We are left with geometrical patterns that disguise their representational origins (Fig. 4.34).

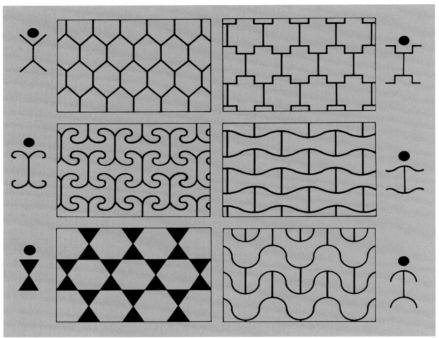

Fig. 4:34: All-over genealogical patterns.

It is more than likely that the patterns used in plaiting, netting, and interlacing were once conceived as generalized genealogical statements. Such is clearly the case with a plaited mat from Tahiti collected on Captain Cook's Third Voyage (Fig. 4.35).

The fact that the original significance of these designs was lost over time does not matter. Even in the earliest times genealogical patterns moved back and forth from the figurative to the abstract.[32] A Hawaiian drum with interlinked humanlike figures (Fig. 4.36A) helps explain a more abstract example, also from Hawaii (Fig. 4.36B).

The same may be said for a vessel from Cameroon that features abstract genealogical patterns on the neck and humanlike ones encircling the body (Fig. 4.37).

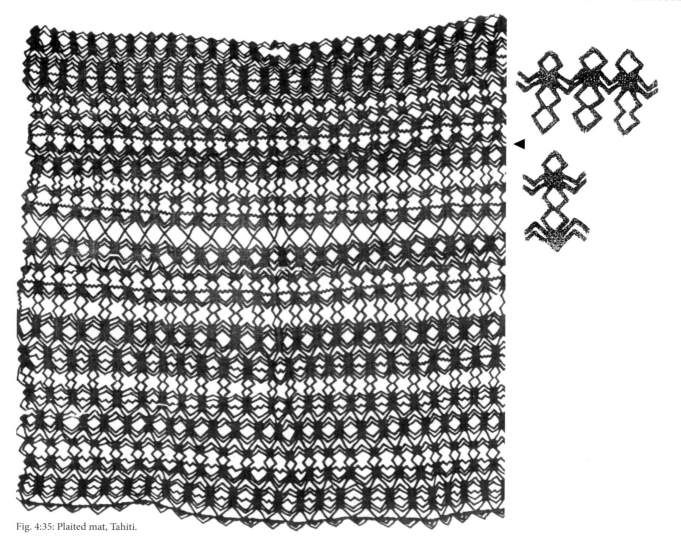

Fig. 4:35: Plaited mat, Tahiti.

Fig. 4:36A: Hawaiian drum.

Fig. 4:36B: Hawaiian drum.

Fig. 4:37: Pottery vessel, Cameroon.

151

Many of the geometrical patterns common to string figures have a similar origin, detectable in patterns like "Ten Men," found in the Caroline Islands (Fig. 4.38).

"Holding Up the Sky," shown here on a stamp from Nauru (Fig. 4.39), copies a common genealogical pattern formed when horizontal bands are cut through the connected bodies that form the over-all pattern (Fig. 4.40). The reason the string figure has this name is that the hands of the excepted figures are raised.

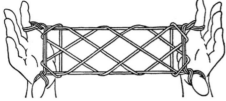

Fig. 4:38: String figure (Ten Men) Caroline Islands.

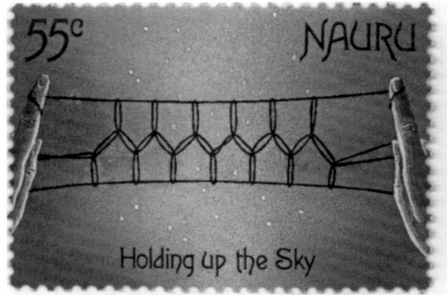

Fig. 4:39: Stamp from with string figure (Holding Up the Sky), Nauru.

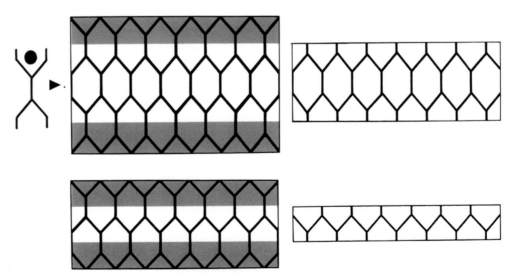

Fig. 4:40: Human figures excerpted from over-all pattern.

We see the same pattern engraved on a bone from the Mesolithic Maglemose culture of Denmark (8000 to 5000 B.C.) (Fig. 4.41) and on a carnelian bead from India dated to megalithic times (Fig. 4.42).

The continuous nature of genealogical patterns made them particularly suitable for cylindrical objects or human limbs. A bamboo tube from New Guinea is encircled with human figures with prominent spines and joint marks (heads) (Fig. 4.43). A Danish Mesolithic engraving from the Maglemose period omits the heads, but leaves the spines and connected limbs (Fig. 4.44).

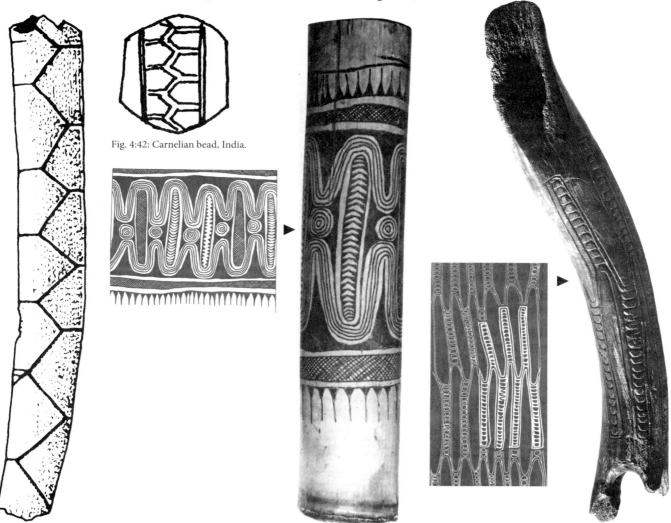

Fig. 4:42: Carnelian bead, India.

Fig. 4:41: Engraved bone, Denmark.   Fig. 4:43: Bamboo tube with detail, New Guinea.   Fig. 4:44: Design incised on antler axe with detail, Denmark.

These encircling patterns moved easily to pottery in Neolithic times. Chalcolithic pottery from Central Europe provides many examples (Fig. 4.45). Note the extra spinal columns beneath the knees resulting from the disruption of what was once a continuous pattern.

Fig. 4:45: Painted pottery cup with detail, Moravia.

153

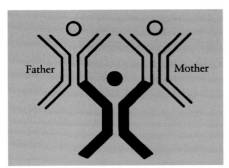

Fig. 4:46: Split pattern emphasizing origin from dual parentage.

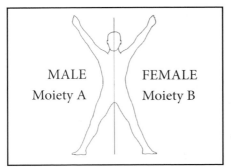

Fig. 4:47: Union of two moieties.

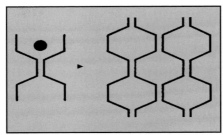

Fig. 4:49: A common split pattern.

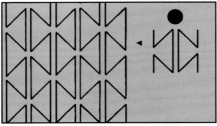

Fig. 4:50: Another common split pattern.

SPLIT PATTERNS

The assumption that each person is composed of two halves, derived from the corresponding halves of each parent, underlies all genealogical iconography (Fig. 4.46).

A vertical bar or blank band separates (or joins) these two sides. This division represents offspring resulting from the union of a male and female from opposing exogamous moieties (Fig. 4.47).[33]

Split patterns were tattooed on bodies, painted or scratched onto clothing, carved on posts or rocks, or painted on pebbles (Fig. 4.48). The zigzags are simply headless, spineless hockers, joined arm to arm and leg to leg. Each row represents one generation.

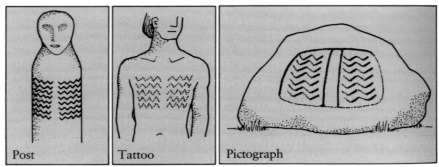

Fig. 4:48: Examples of split patterns.

Split figures are among the most common genealogical patterns (Fig. 4.49 and 4.50).

The Asmat people of West Irian have not only preserved this iconography but understand its significance. They call these designs, *kavé*, and assign the name of a deceased relative to each. Vertical bands of these figures are carved on shields and spears (Fig. 4.51). Each half of a *kavé* is called a *wè-nèt*, after the praying mantis, which it resembles. Humans and mantises are considered interchangeable.

> *Wènèt* may be linked leg-and-arm, to form vertical chains. Two opposing chains, on either side of a spine, represent a lineage. According to Gerbrands, the Asmat explain [the design here] 'as a way of representing graphically the family groups belonging to a particular ceremonial house.'[34]

Schuster collected thousands of examples of split figures from diverse cultures and time periods, including this early example, a limestone pebble fragment from a Paleolithic deposit in the Grotta Romanelli, Italy (Fig. 4.52).[35] The design is hard to make out, but note how the blank parallel line cuts across and interrupts the parallel zigzags.

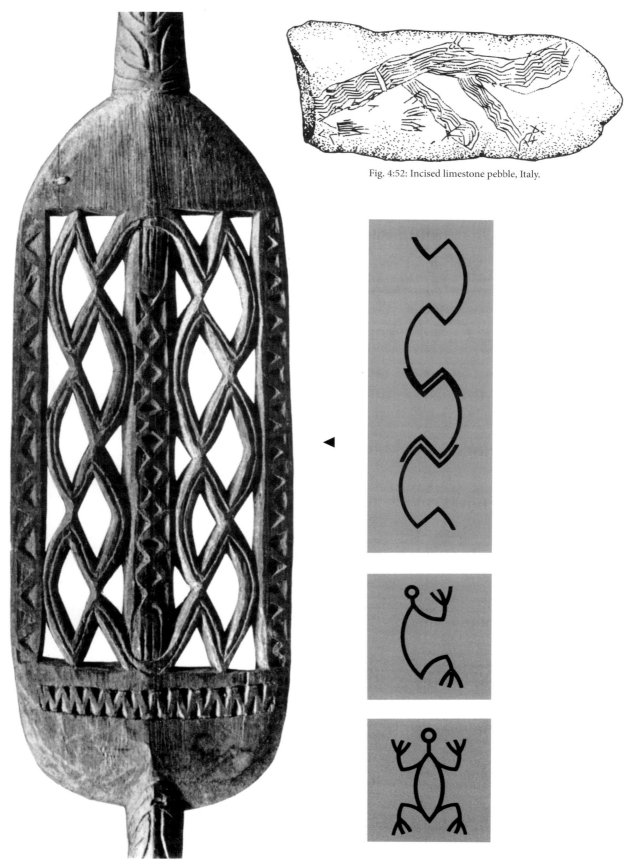

Fig. 4:52: Incised limestone pebble, Italy.

Fig. 4:51: Spear decoration, Asmat, West Irian.

The symbolism of opposites, as well as their original unity in a primordial ancestor, finds expression in diverse cultures and forms. Among the Delaware Indians, the ceremonial house is divided in half (Fig. 4.53). The east is male, associated with red, life, day and the right-hand side. The west is female, black, death, night, and the left-hand side. The center post features an image of the Great Spirit, one side painted red, the other black.[36]

The Bororo of Brazil divide their villages into two halves with the lodges of each moiety on opposite sides.[37]

We have seen the same principle applied in the fiber arts with the most basic example being the knot, which though created from a single strand, both divides and connects.

Fig. 4:53: Interior of Delaware Big House.

QUARTERING

Once a human figure is split vertically to represent exogamous moieties it can be split horizontally to emphasize ascending and descending generations. This produces a quartered figure (Fig. 4.54).

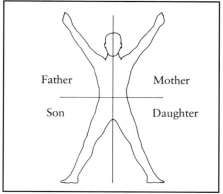

Fig. 4:54: Diagram of a quartered figure.

Quartered designs are exceedingly common in genealogical iconography. A Tukanoan house-post features a single head on a quartered body (Fig. 4.55). Each quarter is filled with genealogical patterns representing the members of the tribe.

> The crossing of the spinal column by a horizontal bar suggests that the body of the tribal ancestor was conceived as having been actually divided into four parts, which must be forever reunited by individual marriages between members of exogamous divisions in order to perpetuate the social fabric of the tribe.[38]

In just this way the symbolism of quartering was extended from the First Ancestor to both society and the cosmos. The same four-fold division acts as the organizing principle for the year (four seasons), city (four quarters), and the world (four directions).

> The belief that the cosmos and society are similarly divided into four parts, as laid out on the body of the Creator, can be found among many peoples. Details vary, but the four-fold division remains constant. In the *Hako* ceremony of the Pawnee Indians, ritual leaders sing and present themselves to 'all the powers of the east, west, south and north.' As they walk, they trace upon the earth the figure of a man, *Tira'wa*, 'the father of all.'[39]

The cross, which produces the quartering, represents the First Man and First Woman crossed in mating. The two lines intersect at the navel, identified as the center of the world and the point where the *axis mundi* passes through the earth. We discussed this symbolism earlier in regard to the warp and woof threads of the loom. It also applies to the drill, which produces fire by imitating the primal act of creation.

Fig. 4:55: Tukanoan house-post, Brazil.

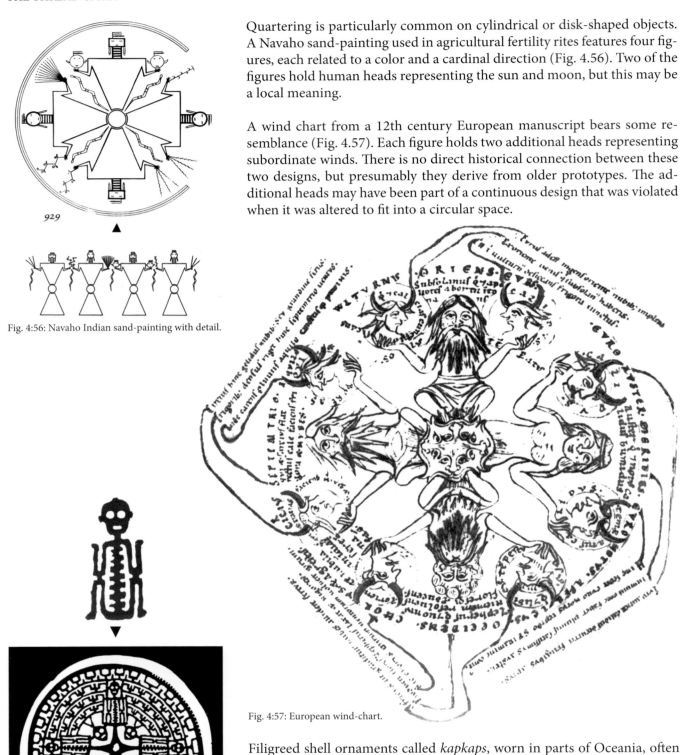

Quartering is particularly common on cylindrical or disk-shaped objects. A Navaho sand-painting used in agricultural fertility rites features four figures, each related to a color and a cardinal direction (Fig. 4.56). Two of the figures hold human heads representing the sun and moon, but this may be a local meaning.

A wind chart from a 12th century European manuscript bears some resemblance (Fig. 4.57). Each figure holds two additional heads representing subordinate winds. There is no direct historical connection between these two designs, but presumably they derive from older prototypes. The additional heads may have been part of a continuous design that was violated when it was altered to fit into a circular space.

929

Fig. 4:56: Navaho Indian sand-painting with detail.

Fig. 4:57: European wind-chart.

Filigreed shell ornaments called *kapkaps*, worn in parts of Oceania, often depict human skeletons, radially arranged, most often in fours (Fig. 4.58).

Fig. 4:58: Shell ornament (*kapkap*) with detail, New Georgia.

Quartered genealogical designs have an ancient provenance: a perforated lid from a grave in Denmark from the Maglemose period with ramiform designs (Fig. 4.59); and an engraved bone disk from Bronze Age Denmark (Fig. 4.60) that share a common design with a Cretan spindle whorl from the same period (Fig. 4.61).

It is impossible to tell if these examples shared a common meaning for the people who made them, but the widespread popularity of such quartered designs over a very long period of time suggests a common underlying significance. Peripheral notching on many of these specimens can also be linked to other notched devices used to count ancestors. Schuster made a separate study of notched disks and collected examples from all over the world.[40]

STACKED FIGURES (RAMIFORMS)

If we bisect our basic genealogical units at the waist, the upper torsos can be stacked to create multi-bodied columns united by a common spine (Fig. 4.62). Most often, a single head serves the whole assemblage.

These designs are often given names based on their resemblance to the local flora and fauna (flying birds, insects, fish bones, etc.), but a comparative analysis reveals an older common meaning.

Schuster referred to these designs as "ramiforms" because of their resemblance to a tree (L. *ramus*—branch, twig, bough). In fact, most genealogical symbolism is based on an analogy with the plant world. We speak of our "family tree" and its "branches" or we search for our "roots." Edmund Carpenter stresses the central role this analogy has played in human culture.

> A single idea underlies all of the evidence offered in this book: equating the image of a tree with the branching of the human race. This correspondence between Tree & Genealogy lies beneath a wide range of phenomena in a wide range of cultures, in fact, Culture. Ultimately it rests on the analogy of plant propagation and the notion of human birth from budding.[41]

Many cultures produce these "tree men," which take a variety of forms including notched posts, shaved sticks, and anthropomorphic ladders. Each tier represents a generation, with the Founding Father or First Couple of the clan or tribe at the top.

Fig. 4:59: Perforated lid, Denmark.

Fig. 4:60: Engraved bone disk, Denmark.

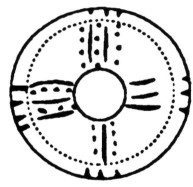

Fig. 4:61: Bronze Age spindle whorl, Cyprus.

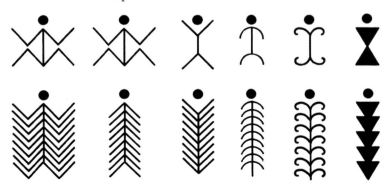

Fig. 4:62: Stacked figures (ramiforms).

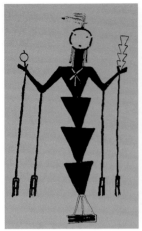

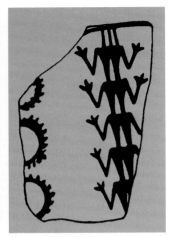

Fig. 4:63: Navaho "cloud-man."   Fig. 4:64: Beothuck Indian staff.   Fig. 4:65: Painted pottery sherd, Iran.

A Navaho example representing one of the four 'cloud-men' (Fig. 4.63) shares a common form with a Beothuck wooden staff from Newfoundland (Fig. 4.64).

Older examples include a painted pottery shard from Iran (3500-3200 B.C.) (Fig. 4.65) and earlier still, these Spanish 'pine-tree men' (circa 4000-3000 B.C.) analyzed by Henri Breuil, which bear a more than passing resemblance to the famous Mesolithic painted pebbles of Mas d'Azil (Fig. 4.67). Schuster was not the first scholar to note the humanlike character of these designs, but he was the first to identify them as genealogical designs.[42]

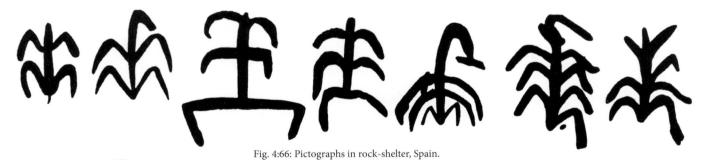

Fig. 4:66: Pictographs in rock-shelter, Spain.

To return to the fiber arts, the same principle underlying stacked figures can be found in mnemonic devices like knotted cords. A rosary is merely a group of stacked figures arranged in a circle. Rosaries embody the idea of a graded ascent into spiritual realms so we should not be surprised to find stacked figures employed as ladders.

Fig. 4:67: Painted pebble, France.

An example from the Metoko serves as a memorial for the dead and includes a ladder-like bottom meant to represent generations (Fig. 4.68).

Likewise, the Garo of Assam, a Tibeto-Burman people, erect memorial posts called *kimas* under the eaves of a deceased person's house, after cremation (Fig. 4.69). Edmund Carpenter explains:

> Each step…is conceived as a headless human figure with free-standing 'limbs'. Collectively these steps symbolize the successive generations of a clan or family, with the 'head' of the family at the top. Ascent of the ladder means identification with each successive ancestor, ultimately with the founder of the lineage. Thus the ladder as a whole represents a genealogy, the mounting of which is an act of ceremonial or ritual significance.[43]

Anthropomorphic ladders occur in eastern Siberia and from Southeast Asia into Melanesia where they share a common religious significance. An American example, from the Mapuche of Chile, is used by female shamans to make a ritual trip to the sky realm (Fig. 4.70). Ananda Coomaraswamy noted the similarity of such practices to Indian ideas about salvation where one climbs the *axis mundi* to achieve union with the Deity.[44]

Fig. 4:68: Metoko notched post, Zaire.

Fig. 4:69: Garo memorial post (kima), India.   Fig. 4:70: Mapuche shaman's ladder, Chile.

The architectural use of heavenly ladders connects genealogical symbolism with cosmology inasmuch as the house is a model of the cosmos. Here a Vietnamese ladder with breasts, representing a female lineage, allows access to an elevated house (Fig. 4.71). The term "house" itself is used to denote a lineage.

A Batak door-post from Sumatra shows the Lord of the Upper World at the top of a ladder of descendents below (Fig. 4.72).

Stairways to Heaven exist in many cultures and in many forms, both small and large. One common version, the notched center post or "king post" supports the roof beams in much traditional architecture, forming a bridge between the lower world and the heavens above. The smoke hole at the top of the dwelling represents the entrance to Heaven. We have only to think of Jacob's ladder or Jack and the Beanstalk, religious and folkloric variations on the same theme.

Fig. 4:71: Anthropomorphic ladder, Vietnam.

Fig. 4:72: Batak door-post, Sumatra.

In a related version of this theme one gets to Heaven by ascending the spine of an ancestor figure, each of whose vertebrae represent an ascending generation. The journey is one through both space and time; a return to one's ultimate source. Some children's games preserve this symbolism.

> Certain hopscotch diagrams suggest a Cosmic Being upon whose body players progress upward, through stages or courts, to the Deity's head at the top [Fig. 4.73]. This is done on a ground drawing, often of anthropomorphic form. The proper route requires that the player land in sequence on each part (joint?) before reaching the Deity's head.[45]

We should remember the warning issued to hopscotch players, "Step on a crack, break your mother's back, step on a line, break your father's spine."

The idea of one head animating many bodies is the very essence of the sutratman doctrine. Let us return to the words of Matthew (23:9): "And call no man your father upon the earth: for one is your Father, which is in heaven."

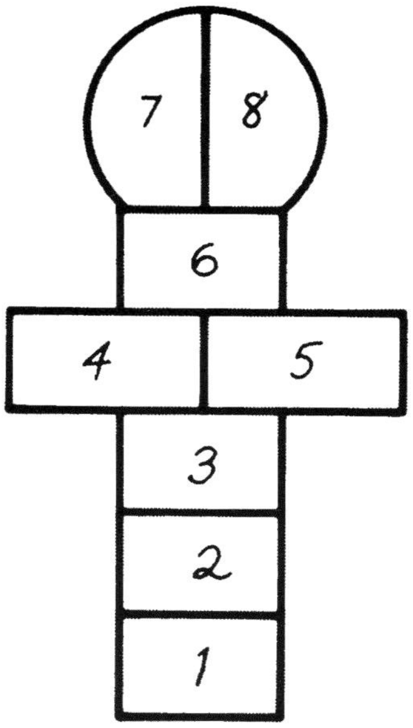

Fig. 4:73: Hopscotch diagram, West Africa.

EXCERPTED ANCESTOR FIGURES

Figures were also excerpted from genealogical patterns and used to decorate bodies, clothing, utensils, dwellings, and cliff facings (Fig. 4.74).

Fig. 4:74: Figures excerpted from genealogical patterns

Fig. 4:75: Excerpted figures elaborated.

Once freed from the constraints of the overall pattern, the figures could be made to look more human by the removal of linkages and the addition of clothing (Fig. 4.75).

163

Fig. 4:76: Cut-out figures forming new patterns.

Motifs that look unique or incoherent usually turn out to be figures excerpted from conventional patterns, reused, and then copied. After enough copying, with attendant omissions and additions, the final figure no longer fits into the original pattern. Dr. Carpenter illustrates how the process takes place (Fig. 4.76).

> For example, cut a vertical swathe from a pattern of hourglass figures with large, hexagonal heads. The resulting band includes two extraneous triangles flanking each hourglass.
>
> Now divide this band horizontally into single hourglass figures. These headless bodies, each with a triangle on either side, may be given new heads and the triangles converted into arms. At least, this is one way it is sometimes done.[46]

Schuster reasoned that these debasements occurred most frequently when seamstresses reused old garments to make new ones, a process he had observed first-hand in China. Even today, peasant-style garments are constructed in tiers, evidence that old material was once cut into strips and reworked to create new garments or repair old ones. Swathes cut from such continuous patterns become cuffs and borders while single figures are used as medallions.

Although it is difficult to ascribe a sex to genealogical patterns, the most common excerpted figure, the hourglass, is normally used to represent the female sex. Of the three hourglass pendants shown here from Hungary and Iran, two have breasts (Fig. 4.77).

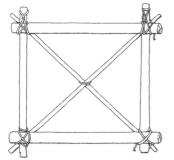

Fig. 4:78: Framework of a Kogi loom.

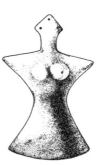

Fig. 4:77: Hourglass pendants: bronze (Hungary), ivory (Iran), and alabaster (Iran).

Hourglass figures are exceedingly common in both Americas as tattoos and petroglyphs. This helps to explain the importance of the figure in Kogi culture and its association with the Mother Goddess (Fig. 4.78).

We can also see that the so-called 'shameless woman' figure is at root an excerpted ancestor figure, whatever other associations she may have acquired over time (Fig. 4.79).

Fig. 4:79: Spindle whorl with "shameless woman" figure.

TAILORED FUR GARMENTS

Let us retrace our steps for a moment and return to sartorial matters—in particular, to the design of fur garments—where we will find the origin of the genealogical iconography we have been discussing.

In 1960, Schuster presented a paper at the Sixth International Congress of Anthropological and Ethnological Sciences in Paris; four years later releasing an expanded version under the title, "Skin and Fur Mosaics in Prehistoric and Modern Times."[47] His opening statement is worth quoting in full.

> The purpose of this paper is to consider a technique of cutting animal skins into decorative patterns, to identify the special character of the patterns produced by this technique, and to establish their influence in the decorative art of prehistoric times (as preserved to us in pottery and other imperishable materials); also to inquire, at least to some extent, into the historical implications of this technique, such as, for example, the question of the type of culture in which it arose, the closely allied question of its antiquity, and the question whether habits and customs associated with this technique may not underlie much of the symbolism of heraldry.[48]

We are first introduced to a design painted on an upright slab from a dolmen in Côta, Portugal, dating from about the third millennium B.C. (Fig. 4.80).

Fig. 4:80: Bronze Age dolmen, Portugal.

Schuster was not the first art historian to write about this design, but his discerning eye focused on two essential features that others had missed, the division of the decorated area into rectangular compartments and the repetition of halves of the central motif—telescoped triangles—at the two sides of each compartment.[49] Applying his wide experience with textiles, he recognized the design as derived from "a garment made by cutting animal skins into certain patterns and re-composing the cut pieces into a 'mosaic.'"[50] He offered another example to support this hypothesis, a robe from the Tehuelche Indians of southern Patagonia, dating from the 19th century (Fig. 4.81).

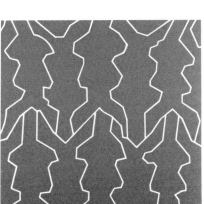

Fig. 4:81: Tehuelche robe, Argentina.

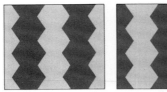

Fig. 4:82: Method for constructing an interlocking design.

1. Take two rectangular sheets of paper of equal size but different color.

2. Place the lighter over darker.

3. Draw three columns of telescoped triangles and two columns of half-triangles.

4. Cut out the design.

5. Rearrange the colors so they alternate, placing the flat side of the half columns on the outer edge to form a rectangle.

Fig. 4:83: Tehuelche Indian robe, Argentina.

Although the specimen was far removed in time and place from the Portuguese dolmen, its method of construction revealed underlying similarities with the painted design. The garment was composed of twelve guanaco skins trimmed in such a way that they fit together in alternately upright and inverted columns of two skins each.[51] In order to achieve a rectangular shape, two of the twelve skins had been split down the middle (along the lines of the animals' backbones) and the split edges of the resulting halves were faced outward.

If we return to the design on the dolmen, the resemblance is clear. Although the animal skins have been replaced by columns of telescoped triangles, several columns of these triangles have been split in the same way as the furs to form the straight outside edges of the design. Schuster suggested an experiment to his readers to help them understand how such designs were made (Fig. 4.82).

This simple mosaic technique has a long history and is known to many cultures. It produces garments that are both beautiful and economical, for no material is wasted. Further, it permits the construction of a wide variety of compartmented, interlocking patterns that can be sewn together to create larger garments. This is clearly the case with the Portuguese dolmen, which was intended to represent a clothed figure.

> Keep in mind that designs found on such megalithic monuments were hardly invented for application to stone, but represented decorated skin garments, copied on stone monuments conceived as clothed effigies of the deceased. Presumably stone monuments were preceded by wooden mortuary effigies, similarly 'clothed' with incised or painted imitations of decorated skin garments. The availability of metal tools may have stimulated & facilitated this transfer of vestimentary designs from wood to stone.[52]

This would account for the sloppiness of the design on the dolmen, which Schuster believed was made by a man imitating the work of a woman.

> Precise accuracy is not necessary: indeed the prehistoric artisan who painted the stela, evidently in haste, introduced many irregularities into the design, giving presumably a rough impression of the original with which he must have been familiar. The carelessness is perhaps to be explained by the mortuary purpose of the monument, for which an approximation of the original was sufficient.[53]

The Tehuelche, a nomadic hunting people who survived into the 19th century, had preserved an ancient method of garment manufacture that dated, in all probability, from Paleolithic times (Fig. 4.83). Although the Tehuelche robe was created in the 19th century, it represented a tradition that was older, in an evolutionary sense, than the design painted on the Portuguese dolmen, which was derived from it. In other words, robes created in the Tehuelche manner were in existence in the New World long before the Portuguese dolmen was erected.

Now we arrive at a matter of singular importance, the similarity of the guanaco skins to human figures.

> Although all of the pelts are identical, their lighter-colored under-bodies form a pattern corresponding roughly to the seams visible on the skin side. By pure coincidence, each pelt looks like a human figure, and the resulting design resembles the most common & basic of all genealogical patterns: an all-over pattern of alternately upright & inverted figures joined limb-to-limb.[54]

Such a view is certainly within reason considering the importance of game animals in a hunting culture and the role of totemism, that mystical affinity between men and animals. The columns of telescoped triangles on the dolmen are simply a more abstract version of the linked animal skins and they share the same anthropomorphic symbolism.

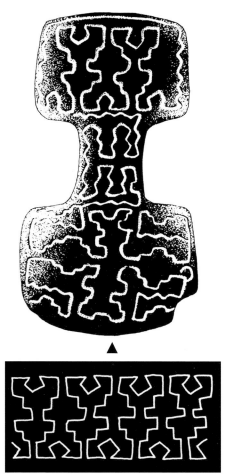

Another example, a stone ceremonial ax from northern Patagonia provides further support for this idea (Fig. 4.84). The design incised on the ax, outlined separately here, is clearly intended to represent a series of interlocked and inverted human figures. It is equally clear that the artist, although working in stone, was familiar with the cutting lines used by seamstresses to produce fur mosaics. Schuster provided a hypothetical reconstruction of the dichromatic skin mosaic that may have served as the model for the incised design.

Fig. 4:84: Stone ceremonial axe with detail, Argentina.

While the splitting of the furs in the Tehuelche robe may have arisen from the need to create a rectangular border, its symbolic character cannot be overlooked, particularly in light of the supporting evidence Schuster was able to gather. In the first place, the Tehuelche not only split the guanaco skins to form the robe, they also simulated the splitting on the reverse or skin side of the robe by painting vertical bands through the centers of the two columns of inverted skins (Fig. 4.85). These bands follow the lines of the animals' spinal columns.

The symbolism connected with splitting was not limited to the Tehuelche and it has a genealogical character wherever it is found.

> Insight into this symbolism is provided by animal sacrifices among certain modern peoples of East Africa. Jensen found that splitting a sacrificed animal along its spine was explicitly associated with the conception of social alignments within a tribe, or with political truces between tribes, for example, in splitting a sacrificed animal to neutralize the bad effects of real or presumed incest, ie of a contravention of marriage regulations.[55]

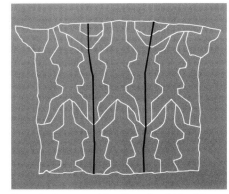

Fig. 4:85: Drawing of the skin side of Tehuelche robe, Argentina.

Jensen also found examples in the Old Testament of practices that, while not specifically related to marriage, involved the sanctity of a contract binding two parties.

> According to Genesis (15:9–10), Abram, following God's direction, divided a heifer, goat & ram 'in the midst, and laid each

Fig. 4:86: Pawnee buffalo robe.

piece one against another.' That evening after a burning lamp 'passed between these pieces' the Lord made a covenant with Abram, saying 'Unto thy seed have I given the land' (15:17–18). Later He spoke of this 'covenant which they made before me, when they cut the calf in twain, and passed between the parts thereof.' (Jeremiah, 34:18).[56]

We saw that knots were also used to verify contracts or unions, particularly in marriage ceremonies.

An analogous example of simulated splitting can be found among the Plains Indians of North America who created robes from the integral hides of large animals, such as bison. One hide equaled one robe.

To prepare a robe like the one pictured here, a woman cut out a long narrow strip from the part that covered the animal's spinal column to split the hide in two (Fig. 4.86). This strip was too tough to be worn and was used instead to make straps and moccasin soles. The two halves of the hide were then stitched together and the resulting seam was covered with an ornamental pattern, sometimes painted, sometimes embroidered over with beads or porcupine quills, called a "blanket strip" (Fig. 4.87). The blanket strip might be removed from a robe and hung separately in a teepee. It played a prominent role in marriage ceremonies where it was referred to as a "marriage belt."

By uniting the two halves of the split robe, blanket strips represented the union of two opposing moieties through marriage. When they were separated from the robe, the symbolism was retained. The sexual symbolism of needles and stitching is also important here since sewing brings about the union of the two skins and by extension, the progeny of the bride and groom. The phallic needle is central to the sutratman doctrine.

Motifs that resemble blanket strips commonly appear as rock art in North America (Fig. 4.88).

Fig. 4:87: Blanket strip.

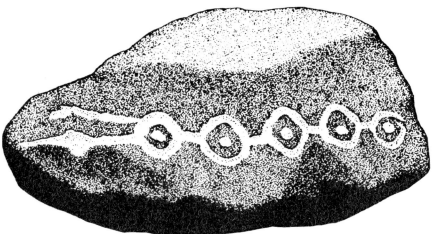

Fig. 4:88: Petroglyph, Nevada.

The resemblance of small animal skins to human figures and their inverted and interlocked placement gave rise to the genealogical iconography we have been discussing.

> The splitting of some of the skins would then imply, on the symbolical level, a splitting of the social fabric. No matter which came first, the social pattern of the robe, the symbolism is, in any case, is as striking as it is natural; and I find it easy to believe that it would have occurred to people who, surely for many millennia in remote prehistoric times, traditionally made and wore such robes.[57]

A question remains, how did the mosaic technique come to emphasize each half of the split with a contrasting color? The skin side of the Tehuelche robe is a single color. On the fur side, however, each skin is dark in the center and light around the edges and this may have suggested the dichromatic symbolism common to mosaic garments and the iconographic patterns derived from them. In fact, complementary mosaics were known to the Tehuelche. Samuel Lothrop found one such *quillango* of guanaco skins, which was painted with a reciprocal pattern on the skin side (Fig. 4.89).

Fig. 4:89: Tehuelche Indian wearing a native robe (*quillango*), Argentina.

169

Fig. 4:90: Pottery vessel, Argentina.

The pattern consists of hourglass figures made in alternating bands: dark bands with white dots opposing light bands with dark dots. The hourglasses are connected at the waists by horizontal bars, meant to represent arms. The fact that the design is painted on the robe rather than being cut from skins and then stitched together is of less importance than the fact that it was applied to the skin side of a fur robe. This particular pattern is so common in tribal art that examples can be found in a wide variety of media, such as this vessel from northern Argentina (A.D. 500) (Fig. 4.90).

Schuster found the last traces of this ancient vestimentary technique and its associated symbolism in the most remote parts of the world. If *homo sapiens sapiens* migrated out of Africa some 100,000 years ago, as is currently believed, and gradually populated the rest of the world, surely Patagonia and Southern Australia mark two ends of the trail. In fact, the same ancient methods of garment designs are shared in both locales (Fig. 4.91).

Fig. 4:91: Tehuelche woman painting a skin robe (left). Australian family of New South Wales (right).

An opossum-skin robe with scratched designs made by the aborigines of southeast Australia bears the same pattern of concatenated human figures found in South America and elsewhere (Fig. 4.92 and Fig. 4.93).

While the Australian garment is not cut from animal furs, it is composed of the same rectangular panels that served as the model for the Portuguese dolmen.

It was Schuster's considered belief that these rare specimens, whose significance he alone understood, represented all that was left of an archaic method of garment manufacture that had survived from the earliest times.

> This is, I think, the best way to account for the prevalence of "endless," or so to speak, "revolving," patterns of concatenated human figures in the decoration of skin robes made and worn by still living (or now dying) "primitive" hunting peoples in southern South America and Australia. Indeed, the designs perpetrated in these traditions may be, in the most literal sense, survivals of the earliest schematic art, still applied as it must have been applied in remote paleolithic times, and still pregnant with the record of man's earliest social consciousness.[58]

Fig. 4:92: Opossum skin robe, Australia.

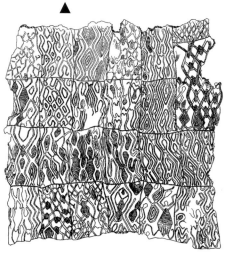

Fig. 4:93: Detail of opossum robe (Fig. 4.92), Australia.

HERALDRY

To summarize Schuster's findings up to this point, there exists a class of designs consisting of interconnected human figures, which we have termed "genealogical patterns." These patterns are found in many cultures and appear on a wide variety of media—textiles, metalwork, clay, wood, and the human body itself—suggesting great antiquity. The idea of using these designs to depict human social relations derived, in all probability, from the imitation of garments created from interlocking animal skins. Lastly—and this is the point we wish to discuss next— these patterns relate to marriage and descent and thus represent a kind of primitive heraldry.

> In order to understand how this could come about, we must remember that the procedures traditionally followed in the manufacture of skin garments, and the designs evolved from these procedures, would inevitably develop differences from tribe to tribe; and it is only natural that these differences would have served, since the remotest imaginable times, especially under nomadic conditions of life, to distinguish members of one tribe from another. Thus garments would have served, from time immemorial, as a means of tribal identification.[59]

Fig. 4:94: Herald's tabard, England.　　　　Fig. 4:95: Painted hide shield, East Africa.

Medieval heraldry shares a common preoccupation with the identification and display of pedigrees. Although heraldic symbolism is far more abstract, it contains traces of its origins. In the first place, heraldic emblems are quartered to symbolize the marital history of the clan or family (Fig. 4.94). This is what genealogical symbolism is all about, relation and descent. Secondly, the presence of animals or parts of animals is reminiscent of totemism.

Thirdly, armorial insignia are displayed on escutcheons in the same way that tribal insignia were displayed on shields covered with animal skins, like the one shown here from East Africa (Fig. 4.95). The Greek *aigis*, a goatskin shield, must have begun in this way. It was associated with Zeus, the Father of gods and men.

An even closer connection can be found in the design of the heraldic device called the "vair," represented by rows of inverted and interlocking cup- or bell-shaped patterns of alternating colors (Fig. 4.96). Vair was a costly squirrel fur worn by the aristocracy and high-church officials in medieval Europe and the design is clearly an imitation of a number of squirrel skins sewn together in the same manner we have been discussing. Jean Guillim's *A Display of Heraldrie* (1611) confirms this observation: "If you observe the proportion of this vaire, you shalle easily discerne the very shape of the case or skinne of little beasts, in them."[60]

Fig. 4:96: Vair pattern.

As fur-bearing animals became harder to find, garments made from them became the exclusive apparel of the elite, who took a special pride in their ancestry.[61] This would account for the depiction of garment patterns on standing stones such as the Cöta dolmen, or this design on a stela from Ellenberg, Germany, dating from the Beaker Culture (2800 to 2400 B.C.) (Fig. 4.97).

Clothing designs were undoubtedly applied to wooden objects as well. Modern examples such as those of the Kamilaroi of Australia provide the evidence (Fig. 4.98). These are robe designs carved onto trees as memorials for the dead.

Fig. 4:97: Stela with vair pattern, Germany.   Fig. 4:98: Dendroglyphs, Australia.

Schuster also found abundant evidence in the form of painted pebbles or small, engraved plaques such as these anthropomorphic schist pendants from Eneolithic Iberia, clothed in heraldic devices (Fig. 4.99).[62]

Fig. 4:99: Anthropomorphic schist pendants, Spain.

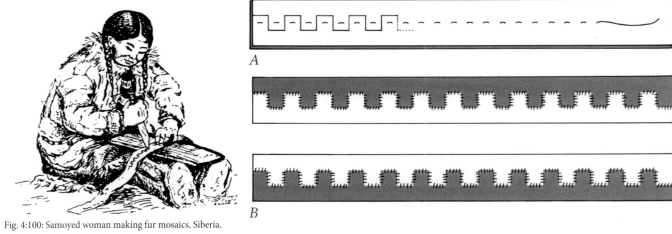

Fig. 4:100: Samoyed woman making fur mosaics, Siberia.

Fig. 4:101: Vogul sewing bag with detail, Siberia.

SIBERIAN MOSAICS

Schuster supported the historical evidence he had gathered about the antiquity of fur and skin mosaics with modern accounts of traditions surviving among Asiatic peoples such as the Kirghiz of Central Asia, the Tavgi-Samoyeds (Nganasan) of northern Siberia, and the Ugrians of the Ob River Basin (Voguls, Mansi, and Ostyaks or Khanti). These groups were still using mosaic techniques to construct their own clothing from fur, reindeer skin, cloth, and felt. The Russian ethnologist A. A. Popov provided a detailed description of the mosaics made by Samoyed women out of reindeer hide (Fig. 4.100).

> Ornaments cut out of hide & cloth with the sharp point of a knife. A piece of hide or cloth of one color is placed on top of a piece of another color, and in order to prevent them from shifting during the cutting, they are tacked together through the middle by a thread, A. The four strips which result from this cutting are then stitched together in such a way that the "teeth" of one strip engage the cutout spaces of the other, B.[63]

While these dichromatic mosaics may not be composed of interlocking animal skins like the medieval vair, many of them exhibit the same anthropomorphic symbolism. A woman's sewing bag from the Voguls of the Ob River Basin shows the same compartmentation found on the Cöta dolmen as well as the same humanlike figures (Fig. 4.101). In this case, instead of telescoped triangles (stacked bodies) we find a series of interlocked figures referred to as "heads" or "skulls" by the Vogul.

One Obugrian design motif used to construct mosaics is referred to as "half-man" or "man-stump" (Fig. 4.102). This stumpy little fellow is completed by being linked to a partner of the opposite color, surely more than a marriage of convenience.

> Of course, in the context of a dichromatic mosaic, the term "half-man" could also be interpreted in other than purely technological terms. If such mosaics convey, as I have proposed, a significant social symbolism, then each "half-man," even if he appears to be complete is not really so until he is united (or, so to speak, reunited, after being cut out of skin) with his marital partner, in the form of an identical figure of the opposite color.[64]

It should also be noted that the "half-stump" has its own genealogical associations. Like a plant cutting, this "human-stump" is capable of procreation as indicated by all the connected figures.

Fig. 4:102: Basic design element: "Half-man."

Fig. 4:103: Neolithic pottery sherd, Croatia.

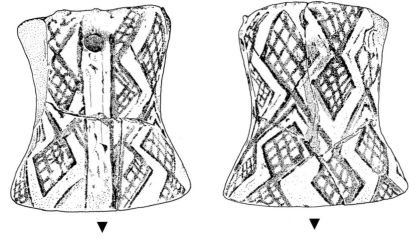

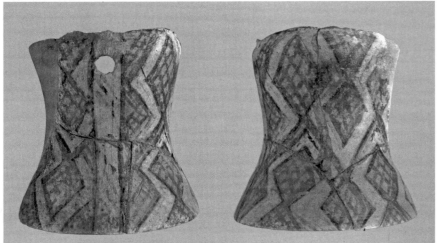

Fig. 4:104: Neolithic vessel base with details, Rumania.

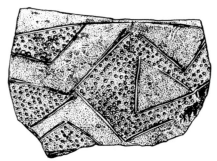

Fig. 4:105: Neolithic pottery sherd, Bosnia.

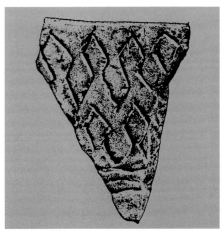

Fig. 4:106: Neolithic pottery sherd, Hungary.

Moving from the present to the past, Schuster compared the central panel of the Siberian fur mosaic with a series of pottery designs taken from four different Neolithic cultures of Central and Eastern Europe (Figs. 4.103, 4.104, 4.105, and 4.106). Some of these designs date from the fourth millennium B.C., two millennia earlier than the Cöta dolmen.

Reciprocal designs are present on all the specimens and three even imitate the dichromaticity of fur mosaics by stippling or by banding alternating elements. The origins of these designs in garment manufacture is more evident in the Moldavian specimen where a vertical split marks the end of one panel and the beginning of another (Fig. 4.104).

As records of social identification, ancestry, and marriage, clothing designs were suitable emblems for a wide variety of personal possessions. In this sense they bear some resemblance to military uniforms, which tell us what branch of the service a person belongs to as well as his or her rank, a matter related to ancestry.

The role of clothing in establishing social identity occupies a central place in human culture, and has since the beginning. God provided Adam and Eve with clothing prior to their expulsion from the Garden of Eden. Dr. Robert Oden has suggested that in the ancient Near East and in many traditional societies, clothing and the act of investiture are traditionally symbolic of status, both of the giver and receiver.

> When an anthropologist investigating the many functions of clothing recently asked an East African why he wore clothes, the later replied, "Because it shows we are human beings." This response is precisely what I am suggesting is the meaning of Genesis 3:21. The investiture of the man and woman with a garment here is not an act prompted by generosity or by a grace that is concerned lest humans become ashamed or cold or both. This investiture is rather a symbolic act that firmly distinguishes humans from the divine.[65]

BIRTH FROM THE KNEE

Let us return to our central theme, the relationship between human joints and ancestors. Schuster had much to say about the matter, all of it directly relevant to the sutratman doctrine.[66]

Examining an earlier example, the Melanesian club, we can see how the heads of the lower figures—descendants, in our genealogical scheme—are placed above the knee of the upper figures—their parents (Fig. 4.107). That is to say, the lower figures are "born" from the knees of the upper. The limbs function as the connections between generations, an idea based on an analogy with the plant world. Strange as this may sound, just such an idea is reflected both in the language, mythology and beliefs of many cultures. The basic notion is that the child originates in the knee of the father and somehow travels into his penis from whence it is "planted" in the female (Fig. 4.108). Let's look at some of the evidence for this unusual idea in which the mysterious process of birth is made to fit, albeit uneasily, into the overall conceptual scheme we have been discussing in one way or another throughout this book.

> Now the importance of limbs as genetic bonds is manifested not only in art, but also in other expressions of human tradition. Throughout many parts of the world we encounter myths and legends about the birth of human beings from the limbs — sometimes from the arms or fingers, more commonly from the legs, and most commonly from the knees. Those born in this way are generally imagined as "the first people"; and the limbs from which they spring are those of an Ultimate Ancestor.[67]

We will begin our abbreviated survey in Africa.

> Among the Masai folk-tales collected by Hollis is one called "The Old Man and the Knee." It relates how an old man, living alone, was troubled with a swelling in his knee which he took for an abscess; but, at the end of sixth months, as it did not burst, he cut it open and out came two children, a boy and a girl.[68]

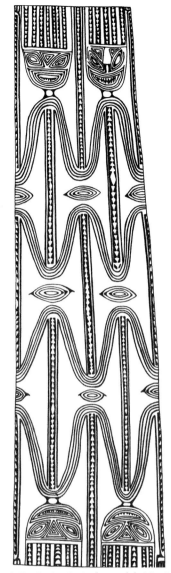

Fig. 4:107: Design incised on a club, New Ireland.

Fig. 4:108: Birth of Dionysos from the knee of Zeus.

An older version of this folktale is preserved among the Nandi.

> Among the Moi clan, there is a tradition that the first Dorobo—again we find the Dorobo looked on as the earliest men— gave birth to a boy and a girl. His leg swelled up one day … at length it burst, and a boy issued from the inner side of the calf, while a girl issued from the outer side. These two in the course of time had children, who were the ancestors of all the people on earth.[69]

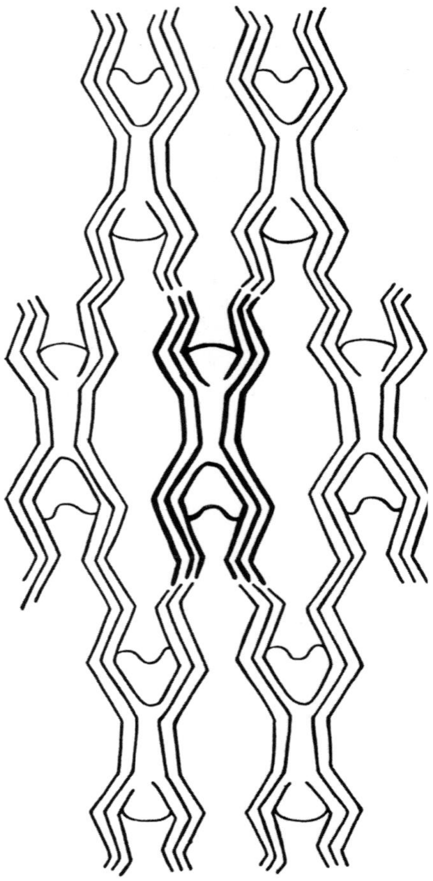

If we remember that legs are the connecting link in the iconography of descent, these ideas may not seem so strange. Some genealogical patterns have multiple, parallel limbs whose extensions connect with figures below them, as seen in these two examples.

The first is taken from a Formosan textile (Fig. 4.109); the second, a female figure copied from a petroglyph in Guiana (Fig. 4.110). A hypothetical reconstruction allows us to see how it might fit within an overall pattern. In either case, the figures remind us of tales of children born from the sinews of their parents. The multiple outlines symbolize the multiple "members" of each generation.

The need to rationalize the male origin of the child led to many variant forms of the myth including an African tale, related by Baumann, about the hero who "slipped out of his mother's womb into her leg and was immediately full grown."[70] The Greeks tell a similar story about the birth of Hephaistos from the hip of Hera. Another tale from the hill-tribes of India demonstrates this tendency to move the source of the child from the father's knee to the mother's.

> Originally the vagina was situated below the knee of the left leg. One day a chicken pecked at it, and it jumped up to a place of safety between the thighs, where it has remained ever since. But it was wounded and blood flows from it every month.[71]

In a Japanese version, a boy called "Knee-Spit" (*Suneko-Tampako*) is born from the knee of an old woman after being instructed by the Boddhissatva Kannon to smear saliva on her knee.[72] The saliva clearly stands for the male semen, which accounts for the transfer of the child, already present in the semen— like the medieval *homunculus*— into the knee of the woman.

A Chinese account of the virgin birth of Hou Chi taken from *The Classic of Poetry* (circa 600 B.C) relates how his mother, Chiang Yuan, conceived by treading in the big toe of God's footprint.[73]

Fig. 4:109: Textile, Formosa.

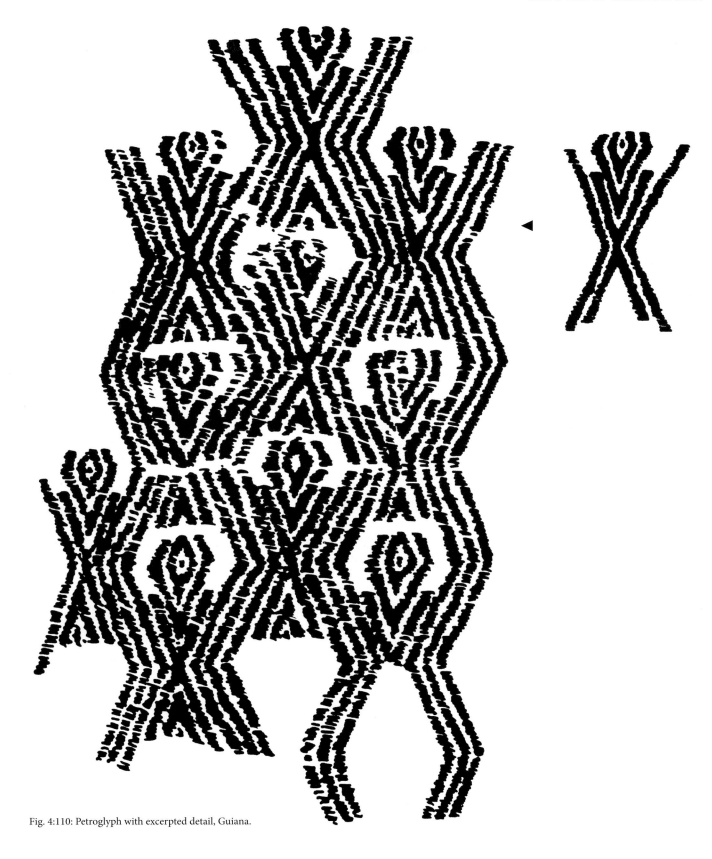

Fig. 4:110: Petroglyph with excerpted detail, Guiana.

A Palaung version from Burma is closest to the original conception of the priority of male over female birth.

> Long, long ago…it was the man and not the woman who bore the children. The man carried the unborn child in the calf of his leg until the time when it was large enough to be born…. Then the man said, …'Take the baby and keep it warm in thy stomach….' He then saw that the woman had taken good care of the child…; so, after that time, he gave over to the woman the care of the children.[74]

The idea is also reflected in the stories of the Yami of Botel Tobago, an island forty-five miles off the southeastern tip of Formosa, and in the Marshall Islands.[75] The Yami rationalize their version of the story by relating that the penes of their ancestors were originally joined to their knees.[76]

Inez de Beauclair, who studied the Yami and corresponded frequently with Schuster, provided supporting evidence.[77] In a Yami folktale a man refers to his great-great grandchild as "the grandchild of the tip of my foot" (*apoko do katchi no ai go*) while his son refers to the same child as the grandchild of my knee (*apoko no tud*). She cites a letter from Dr. Robert Fox (May 1, 1956) of the National Museum in Manila that indicates similar beliefs in the Philippine where the Tagalog designate a great-grandchild as "grandchild of the knee" (*apo sa talampakan*). More detail is provided in Fox's letter:

> The Iloko-speaking people of Luzon (if I remember correctly data which I have collected in the past), have carried this (system of designating generational position by parts of the body) even farther. Likening the generational position of ego to the waist, they define five generations by the shoulders and head (i.e. ascending generations), and by the knees and the soles (i.e. descending generations). This is extremely interesting from the standpoint of social anthropology, for it bounds the bilateral kinship group, as it exists in reality.[78]

Fig. 4:108: Birth of Dionysos from the knee of Zeus.

We have a number of European examples. Most familiar is the myth of the birth of Dionysius from the thigh or knee of Zeus (Fig. 4.108). The Greeks appear to have been as puzzled by this idea as we are and in their version they reversed the order of events to make it appear more plausible. The child is born first to Semele and then sewn into the knee of Zeus. The thread used to suture Zeus' knee is also of some significance and can be related to an initiation ceremony practiced in India up to the present day. Schuster notes that "the Greek epithets *dimhtor* and *dissotokos* meaning "twice born," applied to Dionysius, have their exact counterpart in the Sanscrit *dvija*, applied to a man of any of the first three classes …who has been 'reborn' through investiture with the sacred thread."[79] Zeus uses the same thread to prepare Dionysius for his second birth.

A variant of this theme is central to the medieval Grail motif where the Fisher King is wounded "in his loins" and as a result, his kingdom suffers from drought and desiccation. Dr. Coomaraswamy and others have noted the connection between these stories and Sumerian and Indo-Iranian fertility rites involving the Water of Life, soma, or related concepts involving periodic revivification of the life force.[80] In India, Indra struggles with Vr-tra, the demon of draught. Indra's strength goes into the earth and becomes plants and roots; he is restored by drinking soma.

> Now in the soma sacrifice, the purchase of the soma by the gods from the Gandharva(s) [tree spirits] in exchange for Vak "because the Gandharva is fond of women" (*Satapatha Brahmana* III.2.4) forms the theme of a kind of ritual drama in which a Sudra represents the Gandharva. It is most significant in view of the fact that the offering is primarily to Indra, that the purchased soma is placed by the priest on the sacrificer's right thigh with the formula "Enter the right thigh of Indra," and the sacrificer then rises, saying "With new life, with good life, am I risen after the immortals."[81]

Similar tales are told about Tvastr, Prajapati, and Daksa, gods of fertility "injured in the loins" or paralyzed as punishment for sin.

In Europe, the belief in birth from the father persisted as late as the 18th century. Evidence can be found in Boswell's celebrated *Life of Samuel Johnson*. Boswell offers the following argument during a disagreement with his father over the right of his female relatives to share in the family estate.

> As first, the opinion of some distinguished naturalists, that our species is transmitted through males only, the female being all along no more than a *nidus*, or nurse, as Mother Earth is to plants of every sort; which notion seems to be confirmed by that text of scripture, "He was yet in the loins of his FATHER when Melchisedeck met him;" (Heb. vii. 10) and consequently, that a man's grandson by a daughter, instead of being his surest descendent, as is vulgarly said, has, in reality, no connection whatever with his blood.[82]

Schuster also provides a number of New World examples:

> The theme was current among the Carib Indians of the Antilles, and survives in South America at least among the Chocó and Uitoto of Columbia and the Umatina of south-central Brazil. For each instance here cited, presumably more could be found in surrounding areas.[83]

Despite the variations in these myths, certain elements reappear. Birth from the knee or leg is preceded by a swelling of the affected part, just as the womb swells prior to the birth of a child. Sometimes both knees are involved and a boy emerges from one and a girl from the other; or different races or social divisions spring from each. As Schuster put it, "the vagaries of these legends might be likened to the conventionalization of the artistic patterns which we have studied."[84]

R. B. Onians points out the similarity of these stories to those telling of birth from the head.

> We saw that the story of Zeus engendering a child in his head with-

out the help of a mother was explained by the belief that the head contained the seed. There appears to have been preserved a striking variant in a folk-tale Zakynthos recorded some seventy years ago. It tells how the greatest king in the world in his virtue had resolved never to take a wife, yet would have liked to have children and one day he sat and wept and 'there appeared to him an angel and said he must not weep; he would get a child out of his *atsa*. (This is a rare dialect word for part of the leg. Schmidt renders it *Wade*, i.e. "calf".) Soon after, one of the king's legs swelled and one day as he was hunting he stuck a thorn into it. Then all at once a wonderfully beautiful maiden with all her body armed and carrying lance and helm sprang out of his *atsa*'.[85]

The fact that both the head and the knee were once considered generative organs should no longer surprise us, given their coincidence in our genealogical iconography. Both the head and knees contain fluid, which the ancients likened to the sap of plants and trees. Hesiod and Alcaeus believed that the hot summer dried up men's knees and heads and made them feeble.[86] The head and knee were also thought of as the source of a man's *genius* (Gk. *psyche*), or procreative spirit. Pliny the Elder provides testimony:

> The knees of human beings also possess a sort of religious sanctity in the usage of the nations. Suppliants touch the knees and stretch out their hands towards them and pray at them as at altars, perhaps because they contain a vital principle. For in the joint of each knee, right and left, on the front side there is a sort of twin hollow cavity, the piercing of which, as of the throat, causes the breathe to flow away.[87]

The important role of the knee is also reflected in language. The term for the word "knee" is used alternatively to express concepts like "degrees of kinship" or "generation" in many Indo-European languages and in some non-Indo-European ones as well.

Jacob Grimm, the well-known linguist and chronicler of folklore, identified a large number of kinship terms found in Germanic languages that derived from the names for body parts, including head, nose, cheek, bosom, stomach, lap, womb, side, back, elbow, femur, knee, ankles, and nails.[88] Most familiar are the English words "genealogy," "genus," and "generation," all derived from the Latin *genu* ("knee").

Maurice Cahen provides more specific evidence for the Germanic languages.[89] Using medieval sources, he identified two distinct usages of the term for knee, one relating to a rite of adoption and the other to the calculation of degrees of kinship. In Old Norse, an adopted child is spoken of as having been placed on the knee (*setja i kné*) of his foster father. The compound verb *knésetja* (to adopt) and the substantive *knésetningr* (an adopted son) express the same idea. Cahen provided a number of historical examples of the practice involving Norse kings and cited similar evidence offered by J. Loth for the Irish.[90]

The Norse facts that we have just cited accord perfectly with the Irish facts that held the attention of M. Loth. They bear Hakon "to the knee of Aethelstan" as Cúchulain "to the knee of Fergus." The Scandinavian *knésetningr* and the Irish *glundaltae* both designate the foster child that is placed on the knees of the foster father.[91]

More interesting is the Scandinavian *kné-runnr*, which denotes a family line. The word *runnr* ("runner") has a number of meanings including "course" as well as the shoot of a plant, a meaning that is retained in modern English. The analogy of kinship terms with the plant world is a commonplace in many languages with the attendant notion of relatives as shoots or sprouts branching from a common stock.[92] The notion of a course, path, or line is entirely consistent with the sutratman doctrine where a sequence of knots—and by extension, body joints—can represent related individuals that are united by the continuity of the string. In time, the Scandinavian *kné-runnr* came to have the more general meaning of race, tribe, or family, as did its Anglo-Saxon equivalent, *cnéo-res*.

Loth explored similar matters within the Celtic, Germanic, and Slavic branches of the Indo-European family, adding Assyrian as well, a Semitic tongue.[93] As late as the 16th century the Irish word *glún* ("knee") was used to mean "generation," as in *glún ar ghlún* ("generation after generation"). In Russian we find *kolieno* ("knee") and the plural and distributive forms *koliena* and *pokolienie* for "race," "line," or "branch." Polish gives us *kolano*, meaning either 'knee,' 'generation,' or 'race,' and we find the same associations in Lapp, Finnish, and other Finno-Ugrian languages.[94]

Semitic evidence comes from two sources. The Old Testament has a number of references to the practice of legitimation or filiation, in which the father acknowledged paternity of a newborn by placing it on his knee (Fig. 4.111). In Genesis (50:23) we read:

> And Joseph saw Ephraim's children of the third generation: the children also of Machir the son of Manasseh were brought up upon Joseph's knees.[95]

Loth remarks that this is not an adoption because Manasseh has already been adopted by Jacob. Rather, it is a metaphoric expression by which Joseph recognizes the children as belonging to his race.

The practice of legitimation appears to have played a significant role in the past when not as much importance was attached to biological paternity. The reasons for this are not entirely clear, but certainly the structure of kinship systems must have played a significant role. Aside from the fact that it may be hard to determine who has fathered a child, there must have been times when an appropriate marriage partner was not available. In this case, adoption was a suitable alternative. Add to this the common practice of fosterage (sending a child to a relative to be raised) and you have a more fluid situation than the modern nuclear family. From a religious standpoint, it was the acknowledgment of the child by the father, natural or adoptive, that mattered.

Fig. 4:111: Abraham and Lazarus.

183

The linguist Antoine Meillet summarized the matter succinctly when he noted that the Indo-European root *gen ("knee") is related both to the root *gen, a homonym meaning "beget" (L. gigno)—used to refer exclusively to the parental role of the father—and to a third meaning, "to know," "to recognize" (L. gnosco).[96] He concluded that the third meaning was the original one, and that the word came to mean "beget" when it was used in a more narrow juridical sense: to recognize a child as one's own. The word "genuine" (L. genuinus) reflects the same idea. The genuine child is the one placed upon the father's knee to be named and accepted as his own.[97] The act of legitimation was part of the Roman rite of sublatio (Gk. anaireisthai) during which the newborn was first placed on the ground and then on the knee of the father.

> The custom of placing the child on the ground seems to have been at first a type of homage to Mother Earth. It is on the ground as well that, among the Latins and Germans, the dying were placed. The earth is the mother of men…: they come from her womb and return there. The sublatio consequently appears to be a most general act involving the recognition of the child by the father.[98]

Schuster believed that this practice was in essence a "symbolic return of the child to the place of its prior conception in the male, and thus a repudiation of the conceptive role of the earth-womb."[99] He found further support for this idea in the practice of couvade.

Couvade is a custom observed in many parts of the world in which a father, before, during or after the birth of his child, takes to his bed and behaves as if he, and not his wife, were having the child. This simulated pregnancy and birth may take many forms but often the man adheres to a special diet and imitates the labor pains of his wife. Accounts of this unusual practice are widespread and much has been written on the subject. Tautain, writing in 1896, expressed the belief that the basic principle behind the couvade was filiation or legitimation, an affirmation of paternity.[100]

One significant account of the practice was provided by the Portuguese voyager Soares de Souza, who visited the coast of Brazil in the 16th century.

> When SOARES DE SOUSA asked a Tupinamba husband why he observed dietary and other typical restrictions of the couvade during the pregnancy and parturition of his wife, the man replied: "because the child came out of his loins [lombos], and because all that women can do is to guard the seed in the womb where the child grows up.[101]

What gives meaning to all the elaborate drama of the couvade is the same idea that lies behind the stories about birth from the knees: a conception of the birth process based on an analogy to planting and sowing, where the source of seed in the male is the crucial element. That is to say, the act is intended to emphasize the priority of the male in the procreative act.

DISMEMBERMENT AND CANNIBALISM

Birth from the male knee is related to another cosmogonic myth we discussed earlier, the dismemberment and reconstitution of a cosmic being from which all beings are said to derive. Perhaps the best-known example is the Vedic *Purusha* (Man) who is sacrificed and dismembered to form the world and society.

> The four primary castes of the Indian social system are said to be derived from the body of this being as follows: "The Brahmin (priest) was his mouth, his two arms were made by the Rajanya (warrior), his two thighs the Vaicya (trader and agriculturist), and from his feet the Cudra (servile class) was born." [102]

Division of the body is most commonly into fours, representing the basic social divisions, or into twelves, representing the major joints of the body. It is no coincidence that these numbers have always had mystical significance.

A Russian variant of the Indian myth is found in the *Poem on the Book of Profound Mysteries* in which the social order is similarly derived from the body of Adam. The tsars come from his head, the boyar princes from other parts of his body, and the common people from "the holy knee of Adam."[103]

A less detailed version is provided in Polynesia where Austral Islanders depict their God Tangarora in the act of creating the other gods and man (Fig. 4.112).

Creation of a social order from the *membra disjecta* of a First Ancestor is preserved in the Vedic hymns and the Catholic Mass. Schuster's work helps to place these more abstract ideas within an older and more widespread tradition.

> For it seems likely that stories about birth from the knees or legs, which are found, as we have seen, in widely separated parts of the world, are all ultimately related to such a cosmogonic myth as fragments to a whole. The basic myth of creation by dismemberment is certainly much older than any of the literatures in which it was first recorded; and it seems very likely that such a myth lies at the bottom, or very near the bottom, of all the phenomena studied in this essay. In civilized literary traditions, the cosmic being appears as a mystical abstraction; but among more primitive peoples it seems likely that he was, in the first place, simply a deified ancestor.[104]

Certainly cannibal practices and motives vary from culture to culture. Schuster was interested in those examples in which the distribution of the victim's body parts appeared to have social significance. He found that in many instances there was a special emphasis on the fingers and toes, arms and legs, or hands and feet of the victims, which he believed was due "to something more than a gourmet's interest in a 'joint' of meat."[105]

Fig. 4:112: Tangaroa with rear view, Austral Islands.

Hans Staden, a Hessian mercenary who spent time in Brazil between 1547 and 1555, was captured by the Tupinamba and spent nine months among them. He recounted his adventures in *Wahrhafige Historia* (True Story), published in 1557, illustrated with a number of woodcuts. The one shown here depicts Tupinamban women "racing around the huts of their camp, each carrying one of the freshly dismembered arms and legs of the victim (Fig. 4.113)."[106] Schuster suggests that each limb was associated with a "quarter" of the camp, implying a re-creation of the Tupinamba world through the sacrifice and ingestion of the captive. The Tupinamba also offered the fingertips of their victims to honored guests, as a special treat.

Among the Dieri of southeastern Australia, it is deceased relatives who are eaten, rather than captives, revealing an even closer affinity between body parts and social "members."

> When the body is lowered into the grave, an old man who is the nearest relation to the deceased present, cuts off all the fat adhering to the face, thighs, arms and stomach and passes it around to be swallowed by the relatives. The order in which they partake of it is as follows: — the mother eats of her children, and the children of their mother; a man eats of his sister's husband and of his brother's wife; mother's brothers, mother's sisters, sister's children, mother's parents, or daughter's children are also eaten of; but the father does not eat of his child nor the children of their sire. The relatives eat of the fat in order that they may be no longer sad.[107]

Fig. 4:113: Tupinamba women with body parts.

The significance of this practice is reinforced by the observations of W. Stanner in his report on aboriginal modes of address in northwest Australia.[108] He noted that a number of tribes identify certain relatives by touching various parts of the body, each relative being designated by a different part. He relates this conception to the belief that a twitching in a certain body part foretells the appearance of a relative.

> The Nangiomeri say that twitchings of the thigh mean that mother's brother is likely to appear or that something is happening to him. One informant from this tribe gave me the following list of bodily signs for relatives: right shin, brother; left shin, classificatory brother; groin, mother's brother and sister's son; shoulder, father, father's sister and son; stomach, cross-cousin and father's mother; breast, sister's son; knee, father's father and son's son; buttocks or hips, mother's father; eye, wife's uncle. The lists vary between tribes.[109]

The same connection between body parts and ancestor is found in Ambon and the surrounding Moluccas where it is also associated with cannibalism. Parts of the body are identified with both individuals and the social groups that make up the community at large. That is to say, the community is conceived as a social "body." Villages occupied by clans named by body parts are actually laid out in the shape of a human body.[110]

Among the Kwakiutl, *Dzonokwa*, the cannibal woman of legend and ritual is depicted in the form of feast bowls representing her breast, navel, and knees (Fig. 4.114). The cover serves as her head. Participants in the meal symbolically eat these parts of her body.

If the eating of the body parts of a deceased relative or a sacrificial victim represents the re-creation of the group, we may ask why, among the Dieri, the father is not allowed to eat of his child, nor the child of his father. This same taboo was found among the Aztecs.

> ...after a captive of the Aztecs has been sacrificed, the man who captured him must abstain from eating of him, because of a simulated parental relationship. This is announced ritually at the moment of capture, when the captor says of the captive: "You are the same as my son", and the captive responds, "You are the same as my father." The captor may eat of other sacrificed captives, but not of his own; "for", he says, "should I then eat of myself?"[111]

This is why the sacrificial victim is normally treated as an honored guest before the sacrifice. The prohibition against cannibalism in the direct male line brings us back to matters we have discussed earlier.

Fig. 4:114: Arrangement of Kwakiutl feast dishes, British Columbia.

> Couvade, myth, cannibalism, legitimation and language all perpetrate this one idea: an obsessive preoccupation with the special relation between father and child, based upon the prior activity of the father in the procreative process, and generally symbolized in a fictive male "womb."[112]

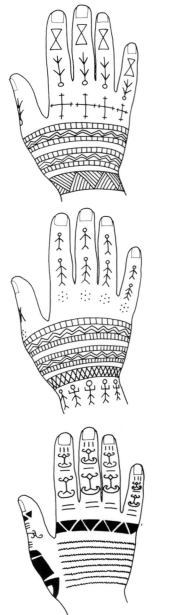

Fig. 4:115: Tattooed hands, Taiwan (2) and Borneo.

Fig. 4:116: Tlingit charm, Alaska.

FINGERS AND ANCESTORS

It was once widely believed that the fingers possess a genetic potency like the cuttings from a plant. A story is told in Papua, New Guinea about a man who was dismembered and eaten, except for one finger. The next morning he reappeared alive.[113] A similar story from the Bacairi of Brazil relates how the first Bacairi woman became pregnant by swallowing the finger-bones of dead Bacairi Indians. She herself was subsequently dismembered and eaten.[114]

The procreative power of the fingers is in large part a reflection of their association with ancestors. This accounts for the frequency of finger tattooing, in which the hands are used as a kind of kinship chart. In Taiwan and Borneo human figures are tattooed on phalanges (Fig. 4.115) while the Tlingit of Alaska explain the eye-like grooves on this charm as 'spirits emerging from the knuckles (Fig. 4.116).'[115] We should recall the words of Thalbitzer, quoted earlier that "according to Eskimo notions, in every part of the human body (particularly in every joint, as for instance, in every finger joint) there resides a little soul."[116]

None of this should be surprising given the association we have seen between ancestors and counting systems. In Schuster's words:

> It may be regarded as a safe conjecture that this association arose through the use of the fingers as digits in counting relatives for purposes of social classification; and we may suppose that this numerative function of the fingers led, at a very early time, to their identification with certain relatives or classes of relatives.[117]

Echoes of these ideas remained as long as the hand was used for mnemonic purposes. Here for example, an illustration from an early printed work, *Schatzbehalter der wahren Reichtümer des Heils* (The Treasure Chest of Salvation), used for memorizing the Apostles' Creed (Fig. 4.117).[118]

The belief in the potency of fingers can be most clearly seen in the worldwide practice of finger mutilation, in which a finger or part of a finger is sacrificed when a close relative is ill or has died. This sacrifice rests on a deeply felt principle of identification: for each joint a relative, for each relative a joint. Finger amputation is clearly related to the notion that individuals are in some way composed of the spirits of their ancestors, who reside in their finger joints.

Fig. 4:117: Finger mnemonic for memorizing the Apostle's Creed.

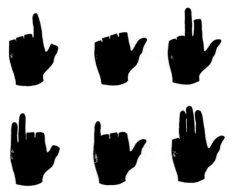

Figure 4:118: Images of hands with missing finger joints, France.

We know the practice of finger amputation is very old from the silhouettes of hands with missing fingers or parts of fingers depicted on the walls of caves in France and northern Spain some 20,000 years ago (Fig. 4.118). Hand prints are also found on rock paintings in Texas and in caves in southern Patagonia, but these cannot be dated (Fig. 4.119).[119]

We also find handprints on cave walls in both the Old and New Worlds as well as in Oceania and Australia. It is possible these marks were left to commemorate the attendance of individuals at a ritual or ceremony; a kind of primitive guest book (Fig. 4.120).

Figure 4:119: Petrogylphs, Patagonia.

Fig. 4:120: Pictograph, Arizona.

We have seen that figures of animals were joint-marked in the same way that human bodies were. Eskimo myth encapsulates this complex relationship.

> Of the myths that are told by Eskimos from Greenland to Siberia, none is more important than the myth of Sedna. Sedna is variously a daughter, orphan or mother sacrificed to save the community. In this sacrifice, her first, second & third finger-joints are cut off. These fall into the sea to become the seal, walrus & whale upon whom the Eskimo depend for survival. Sedna controls these sea mammals and thus holds the power of life and death over the living. Since these animals derive from her, hunting them is a holy occupation and eating them is a communion tantamount to eating the First One.[120]

Many hunting peoples divide the carcasses of game animals according to a social scheme. Certain parts of the meat are reserved for certain relatives. The successful hunter identifies with a specific part of the game animal, which he may or may not eat.

> An Eskimo boy, after his first kill, formally distributes appropriate 'joints' to appropriate relatives. After that, the custom is followed without formality. Relatives who didn't participate in the hunt, who may not even be on good terms with the successful hunter, nevertheless can lay claim to 'their' portion—and I've seen them do so.[121]

The butchering, division, and consumption of game animals and the association of their bodies with human social groupings reflects the same spiritual affinity (totemism) between animals and humans symbolized in the construction of fur garments.

THE BODY AS A LIVING KINSHIP CHART

If kinship relations were first registered using the joints of the fingers, this model could have been easily extended to the other joints of the body. This would account for the widespread evidence of joint marking found in so many ancient and tribal cultures. The basic idea is that the structure of a person's body corresponds to the social order and may be thought of as a living kinship chart. We have seen the same idea expressed in our genealogical iconography and need not go far into the past to find examples.

We can start with a 14th century German manuscript known as the *Sachsenspiegel*, a legal code that includes illustrations of joint-marked humans intended as memory devices, helpful for determining the sequence of relations governing the rights of inheritance (Fig. 4.121).

> The father and the mother stand in the head, full brothers and sisters in the neck, first cousins at the shoulders, second cousins at the elbows, third cousins at the wrists, fourth, fifth, and sixth cousins at the joints of the fingers. Finally come the nails, at which would stand the seventh cousins…[122]

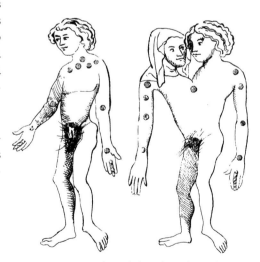

Fig. 4:121: Genealogical chart from the *Sachsenspiegel*. Germany.

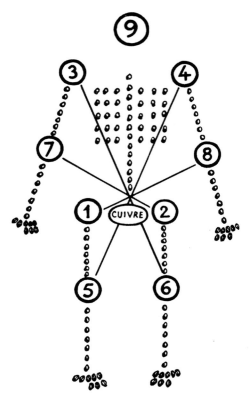

Fig. 4:122: Drawing of Dogon kinship chart, Mali.

While the medieval jurists who compiled this manuscript were many centuries removed from their tribal ancestors, they called on an image of ancient vintage, one that would have been meaningful to the unlearned. The basic principle is simple: the relationship is more remote the farther you are from the head. Despite the logic of this arrangement, Schuster believed this system represented an inversion of the actual historical development in which the joints of the fingers would have been used first and then the joints of the body.

A similar chart is found among the Dogon people of West Africa that is closer to the original tradition, for it uses the whole body to express kinship relations (Fig. 4.122). The French anthropologist Marcel Griaule relates the story behind the diagram in his remarkable book, *Conversations With Ogotemmêli*. In Dogon cosmology, a mythical seventh ancestor organizes the world by vomiting forth *dougé* stones in the outline of a man's soul. The blind elder Ogotemmêli explains:

> He placed the stones one by one, beginning with the one for the head, and with the eight principal stones, one for each ancestor, he marked the joints of the pelvis, the shoulders, the knees and the elbows. The right-hand side came first; the stones of the four male ancestors were placed at the joints of the pelvis and shoulders, that is, where the limbs had been attached, while the stones of the four female ancestors were placed at the other four joints.

'The joints,' said Ogotemmêli 'are the most important part of a man.'[123]

The purpose of this diagram is to illustrate marital relationships of the ancestors of the eight clans composing the society. Griaule added numbers to the diagram to indicate the relative social rank assigned by the Dogon. Large stones mark the primary joints on the diagram (shoulders, elbows, hips, and knees). Males and females of opposite clans intermarry according to the lines connecting the numbers diagonally across the center of the body. The ninth stone, marking the head, represents the chieftaincy of each clan.

In the Dogon scheme, these *dougé* stones represent both the individual soul and the social structure at large. Further, they are covenant-stones, worn around the necks of totemic priests. They act as pledges of the affection of the eight original ancestors and as repositories of their life force that will sustain future generations.[124]

Both the *Sachsenspiegel* and the Dogon chart bring us as close to the origins of the sutratman doctrine as we are likely to get.

> The human body may serve as an image of human society in more than its joints. It must always have been obvious that joints are nothing more than locations where bones connect and that they disappear with the dissolution of the flesh, while bones remain. I presume that joints were first conceived as symbolizing marital unions between 'members' of the social order as represented by bones.[125]

Not surprisingly, we find the term "bone" used to refer to relationships in the male line and the term "flesh" for those in the female line in many kinship systems, particularly those involving cross-cousin marriage. The Batak of Sumatra, for example, use the Malay word *tulang* (bone) for relatives related through the male line (agnate).[126] We may also recall our Balinese doll (*ukur-kepeng*) made to represent the skeleton of the deceased, as indicated by its jointed composition (Fig. 4.123). It is made of white yarn (the nerves) and "black" Chinese coins (the bones).

There is another vital point that will help us understand the symbolism of the fiber arts. The human body forms a nexus between the utilitarian and the spiritual, a subject we approached in more abstract terms earlier in this book. Joints are useful as mnemonic devices for keeping track of social relations, but only because of their deeper spiritual significance, revealed in practices like finger amputation that are almost inconceivable to us.

Yet there is much more here, matters of identity that we may never fully understand. In a world where people lived very brief lives, the continuity of the social structure meant everything. Social roles are temporary assignments. People die and others replace them at their posts. The roles remain. "The king is dead, long live the king." I am composed of the spirits of my ancestors who reside within me and keep me together. They occupy the same place in my body that they occupied within the social structure. In effect, I will live on in spirit as long as the social structure remains in place.[127]

Fig. 4:123: *Ukur-kèpèng*, Bali.

THE BONDS OF KINSHIP
The idea that human limbs represent social connections is a metaphor drawn from observation of the plant world. From a single stock grow the roots and branches that form human society. The stock or World Tree is formed from the body of a First Ancestor. We have only to recall the words of Jesus: "I am the vine, ye are the branches. He that abideth in me, and I in him, the same bringeth forth much fruit: for without me ye are nothing" (John 15:5). The Tree of Jesse depicts this ancient idea.

Here the tree grows from the shoulder of a sleeping Jesse, surrounded by the Old Testament prophets who foretell of Christ's coming (Fig. 4.124). From the branches come Christ's ancestors, the twelve Kings of Judah, and at the top the Virgin Mary with Child, symbolizing the fruit of the tree. But the Tree of Life is older than Christ, who is but one efflourescence of his Father, like the Buddha before him. As Ananda Coomaraswamy and other scholars have shown, the Tree of Jesse has older eastern parallels, most notably depictions of the Brahma, referred to as "lotus born" or "navel born."[128]

Fig. 4:124: Drawing of the Tree of Jesse.

An 8th century monument from Elura, India, depicts the birth of Brahma from a lotus, arising from the navel of Narayana, the supreme deity of the later Vedic period, represented as reclining on the cosmic waters (Fig. 4.125). This tradition is very old in India and certainly predates the coming of the Aryans.

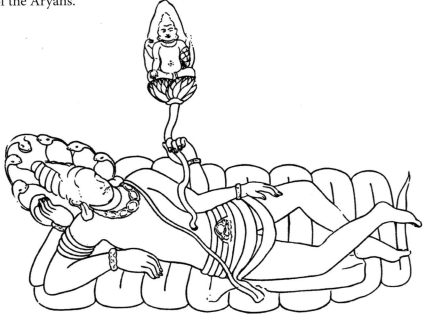

Fig. 4:125: Birth of Brahma from a lotus, India.

Whether the Tree of Jesse motif passed from the East to the medieval West, as the French art historian Emil Mâle supposed, is of minor historical importance since the idea common to both conceptions, the Tree of Life and the related notion of the Water of Life, are far older than either of these particular expressions of it.[129]

The differences between these two images are not as great as someone unfamiliar with the iconography might suppose. Both figures are sleeping or recumbent, a reference, at least in India, to the interval between each cycle of creation. The manifested God, in contrast, stands erect, in the form of a man, tree, pillar, or lingam.[130] The fact that the tree springs from the shoulder of the sleeping Jesse rather than from the navel is also a minor issue. In earlier versions the stem appears in Jesse's hand or rising from his navel. Indian examples also vary, as in the case of this carving from Amaravati (c. A.D. 200) depicting a rhizome with vine and lotus elements emerging from the mouth of a *yaksa* (Fig. 4.126).[131]

The source of the vine in the mouth may be a reference to the life breath (*mukhya prana*) that animates all living things or to the saliva, associated with the Water of Life, or more properly with the *rasa* (vital force, quintessence) found in all liquids.[132] The representation of the Tree of Life as a rhizome is frequently found in what is called the Plant Style.

> So now it will be found that the special formulae of the Plant Style are only explicable in the light of the innumerable passages in Vedic literature in which the Water Cosmology is referred to. It follows,

Fig. 4:126: Carving of *yaksa*, India.

of course, that the Plant Style did not come into being for the first time about 200 B.C., but that the Sungha reliefs are simply the oldest monuments we possess of what is really a very ancient style. This is not surprising in itself; it is merely a special case of the general argument for the long pre-Maurya antiquity of the earliest Indian animal, plant, geometric, and architectural formulae as met with in Maurya, Sunga and later reliefs.[133]

Coomaraswamy was well aware that these forms of expression were to be found in Indo-Iranian culture generally, and as far back as Sumerian times. Water is necessary for life and the ever-flowing vase is an ancient and widespread symbol of the endless fecundity of the Godhead. It is directly related to the Plant Style and the Tree of Life motif.

The vase of plenty (Sk. *purna kalasa*) is one of the most common symbols in Indian art, also found in Persian carpet designs and in the art of the Renaissance. In Indian renditions, it is typically a flower vase with symmetrically placed overflowing leaves, such as this example from Amaravati (c. A.D. 200) (Fig. 4.127).

The use of wavy lines to represent water is another related symbol of great antiquity. Although clearly meant to represent the ripples that appear on moving water, the wavy lines have an older but not unrelated provenance.

A number of Chinese embroidery designs collected by Carl Schuster show various types of vases, some containing plants, but all marked with a wavy line or lines to indicate water (Fig. 4.128A). The last example, a zigzag ornament on a European Neolithic ceramic vessel brings us closer to the source of the iconography (Fig. 4.128B).

> The M- and W- marks which occur so frequently on archaic Greek pottery and in predynastic Egyptian art have been interpreted by Herbert Kühn (in the appendix to Carl Hentze '*Mythes et Symboles lunaires*,' Antwerp, 1932, pp. 245 ff.) as signs for water, and, by extension, for fertility. Kühn attaches this symbolism also to the zigzag ('*Winkelband*') which occurs conspicuously on the neolithic banded pottery of Central Europe…the same ornament seems to have been taken over by artisans of the bronze age and the Halsatt [*sic*] period. Kühn observes: "That these markings occur on vessels certainly cannot be due to chance, since vessels were made for the express purpose of containing fluids—water or milk—and it would be natural for people to have decorated them with the spell for 'water,' in the desire to have them always full."[134]

Writing in 1936, Schuster was supporting the comments of Kühn with his own Chinese examples, but he had yet to understand the full significance of the symbolism. That was to come later when the zigzags, M's, and W's revealed themselves as the remnants of interlinked human figures derived from our genealogical iconography.

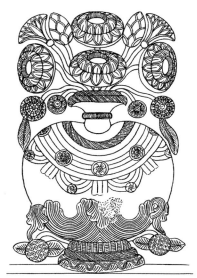

Fig. 4:127: Vase of plenty (*purna kalasa*), India.

Fig. 4:128A: Embroidery designs showing the water symbol, China.

Fig. 4:128B: European Neolithic ceramic vessel.

These headless hockers, severed at the waist and lacking a spine, were arranged in columns to represent generations (Fig. 4.129). They are among the most common of all genealogical patterns and it is appropriate that they should come to represent the Water of Life given their association with plant life, genetic linkage, and continuity. In this way, they formed a connection between the older 'geometric' art and the later Plant Style. The symbolism remained intact even though its figurative origin was forgotten.

Fig. 4:129: Origin of the water symbol.

A Sumerian overflowing-vase design combines multiple vases linked by wavy water symbols (Fig. 4.130). The design resembles a genealogical diagram in which human figures in the form of vases—the body as "vessel" being a common analogy—are linked by water symbols in place of arms and legs.[135]

Fig. 4:130: Sumerian overflowing vases connected with water symbols.

Two motifs from a Spanish cave painting in Almeira (c. 4000 B.C. to 3000 B.C.) provide even earlier evidence for the Tree of Life (Fig. 4.131). Abbé Breuil described them as follows:

A basic figure in the form of two triangles or two thickened chevrons joined at the points (certainly the scheme of a woman) has attached to one, two, or all four of its corners certain appendages, generally curvilinear, which burgeon at the ends into smaller figures similar or analogous to the main one. Apparently we have to do with the representation of a mother with her progeny, a sort of female Tree of Jesse — in which the human elements are reduced to a triangle or a thickened chevron.[136]

Fig. 4:131: Neolithic pictograph, Spain.

Schuster identified them as genealogical patterns, though poorly executed, of the type we discussed earlier in which linkages are formed between the limbs to provide an over-all design.

He compared them to a series of interlinked human figures carved on the earth at an aboriginal initiation ceremony by the Kamilaroi of New South Wales, Australia (Fig. 4.132). Here too, the linkages were sloppy, as in the previous example. R.H. Matthews, the man who recorded the ceremony in 1898, was told they represented the men who were present with Baiamai, the Creator of the Kamilaroi, at his first camp.[137] That is to say, they were ancestor figures whose links were meant to represent genetic bonds.

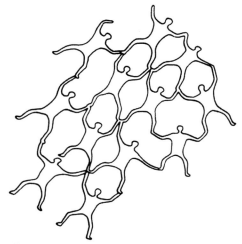

Fig. 4:132: Figures carved in the earth, Australia.

A panel from an Australian opossum-skin robe collected by the Wilkes expedition (1839-1841) shows the same design of concatenated human figures (Fig. 4.133).

As Edmund Carpenter wrote: "What distinguishes genealogical patterns from mere representations of human figures is the continuous limbs. These can only be symbolic; nothing like them exists in nature."[138] These linkages can be depicted in any number of ways, from netting and basketry to people holding hands while dancing, but the most common is the equation of plants and human limbs.

The rhizomes of the Plant Style recall the Scandinavian expression *kné runnr*, in which the generations of men are likened to a periodically renascent plant or vine, originally associated with the seed in the knee. It is curious that the English word "runners" can also refer to the small intestine of a domestic animal, which we related earlier both to divination and the labyrinth. This might seem fortuitous were the ideas of genealogical connectedness and the wandering path of the labyrinth or maze not also linked by certain designs showing interlinked human figures, created by means of a continuous line, whose bodies form a maze-like path to the other world.

A pictograph from Patagonia, composed of five genealogical figures, provides a suitable example (Fig. 4.134).

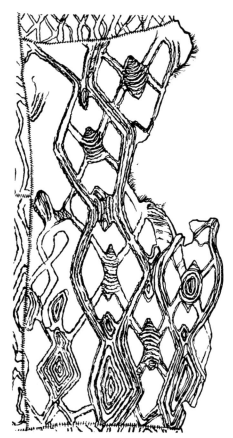

Fig. 4:133: Design on a painted skin robe, Australia.

> Its basic element, repeated four times at the top, is simply a headless, directionless human figure. At the left, an erect figure links limbs (arms-legs) with four diagonally adjacent, horizontal figures to form a Biaxial Pattern: ego in the center, ego's parents above, ego's offspring below. The headlessness of each figure facilitates 'reading' this composition in any direction, depending upon the observer's point of view (somewhat as kinship terminology varies with the speaker's identity).[139]

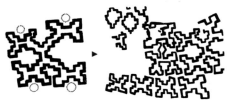

Fig. 4:134: Design painted on a cave wall, Argentina.

197

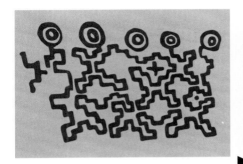

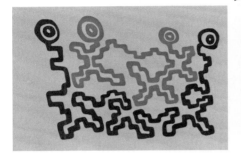

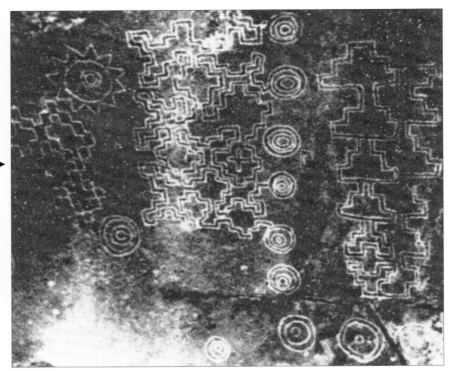

Fig. 4:135: Rock painting with details, Argentina.

A related example, also from Patagonia, takes the form of a picture puzzle (Fig. 4.135). Schuster identified it as a maze composed of human figures.[140] The four circles at the top (the fifth is superfluous) were intended to serve as points of departure and arrival in the construction of the maze. The design was intended as an exercise for a novice. The goal: to supply bodies for the heads by connecting them with two lines that never cross. Notice also the unconnected cross looking strangely out of place.

This same cross occurs in the labyrinth, where the two lines do cross (Fig. 4.136), and in the Malekulan sand drawing, where they don't (Fig. 4.137).

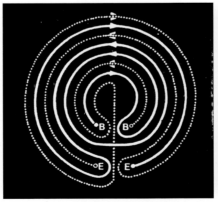

Fig. 4:136: Hypothetical method for drawing the labyrinth.

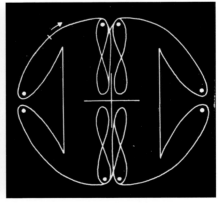

Fig. 4:137: Continuous-line drawing, New Hebrides.

This little exercise of ingenuity is a culture historical document of the greatest interest; for the idea of a maze connecting two points of departure and two points of arrival by means of two lines which never cross is hardly likely to have been conceived without knowledge of another design—that commonly called "the labyrinth", in which essentially the same puzzle is layed out [*sic*] on a circular plan.[141]

Let us also compare our wooden spindle whorl from the Barreales culture of Argentina that contained two human-headed patterns in inverse relation to one another (Fig. 4.138).

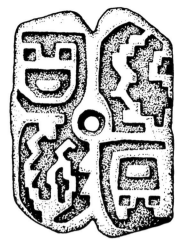

Fig. 4:138: Wooden spindle whorl (Argentina).

Its twirling was believed to facilitate the passage of the soul into the next world, the same objective that lies at the root of the labyrinth and the Patagonian examples. Both the Malekulan sand drawing and the Cahuillan and Gilbertese string figures were said to serve the same purpose.

We can also compare all these designs to the fret style we saw earlier on a Patagonian stone ax from Nequén, Argentina (Figs 4.139). Once again, we find a series of reciprocal human-like figures composed of a single line, incised in this case, but clearly derived from the cutting line used to create fur garments.

All these designs bring together the themes we have discussed in the course of this book, from the continuous line to the spindle whorl. The path to the other world is guarded by a monster, whose body itself forms the path. This monster is really a joint-marked ancestor figure derived from a genealogical pattern. The joints represent the heads of adjoining figures. Tracing a line from joint to joint on this figure, or passing through its joint-marked body, is equivalent to tracing one's ancestry by touching one's relations in sequence.

The connections within my body hold me together. The same connections hold society together. I represent the social order in miniature. This is what our genealogical diagrams are about. They translate society into me and me into society.

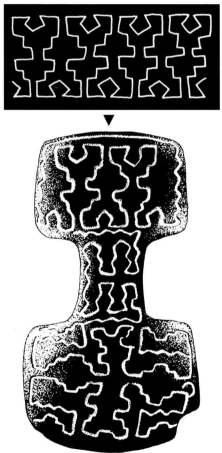

The essence of the sutratman doctrine is the idea that there is but one life that unites all members, like a single thread that makes a whole cloth. We all owe our existence to this single Spirit. Kinsmen are conceived quite graphically as heads, joints, or knots, and relatedness by links of various kinds. But these links that unite individuals and the social order are temporary and must be continually renewed. This renewal, which lies at the heart of many of the rituals described in this book, ensures rebirth, and a continuance of the social order. The lesson our ancestors saw in nature is clear: all matter dies but is reborn, because the Spirit that gives it life is eternal.

Fig. 4:139: Stone ceremonial axe with detail of fret-style design, Argentina.

ENDNOTES

1. Edmund Carpenter and Carl Schuster, *Social Symbolism in Ancient and Tribal Art*, vol. 1, bk. 1, pp. 39-40.

2. Schuyler Cammann, in Edmund Carpenter and Carl Schuster, ibid., p. 13.

3. The two men met in Cambridge, Massachusetts in the early 1930s and exchanged a number of letters over the years. See the *Selected Letters of Ananda Coomaraswamy*, pp. 220-221, for one example.

4. Edmund Carpenter and Carl Schuster, op. cit., vol. 1, bk. 1, p. 36.

5. Schuster, "A Comparative Study of Motives in Western Chinese Folk Embroideries," p. 22. Cf., "Peasant Embroideries of China" for a non-scholarly account of the subject. See also, *Blue and White. The Cotton Embroideries of Rural China*. The editorial remarks in this last work may be safely ignored.

6. Ibid., p. 25. This fact will be of no surprise to students of folklore where a similar typology exists that crosses both ethnic and national boundaries. Such practices are rooted in the dictates of memory. See Albert Lord's *The Singer of Tales* for a close discussion of this fundamental issue.

7. See Schuster, "The Triumphant Equestrian."

8. Schuster, "Joint Marks: A Possible Index of Cultural Contact Between America, Oceania, and the Far East," p. 3.

9. Schuyler Cammann in Edmund Carpenter and Carl Schuster, op. cit., vol. 1, bk. 1, pp. 16-17.

10. The topic would be taken up again some two decades later at a conference at Columbia University where Schuster also presented a paper, "Relations of a Chinese Embroidery Design: Eastern Europe and Western Asia, Southeast Asia (the Dong-Son Culture) and Melanesia." It was published posthumously in 1972 in a three-volume collection of the conference proceedings, *Early Chinese Art and its Possible Influence in the Pacific Basin*.

11. Schuster, "Joint Marks: A Possible Index of Cultural Contact Between America, Oceania, and the Far East," p. 5.

12. Schuster noted that it was difficult to separate human and animal forms in South American art and the same made be said for tribal art generally.

13. Schuster, "Joint Marks," op cit., p. 24.

14. Ibid., p. 17.

15. Ibid., p. 17, ft. 18.

16. Ibid., p. 18, ft. 21.

17. Helge Larsen, "The Ipiutak Culture: Its Origins and Relationships." For an introduction to Animal Style art, see Bunker, Chatwin, and Farkas, *"Animal Style" Art from East to West*. See also, Edmund Carpenter and Carl Schuster, op. cit., vol. 1, bk. 4, app. 1.

18. Schuster, "A Survival of the Eurasiatic Animal Style in Modern Alaskan Eskimo Art," p. 39.

19. Ibid., p. 37.

20. See Marius Barbeau, "The Old World Dragon in America."

21. Edmund Carpenter and Carl Schuster, *Social Symbolism in Ancient and Tribal Art*, vol. 1, bk. 4, p. 961, ft. 210.

22. Ibid., p. 961, ft. 210.

23. Edmund Carpenter and Carl Schuster, op. cit., vol. 1, bk. 4, p. 915.

24. Schuster, "Joint Marks: A Possible Index of Cultural Contact Between America, Oceania, and the Far East," p. 15.

25. Ibid., p. 16.

26. Edmund Carpenter and Carl Schuster, *Social Symbolism in Ancient and Tribal Art*, vol. 1, bk. 3, p. 821.

27. Ibid., vol. 1, bk. 1, pp. 42-43.

28. The work was part of a series published by the Museu Paulista in Sao Paulo. Schuster reprinted the article by itself for distribution to other scholars.

29. Schuster, "Genealogical Patterns in the Old and New Worlds," p. 7.

30. Edmund Carpenter and Carl Schuster, op. cit., vol. 1, bk. 1, p. 47.

31. Ibid., p. 51.

32. The same process took place with counting systems, which were once a concrete means for counting relatives or generations and only gradually took on a more abstract character suitable for divination, arithmetic, and commerce.

33. Herein lies the distinction between gender and sex. Gender is a classification system. Sex is about physical characterization. Note that each moiety contains both men and women. The neuter gender, where it exists, represents the spirit world.

34. Edmund Carpenter and Carl Schuster, op. cit., vol. 1, bk. 2, p. 420.

35. Schuster believed that the sloppiness of some of these designs—particularly apparent on cave walls and incised stones—was due to the fact that they were created by men. Genealogical patterns originated in clothing design and tattooing, women's work. Men were familiar enough with these patterns to sketch them but not comfortable enough to do them justice. They may also have been in a hurry, making these notations a kind of shorthand.

36. Edmund Carpenter and Carl Schuster, op. cit., vol. 1, bk. 2, p. 556.

37. Ibid., vol. 1, bk. 2, p. 557. See also, Claude Lévi Strauss, *Tristes Tropiques*, ch. 22.

38. Edmund Carpenter and Carl Schuster, *Patterns That Connect*, p. 165. Houseposts and pillars often represent ancestors. Note the English expression, a "pillar of the community." The classical column has its roots in this tradition. See Joseph Rykwert, *The Dancing Column: On Order in Classical Architecture*.

39. Edmund Carpenter and Carl Schuster, *Social Symbolism in Ancient and Tribal Art*, Vol. 1, Book 2, p. 561.

40. See Edmund Carpenter and Carl Schuster, op. cit., vol. 1, bk. 2, ch. 11.

41. Edmund Carpenter, *Patterns That Connect*, p. 14.

42. In particular, the work of Hugo Obermaier, Gutorm Gjessing, G. H. Luquet, and the more famous Henri Breuil, among others. See Edmund Carpenter and Carl Schuster, *Social Symbolism in Ancient and Tribal Art*, vol. 1, bk. 3, ch. 8.

43. Carl Schuster and Edmund Carpenter, *Patterns That Connect*, p. 73.

44. See A.K. Coomaraswamy, "Svayama-trnna: Janua Coeli" (Door of Heaven) in Lipsey, *Collected Works*, vol. 1. It is likely that the many-armed figures of Hindu iconography were once ramiforms.

45. Edmund Carpenter and Carl Schuster, *Social Symbolism in Ancient and Tribal Art*, vol. 3, bk. 1, p. 186. The hopping movement of the players is a kind of horizontal climbing. Hopscotch combines the ramiform or ladder-climbing pattern with the symbolism of dismemberment and reintegration. The hopscotch board also acquired astronomical and calendrical associations in the course of time. The stone that is tossed represents the sun, which must pass through the signs of the zodiac, one by one, to complete the year. This is an important connection because it lets us see how the older idea of dismemberment forms the substructure for later astronomical/astrological speculations.

46. Edmund Carpenter and Carl Schuster, ibid., vol. 1, bk. 1, p. 187.

47. In *Festschrift für Ad. E. Jenson*, Munich, 1964, pp. 559-610.

48. Ibid., p. 559.

49. Henri Breuil had earlier described the two upper elements as "Almerian idols," known from other Iberian rock shelters, also noting the telescoped designs that he described as multiplied heads or torsos.

50. Schuster, *Festschrift*, op. cit., p. 560.

51. The guanaco (*Lama guanicoe*) is a small South American lama, resembling a deer, with a soft, thick, fawn-colored coat.

52. Edmund Carpenter and Carl Schuster, op. cit., vol. 2, bk. 3, p. 582. We still speak of "dressing" (erecting, setting up) a stone.

53. Schuster, *Festschrift*, op. cit., p. 561.

54. Edmund Carpenter and Carl Schuster, op. cit., vol. 2, bk. 2, p. 304.

55. Ibid., p. 313. The work cited is Alfred Jensen, "Beziehungen zwischen dem alten Testament und der nilotischen Kultur in Afrika," in *Culture in History, Essays in Honor of Paul Radin*, pp. 449-466, New York, 1960.

56. Edmund Carpenter and Carl Schuster, op. cit., vol. 2, bk. 2, p. 313.

57. Schuster, *Festschrift*, op. cit., p. 565.

58. Schuster, *Essays in Pre-Columbian Art and Archeology*, p. 447.

59. Schuster, *Festschrift*, op. cit., p. 567.

60. Quoted from, Edmund Carpenter and Carl Schuster, op. cit., vol. 2, bk. 2, p. 367.

61. The glass slipper that fits on Cinderella's foot in the Walt Disney version of this widespread folktale was originally a fur (vair) slipper. The two words are homonyms in French (*le verre, le vair*) confused by oral transmission of the story. A fur slipper is more appropriate—albeit less cinematic—since it reveals Cinderella's aristocratic origins.

62. For numerous North American examples see Schuster, "Incised Stones from Nevada and Elsewhere."

63. Edmund Carpenter and Carl Schuster, op. cit., vol. 2, bk. 2, p. 319.

64. Schuster, *Festschrift*, op. cit., p. 597.

65. Robert Oden, *The Bible Without Theology*, pp. 103-104.

66. See Schuster, "Genealogical Patterns in the Old and New Worlds," passim.

67. Ibid., p. 82. Stith Thompson's *Motif Index of Folk Literature* lists the following related themes: birth from a person's head; a man's thigh; a woman's thigh; an arm; an eye; a shoulder; a knee; a plant; a twig; a tree; a flower; a fruit.

68. Alice Werner, in *Mythology of All Races*, vol. 7: *African Mythology*, p. 156.

69. Ibid. In the Judeo-Christian tradition, Adam is also conceived as a First Ancestor who gives birth to both man and woman as we read in Genesis 5:2: "Male and female created he them; and blessed them, and called their name Adam, in the day when they were created." This is fully in keeping with the metaphysical notion that all opposites derive from a unity pre-existing *in divinis*. The Sunday school version of the story confuses Adam the Man (the form of humanity) with a male Adam.

70. Werner, op. cit., p. 103, ft. 141.

71. Ibid., p. 103, ft. 141.

72. Ibid., p. 83, ft. 106a.

73. Anne Birrell, *Chinese Mythology*, pp. 116-117.

74. Schuster, "Genealogical Patterns," op. cit., p. 84, ft.106a.

75. Ibid., p. 83.

76. Ibid., p. 103, ft. 142.

77. See de Beauclair, "Three Genealogical Stories from BOTEL TOBAGO: A Contribution to the Folklore of the Yami," reference 10. For the prevalence of genealogical symbolism among the Yami, see Edmund Carpenter and Carl Schuster, op. cit., vol. 1, bk. 1, pp. 206-207.

78. Schuster, "Genealogical Patterns," op. cit., pp. 95-96, ft. 130.

79. Schuster, ibid., p. 103, ft. 141.

80. See Ananda Coomaraswamy, *Yaksas*.

81. Ibid., pp. 131-132. These ancient beliefs are related to the Indian *lingam* cult in which the ritual "erection" of the lingam symbolically brings about the reunion of Shiva's lost member with the rest of his body. Coomaraswamy (p. 135) compares this act to the ritual task of the "welding of the sword" in the Grail legend.

82. *The Life of Johnson*, p. 587, ft. 2.

83. Schuster, "Genealogical Patterns," op. cit., p. 83.

84. Ibid., p. 85.

85. R. B. Onians, *The Origins of European Thought*, pp. 178-9. For his comments on the genius and the sanctity of the head, see chapter 2 and passim.

86. Ibid., p. 177. See also, footnote 9 on the same page where Onians discusses the analogy between human body fluids and plants.

87. *Natural History*, XI, 103, 250. Cf. Apuleius, *The God of Socrates*, XV, 152.

88. Schuster, "Genealogical Patterns," op. cit., p. 100. The Grimm work cited is

Deutsche Rechtsalterthümer, Leipzig, 1899.

89. Maurice Cahen, "'Genou', 'Adoption' et 'Parente' en Germanique."

90. J. Loth, "Le Mot Désignant Le Genou au Sens de Génération Chez les Celtes, les Germains, Les Slaves, Les Assyriens."

91. Cahen, op. cit., p. 57, my translation.

92. In the same manner, the stem between two nodes (*kné*) of a plant is referred to by the Scandinavian word *leggr* ("leg").

93. J. Loth, op. cit.

94. R. B. Onians, op. cit., p. 176.

95. The situation is slightly different in Genesis (30:3) where Rachel adopts the children of her servant Bilhah when she cannot conceive with Jacob. See Loth (p. 145). Some scholars believe that this passage suggests that women once gave birth sitting on the knees of their husbands or other assistants but this does not seem feasible. The expression is more likely metaphoric. See Beneviste, pp. 52-53 for a comment on this issue.

Another reference to the practice can be found in Job (3:12) where he curses his birth. And let us add Boswell's New Testament reference quoted earlier, Hebrews (7:10).

96. Antoine Meillet, "LAT. genuinus." R. B. Onians (op. cit., p. 176) was not convinced by this argument. "His suggestion of a 'purely juristic' meaning in this idea of recognition (curiously surviving in so limited a sphere and with so little trace of that meaning in the terms in question), and his denial of connection with the physical process of generation, are more than bold. Consider e.g. the traceable uses of *gigno, genius, genialis, genitalis*, etc., and of the Greek cognates of *gonu: geinomai, gignomai, goneus, gonos, gonh, gonar* (= 'womb', Lacon.), etc. Moreover, he offers no hint why the jaw should have been referred to with this same adjective *genuinus* and *genus*, etc. …"

97. Failure to recognize the child would mean that it would be abandoned or killed rather than "raised." This was the fate of the children of Kronos in Hesiod's *Theogony*, who were devoured once they were taken from the womb of their mother and placed

on his knees. Schuster (op. cit., p. 101, ft. 138) notes that "there is no pronoun in the original specifying whose knees are meant and the passage is generally translated with 'her' (i.e., the mother's knees)." Benveniste (p. 52) translates the passage using "his" with the understanding that the rite of legitimation is involved.

98. Carpenter, *Patterns That Connect*, p. 191, translating Loth, op, cit., pp. 151-152.

99. Schuster, "Genealogical Patterns," op. cit., p. 105, ft. 145.

100. For a general introduction to the subject, see Warren Dawson, *The Custom of the Couvade*. The value of the work is documentary as it has little to say about the meaning of the practice. See p. 186 for Tautain's comments; cf. Schuster, "Genealogical Patterns," op. cit., p. 104.

101. Ibid., p. 102, quoting from Gabriel Soares de Sousa's "Tratado descriptivo do Brasil em 1857". *Revista do Instituto Historico e Geographico Brasiliero*, Vol. 14, Rio de Janeiro, 1851, pp. 1-365.

102. Schuster, "Genealogical Patterns," op. cit., p. 86, quoting from *Rg Veda* X, 90.

103. Ibid., p. 86.

104. Ibid., p. 87.

105. Ibid., p. 87.

106. Ibid., p, 87.

107. Schuster, "Genealogical Patterns," op. cit., p. 96, quoting from Alfred Howitt, *The Native Tribes of South-East Australia*.

108. Stanner, "Aboriginal Modes of Address and Reference in the North-West of the Northern Territory." Quoted from Schuster, "Genealogical Patterns," op. cit., p. 95.

109. Ibid., Stanner also notes the close connection between relatives and counting systems. "This is commonly done when silent communication is for some reason necessary, but often it simply accompanies the mention of a relative, much as many aborigines when counting on their fingers raise each finger to their lips as the numerals are ticked off."

110. Schuster, "Genealogical Patterns," op. cit., p. 97, ft. 132. The Ambonese practices

brings to mind the once common division of the social body into twelve tribes, or the country into twelve districts, found among the ancient Greeks, Hebrews, and Celts.

111. Ibid., p. 98, quoting from Ewald Volhard, *Kannibalismus* (1939). Vohard in his turn is quoting from the historian and priest Father Bernardino de Sahagún, author of the *Florentine Codex* (The General History of the Things of New Spain).

112. Ibid., p. 106.

113. Carpenter and Schuster, *Social Symbolism in Ancient and Tribal Art*, vol. 1, bk. 3, p. 752.

114. Schuster, "Genealogical Patterns," op. cit., p. 88.

115. Carpenter and Schuster, op. cit., vol. 1, bk. 3, p. 872.

116. Schuster, "Joint Marks: A Possible Index of Cultural Contact Between America, Oceania, and the Far East," p. 18, ft. 21.

117. Schuster, "Genealogical Patterns," op. cit., p. 90.

118. See Sherman, *Writing on Hands. Memory and Knowledge in Early Modern Europe*, pp. 153-155.

119. Carpenter and Schuster, op. cit., vol. 1, bk. 3, p. 756. It is peculiar that anthropologists continue to puzzle over the significance of missing fingers in Paleolithic art. Schuster noted the extensive literature on the topic (op. cit., p. 89, ft. 121) and the practice of finger amputation was still being practiced in New Guinea in recent times. See the *New York Times* (March 11, 2001, p. 8) for an article on the Dani.

120. Carpenter and Schuster, *Patterns That Connect*, p. 146.

121. Carpenter and Schuster, op. cit., vol. 1, bk. 3, p. 879.

122. Schuster, "Genealogical Patterns," op. cit., p. 92.

123. Marcel Griaule, *Conversations With Ogotemmêli*, p. 50. See also, Griaule and Dieterlin, *The Pale Fox*.

124. In this sense they are similar to the *churingas* of the Australian Bushmen. See

Edmund Carpenter, *Social Symbolism in Ancient & Tribal Art*, vol. 2, bk. 5, pp. 1195-1201. Cf. René Guénon on sacred stones in *The Lord of the World*, Ch. 9.

125. Schuster, "Genealogical Patterns," op. cit., p. 94.

126. Ibid., p. 94, ft. 120.

127. Such a view of life and society touches on the crucial matters of reincarnation and rebirth. Despite what is written in the popular press, none of the major religions believe in reincarnation, only in transmigration. Transmigration involves God alone, who vivifies and leaves bodies at will. This is clearly part of the ancient view since the older idea seems to be a primal ancestor from whom all were derived. That many peoples have believed in the physical reincarnation of individuals is beyond doubt, but it is unlikely that the distinction between an individual identity and a social identity could have meant much until later in history when tribalism was beginning to break down. The Indian doctrine of progenitive rebirth, in which a man in his vocational nature is "reincarnated" in his descendants who inherit his functions and responsibilities, comes closer to the original notion; likewise, the idea of initiatic rebirth, which is restricted to a living individual who takes on a new life. Dr. Coomaraswamy began a book on the subject of reincarnation, but regrettably never completed it. The unfinished manuscript can be found in the Firestone Library at Princeton University.

128. See Coomaraswamy, "The Tree of Jesse and Indian Parallels and Sources." Cf. Coomaraswamy, *Yaksas*, for a full discussion of the Tree of Life, Water Cosmology, and Grail motifs.

129. "Née en Orient, l'iconography chrétienne nous est arrivée toute faite." Quoted from Coomaraswamy, "The Tree of Jesse and Indian Parallels and Sources," p. 219.

130. The sexual and reproductive energies associated with the emergent God are clearer in India, Greece, and Rome, but not absent in the Christian Middle Ages. See Leo Steinberg, "The Sexuality of Christ in Renaissance Art and in Modern Oblivion."

131. Coomaraswamy, "The Tree of Jesse and Indian Parallels and Sources," plate 53c. The term *yaksa* may refer to Brah-

man or other universal deities, tutelary deities of kingdoms or clans, deceased ancestors, or local tree spirits of good or bad character. In general, the *yaksa* represents the immanent Spirit that dwells within us all. *Yaksas* are associated most closely with vegetation, fertility, and the Water of Life.

132. See Coomaraswamy, *Yaksas*, p. 112, ft. 7.

133. Ibid., p. 100.

134. Schuster, A Prehistoric Symbol in Modern Chinese Folk Art," p. 201. (The normal spelling of the period referred to is Hallstatt or Hallstadt.)

135. Coomaraswamy discusses another Jaina vase of plenty with "eyes," possibly once joint marks, which he says, "might be regarded as the survival of an older anthropomorphic vase, such as those that have been found at Troy." *Yaksas*, pp. 164 and plate 56b.

136. Quoted from Schuster, "Genealogical Patterns in the Old and New Worlds," p. 72.

137. Ibid., p. 80.

138. Carpenter and Schuster, *Social Symbolism in Ancient and Tribal Art*, vol. 1, bk. 3, p. 721.

139. Ibid., vol. 3, bk. 1, p. 235.

140. Schuster, "Genealogical Patterns," op. cit., p. 50. He credits Prof. Osvaldo Menghin with first recognizing the design "as a maze of continuous lines which nowhere cross."

141. Ibid., p. 50.

AFTERWORD

Your Messiah is a friend of all mankind.
Mine speaks in parables to the blind.

William Blake

I have closed this extended work of translation with the words of William Blake. People who think in images are often at odds with the rationalism that governs daily life. Blake lived in an age when this conflict came to a head, when the dramatic and mimetic elements of social life were being displaced by a new scientific and economic order. As an artist and a religious man he understood that images and words had a common origin. He also understood the "eternality" of doctrine—that the symbolism of rotating devices was meaningful to people long before the Buddha set the Wheel of Law in motion. The great religions inherited the remnants of this ancient symbolism and tried to pass it on, if only in a more attenuated and moralized form. Blake tried to translate this *philosophia perennis* in a manner suitable for his own age, but few if any were listening.

The anthropologist and cybernetician Gregory Bateson spent much of his life thinking and writing about the problems involved in communication and he liked to distinguish the truths of logic from the truths of metaphor in the following manner. He began with the classical "Syllogism in Barbara," which states:

    Men die;
    Socrates is a man;
    Socrates will die.

He followed this with one of his own, the "Syllogism in Grass."

    Men die;
    Grass dies;
    Men are grass.

This is a metaphor, of course, and not a syllogism. It commits the logical error referred to as "affirming the consequent," as Bateson well knew. What was of importance to him was the difference between these two formulations, not the dictates of classical logic.

> It's really very simple—in order to make syllogisms in Barbara, you must have identified classes, so that subjects and predicates can be

1. Gregory Bateson, *Angels Fear*, p. 27.

2. Carl Schuster, "Genealogical Patterns in the Old and New World," p. 85.

3. For example, see Lakoff, *Women, Fire, and Dangerous Things* and Lakoff and Johnson, *Metaphors We Live By.*

differentiated. But, apart from language, there are no named classes and no subject-predicate relations. Therefore, syllogisms in grass must be the dominant mode of communicating interconnections of ideas in all preverbal realms.[1]

Formal logic arrives late in human history, and useful as it is, cannot compare with the central role that metaphor plays in structuring human thought. We think in stories, and stories are metaphors, as are dreams, poetry, and art. The beauty of stories, Bateson explained, is that all the relations get into the picture at once, so they pull on each other in the right way. Stories don't need to be factual as long as the relations within the story are consistent. As Nietzsche put it when speaking about numbers, "No more fiction for us: we calculate; but that we may calculate, we had to make fiction first."

We have seen how philosophy began with images, a fact that led Dr. Coomaraswamy to write: "to have lost the art of thinking in images is precisely to have lost the proper linguistic of metaphysics and to have descended to the verbal logic of 'philosophy.'" Carl Schuster came to the same conclusion about the genealogical system he discovered.

A fascinating question is that which came first: the idea or its projection in art. Perhaps both came into being at once: for man thinks in images. It is, at any rate obvious, that the genealogical diagram or pattern must have played an important, perhaps an indispensable, role in the perpetuation if not in the conception of the genealogical idea.[2]

There is nothing strange or mystical about traditional symbolism, but it must be approached on its own terms, free of the prejudices of psychology and misplaced notions about the psychic unity of mankind. It is, in essence, the way our minds work in the absence of writing and other complex communications media. The common intellectual environment that humans developed based on books and reading is the result of historical events we can trace. Traditional symbolism created a similar worldwide "intellectual" environment. It spread with the dispersal of people, probably from a central location in Africa. This is conjecture of course, but Schuster found more than enough evidence to support his claims and modern archeology, linguistics, and the study of mitochondrial DNA are beginning to provide supporting evidence. There is also the work of cognitive scientists, who are beginning to tease out the central role of metaphor in human cognition and language.[3]

Metaphors are a means of understanding one thing in terms of another and the physical world provides any number of models. The branching of trees is a fine analogy for the division of families into groups and subgroups. The growth, death and rebirth of plants provide a parallel to human generation and regeneration. The role of sunlight and water in fostering life endows them with a special symbolic potency. But this merely scratches the surface. For our ancestors, natural or artificial objects were not symbols of a higher reality, but actual manifestations of it. All traditional arts are created in the likeness of a model or prototype, but they don't tell us what the model looks like, because it is invisible. Rather, the invisible world is understood through the visible, the inaudible through the audible.

We've done our prehistoric ancestors a disservice by underestimating their intelligence and then covering our own ignorance with a veil of sentimentality or with projections of our own interests or prejudices. They were as intelligent as us and what they accomplished rivals anything we have produced. The order, beauty, and utility of knots, basketry, weaving, jewelry, and tiling provides silent testimony. Further, the thoughts and accomplishments of the world's great civilizations were built on an ancient substructure invisible to us until now.

Symbolism allowed people to communicate in the past. The ancients understood each other better than we understand them because they could 'read,' in one fashion or another, this common language that extended back into prehistory. Despite their limited knowledge of history, Ficino and Pico were more in tune with Plato than modern commentators are. They were believers, which is the last thing scholars are interested in, being skeptics by training.

When understanding of the great tradition waned, it was taken over by kooks, with the exception of a few unusual individuals whose works were largely ignored. It fell to great scholars like R. B. Onians, René Guénon, Ananda Coomaraswamy and Carl Schuster to resurrect the *philosophia perennis* using the comparative method, long since rejected by the academic world in favor of a narrow and provincial specialism.

With the rise of electronic media, the distortions of writing and print suddenly became clear and the structures governing oral culture emerged in all their integrity. The French Jesuit Marcel Jousse was the first scholar to try to formulate the principles of organization underlying oral cultures and his work directly influenced the young Harvard scholar Milman Parry. It was Parry and his student Albert Lord who made the decisive break with the culture of literacy with *The Singer of Tales*, a detailed study of oral composition.

Folklore tells us that the door to the other world has deadly jambs, set to crush all but those who enter in the nick of time—that briefest of intervals between the end of one day and the beginning of another. During the 1960s just such a moment occurred, when two worlds came briefly into alignment. Marshall McLuhan and a few colleagues crossed this threshold and returned with fantastic stories about media galaxies that pass through one another without collision, but whose gravitational fields produce unanticipated and disquieting effects. Stories about how the past we read about was more like a dance or a song; and tales of lost worlds whose inhabitants walked backwards into the future.

But the door closed quickly. The culture of literacy disappeared overnight. Like a man ascending gradually from the depths of sleep who experiences a startling clarity of vision at a point just below consciousness, only to descend again suddenly into the dream world. Today our best students sit silently before the great works of the past, untrained in the intricacies of reading and writing and no longer able to participate. They inhabit another world entirely and see no reason to undergo such rigorous training.

What role is left for the scholarship McLuhan so dearly loved and which helped make his clairvoyance possible? He had hoped that the insights provided by electronic media would light up the past and reveal the differing symbolic environments within which ideas arise. This was not to be. Writing is no longer the path for the culture but a monastic vocation for the few. What was once an unseen environment reveals itself as an inner landscape produced by a particular form of sensory conditioning, surviving only as an archaic technique for understanding the world, made all the more powerful by its obsolescence.

This is all to be regretted and not without a touch of irony, for the world of our prehistoric ancestors, who knew neither reading nor writing is no longer accessible without these skills. Carl Schuster arrived at the eleventh hour to gather what was scattered. His work may be the most important contribution made in the humanities in the last century, for this is where we have been, who we have been, and in some measure, who we still are.

BIBLIOGRAPHY

BOOKS

Amsden, Charles. *Navaho Weaving: It's Technique and History*. New York, Dover, 1991.

Anati, Emmanuel. *Camonica Valley*. New York, Alfred Knopf, 1961.

Andrews, John F., ed. *William Shakespeare. His World. His Work. His Influence*. Three vols. New York, Charles Scribner & Sons, 1985.

Apuleius. *The God of Socrates*. Heptangle Books, Gillette, New Jersey, 1993.

Bain, George. *Celtic Art. The Methods of Construction*. New York, Dover, 1973.

Baker, Muriel, and Lunt, Margaret. *Blue and White. The Cotton Embroideries of Rural China*. Charles Scribner and Sons, New York, 1977.

Barber, Elizabeth W. *Prehistoric Textiles*. Princeton, N.J., Princeton University Press, 1991.
_____. *Women's Work*. New York, W. W. Norton & Co., 1994.

Bateson, Gregory. *A Sacred Unity*. New York, Harper Collins, 1994.

Bateson, Gregory, and Mead, Margaret. *Balinese Character*. New York, New York Academy of Sciences, 1942.

Bede. *The Ecclesiastical History of the English People*. Washington Square Press, New York, 1968.

Bennet, George and Tyerman, Daniel. *Journal of Voyages and Travels by the Rev. Daniel Tyerman and George Bennet, Esq*. Three vols. Boston, Crocker and Brewster, 1832.

Beowulf. Translated by Howell D. Chickering, Jr., New York, Anchor Books, 1977.

Bernal, Martin. *Black Athena*. Two vols. Rutgers University Press, 1987.

Bunce, Frederick W. *An Encyclopedia of Hindu Deities, Demi-Gods, Godlings, Demons and Heros*. Three vols. New Delhi, India. D.K. Printworld, Ltd., 2000.

Birrell, Anne. *Chinese Mythology*. Johns Hopkins University Press, 1993.

Blake, William. *The Complete Poetry and Prose of William Blake*. New York, Anchor Doubleday, 1988.

Boswell, James. *The Life of Samuel Johnson*. Everyman's Library, Alfred A. Knopf, New York, 1992.

Budge, E. A. Wallis. *Osiris and the Egyptian Resurrection*. Two vols. New York, Dover Press, 1973.

_____. *The Gods of the Egyptians*. Two vols. New York, Dover Press, 1969.

Burnett, John. *Early Greek Philosophy*. New York, Meridian, 1957.

Burns, Robert. *The Complete Poetical Works of Robert Burns*. Boston, Houghton Mifflin, 1897.

Canteins, Jean. *Sauver Le Mythe*. Paris, Editions Maisonneuve & Larose, three vols. Vol. 1: *Le Potier Démiurge*, 1986. Vol. 2: *Les Barrateurs Divins*, 1987. Vol. 3: *Dédale et Ses Oeuvres*, 1994.

Cargill, John. *The Celtic Cross and Greek Proportion*. Chicago, Charles G. Blake Co., 1930.

Carpenter, Edmund, and Carl Schuster. *Materials for the Study of Social Symbolism in Ancient and Tribal Art*, three vols. New York, Rock Foundation, 1986-1988.
____. *Patterns That Connect*. New York, Harry N. Abram, Inc., 1996.

Claiborne, Robert. *The Roots of English: A Reader's Handbook of Word Origins*. Times Books, 1989.

Cook, A. B. *Zeus: A Study in Ancient Religion*, vol. II. New York, Biblo & Tannen, 1965.

Coomaraswamy, Ananda K. Coomaraswamy: *Selected Papers/His Life and Work*, three vols. Edited by Roger Lipsey. Princeton, N.J., Princeton University Press, 1977. Bollingen Series, Vol. LXXXIX.
____. *The Bugbear of Literacy*. London, Dennis Dobson Ltd., 1943.
____. *The Christian and Oriental Philosophy of Art*. New York, Dover Press, 1956.
____. *The Transformation of Nature in Art*. New York, Dover Press, 1956.
____. *On the Traditional Doctrine of Art*. Ipswich, Golgonooza Press, 1977.
____. *Selected Letters of Ananda Coomaraswamy*. Oxford University Press, 1988.
____. *What is Civiliztion? and Other Essays*. Great Barrington, MA., Lindisfarne Press, 1989.
____. *Time and Eternity*. New Delhi, Munshiram Manoharlal, 1993.
____. *Yaksas: Essays in the Water Cosmology*. Edited by Paul Schroeder. New Delhi, Oxford University Press, 1993.
____. *Guardians of the Sundoor*. Edited by Robert Strom. Louisville, Kentucky, Fons Vitae, 2004.

Coomaraswamy, Ananda K. and Sister Nivedita. *Myths of the Hindus and Buddhists*. New York, Dover, 1967.

Covarrubias, Miguel. *Island of Bali*. New York, Alfred Knopf, 1937.

Crepereia Tryphaena. Milan, Italy, Gruppo Editoriale Fabbri, 1983.

Crewe, Lindy. *Spindle Whorls*. Jonsered, Sweden, Paul Aströms Förlag, 1998.

Curtius, Ernst Robert. *European Literature and the Latin Middle Ages*. Princeton, N.J., Princeton University Press, 1953. Bollingen Series, Vol. XXXVI.

Dalyell, J. G. *The Darker Superstitions of Scotland*. Edinburgh, Waugh & James, 1834.

Dantzig, T. *Number—The Language of Science*. New York, Doubleday, 1954.

Das Hausbuch der Mendelschen Zwölfbrüderstiftung zu Nürnberg. Facsimile of the original. Two vols. Bruckmann, Munich, 1965.

Dawson, Warren R. *The Custom of Couvade*. Manchester University Press, Manchester, England, 1929.

Day, Cyrus L. *Quipus and Witches' Knots*. Lawrence, Kansas, University of Kansas Press, 1967.

Deacon, Arthur B. *Malekula: A Vanishing People in the New Hebrides*. London, 1934.

The Discoveries of John Lederer. Edited by William Cumming. Charlottesville, Virginia, University of Virginia Press, 1958.

Dogra, Ramesh and Urmila. *Hindu and Sikh Wedding Ceremonies*. New Delhi, Star Publications, 2000.

Donovan, Claire. *The Wincester Bible*. London, British Library, 1993.

Eliade, Mircea. *Images and Symbols*. New York, Sheed and Ward, 1969.
____. *Shamanism. Archaic Techniques of Ecstasy*. Translated by Williard Trask. Bollingen Series LXXVI, Princeton University Press, 1964.

Findley, Palmer. *Priests of Lucina: the Story of Obstetrics*. Boston, Little Brown & Co., 1939.

Flint, V. *The Rise of Magic in Early Medieval Europe*. Princeton, N.J., Princeton University Press, 1991.

Frazer, J. G. *The Golden Bough*. Two vols. London, Macmillan, 1890.

Furst, Peter and Jill. *North American Indian Art*. New York, Rizzoli International Publications, 1982.

Gantz, Timothy. *Early Greek Myth. A Guide to Literary and Artistic Sources*. Johns Hopkins University Press, Baltimore, Maryland, 1993.

Garcilaso de la Vega. *Royal Commentaries of the Incas and General History of Peru*. Two vols. Translated by Harold Livermore. Austin, University of Texas Press, 1966.

John Gay. *Poetry and Prose*. Edited by V. Dearing. Oxford University Press, 1974.

Gerdes, Paulus. *Une Tradition Géométrique En Afrique. Les Dessins Sur Le Sable*. Three vols. Paris, L'Harmattan, 1995.

Giedion, Siegfried. *Mechanization Takes Command*. New York, W. W. Norton & Co., 1969.

Ginzburg, Carlo. *Ecstasies: Deciphering the Witches' Sabbath*. New York, Pantheon, 1991.

_____. *The Cheese and the Worms*. Translated by John and Anne Tedeschi. New York, Penguin, 1982.

Griaule, M. *Conversations with Ogotemmêli*. London, Oxford University Press, 1965.

Griaule, M. and Dieterlan, G. *The Pale Fox*. Translated by Stephen C. Infantino. Chino Valley, Arizona, The Continuum Foundation, 1986.

Guénon, René. *The Esoterism of Dante*. Translated by C. B. Bethell. Ghent, New York, Sophia Perennis et Universalis, 1996.
_____. *Fundamental Symbols*. Translated by Alvin Moore. Cambridge, U.K., Quinta Essentia, 1995.
_____. *Symbolism of the Cross*. Translated by Angus Macnab. Ghent, New York, Sophia Perennis et Universalis, 1996.
_____. *The Great Triad*. Tranlated by Peter Kingsley. Cambridge, U.K., Quinta Essentia, 1991.
_____. *The Lord of the World*. Tranlated by A. Cheke, A. Blake, C. Shaffer and O. Nottbeck. Moorcote, U.K., Coombe Springs Press, 1983.

Handbook of American Indians. Two vols. Edited by Frederick Hodge. Washington, D.C., Bureau of American Ethnology, 1910.

Handbook of South American Indians. Seven vols. Washington, D.C., Bureau of American Ethnology Bulletin 143, US Government Printing Office, 1946-1959.

Harris, Joel Chandler. *Uncle Remus his Songs and Sayings*. Illustrations by Frederick Church and James H. Moser. New York, Appleton & Co., 1886.

Harrisson, Tom. *Savage Civilizaton*. New York, Alfred A. Knopf, 1937.

Herodotus. *The Histories*. Translated by Aubrey de Sélincourt. New York, Penguin, 1954.

Hocart, A. M. *The Life-Giving Myth*. New York, Grove Press.

Hoffman, Marta. *The Warp-Weighted Loom*. Oslo, Universitetsforlaget, 1974.

Homer. *The Odyssey*. Translated by Robert Fitzgerald. New York, Anchor Press, 1963.

Howitt, Alfred William. *The Native Tribes of South-East Australia*. London, 1904.

Ifrah, Georges. *From One to Zero*. Translated by Lowell Bair. New York, Viking Penguin, 1985.

Jayne, Caroline Furness. *String Figures and How to Make Them*. New York, Dover, 1962.

Jyotsna, Maurya. *Distinctive Beads of Ancient India*. Archaeopress, British Archaeological Reports International, Series 864, Oxford, England, 2000.

Jolly, C. and White, R. *Physical Anthropology and Archeology*. New York, McGraw Hill, 1995.

Joseph, B. L. *Shakespeare's Eden*. London, Blandford Press, 1971.

Kaplan, Aryeh. *Tzitzith: A Thread of Light*. NCSY/Orthodox Union, New York, 1984.

Knight, W. F. Jackson. *Cumaen Gates: A Reference of the Sixth Aeneid to the Initiation Pattern*. Oxford, Basil Blackwell, 1936.
____. *Vergil. Epic and Anthropology*. Barnes & Noble, New York, 1967.

Kristeller, Oskar. *The Philosophy of Marsilio Ficino*. Translated by Virginia Conant. New York, Columbia University Press, 1943.

Lakoff, George. *Women, Fire, and Dangerous Things*. Chicago, University of Chicago Press, 1987.

Lakoff, George, and Johnson, Mark. *Metaphors We Live By*. Chicago, University of Chicago Press, 1980.

Lawlor, Robert. *Sacred Geometry*. New York, Thames and Hudson, 1982.

Layard, John. *Stone Men of Malekula*. London, Chatto & Windus, 1942.

Leupold, Jacob. *Theatrum Arithmetico-Geometricum*. Leipzig, C. Zunkel, 1727.

Lévi-Strauss, Claude. *Tristes Tropiques*. Translated by John and Doreen Weightman. Penguin Books, 1992.

Locke, L. L. *The Ancient Quipu or Peruvian Knot Record*. New York, American Museum of Natural History, 1923.

L'Orange, Hans Peter. *Studies on The Iconography of Cosmic Kingship in the Ancient World*. New Rochelle, New York, Caratzas Brothers, 1982.

Lord, Albert B. *The Singer of Tales*. Cambridge, MA., Harvard University Press, 1960.

Lumholtz, Carl. *Symbolism of the Huichol Indians*. New York, Memoirs of the American Musuem of Natural History, vol. III (1900-1907).

MacDonald, D. B. *The Hebrew Philosophical Genius*. Princeton, Princeton University Press, 1936.

Magnin, Charles. *Histoire des marionnettes en Europe: depuis l'antiquité jusqu'a nos jours*. Paris, Michael Lévy fréres, 1852.

Marcus Aurelius. Loeb Classical Library. Translated by C. R. Haines. Cambridge, Massachusetts, Harvard University Press.

Mason, Otis. *Aboriginal Indian Basketry*. Glorieta, New Mexico, Rio Grande Press, 1984.

Maiuri, Amadeo. *The Phlegraean Fields: from Virgil's tomb to the grotto of the Cumaean sibyl*. Translated by

V. Priestly. Rome, Instituto poligrafico dello Stato, 1947.

Matthews, W.H. *Mazes and Labyrinths.* New York, Dover Press, 1970.

Mead, G. R. S., *Thrice Greatest Hermes*, York Beach, Maine, Samuel Weiser, Inc., 1992.

Menninger, Karl. *Number Words and Symbols.* Translated by Paul Broneer. Cambridge, MIT Press, 1969. Also, Dover Publications, paperback edition, New York, 1992.

Mercante, Anthony. *Encyclopedia of World Mythology and Legend.* Facts on File, New York, 1988.

Merh, Kusum P. *Yama—The Glorious Lord of the Other World*, New Delhi, D.K. Printword Ltd., 1996.

Michell, John and Rhone, Christine. *Twelve-Tribe Nations and the Science of Enchanting the Landscape.* Grand Rapids, Michigan, Phanes Press.

Moon, Parry. *The Abacus.* London, Gordon & Breach, 1971.

Moon, William Least Heat. *Blue Highways.* New York, Fawcett Crest, 1982.

Needham, J. *Science and Civilization in China.* Cambridge, Cambridge University Press, 1954.

Nordenskiöld, E. *The Secret of the Peruvian Quipus.* New York, AMS Press Reprint, 1979.

Oden, Robert. *The Bible Without Theology.* Urbana and Chicago, University of Illinois Press, 2000.

Olaus, Magnus. *Historia de Gentibus Septentriorialibus.* Reprint of the 1555 edition. Copenhagen, Denmark, Rosenkilde & Bagger, 1972.

Onians, Richard B. *The Origins of European Thought.* New York, Cambridge University Press, 1951.

Opler, Morris E. *Myths and Tales of the Jicarilla Apache Indians.* Lincoln, Nebraska, University of Nebraska Press, 1938.

Ovid. *Fasti.* Translated by J. G. Frazer. New York, Putnam and Sons, 1931.
_____. *Metamorphosis.* Translated by Rolfe Humphries. Norman, University of Oklahoma Press, 1972.

Panofsky, Erwin. *Albrecht Dürer*, 3rd edition, two vols. Princeton, Princeton University Press, 1948.

Petronius. *The Satyricon and the Fragments.* Translated by J. P. Sullivan. New York, Penguin, 1965.

Pliny. *Natural History.* Loeb Classical Library. Translated by W. Jones and H. Rackham. Cambridge, Massachusetts, Harvard University Press.

Plato. *Laws.* Loeb Classical Library. Translated by R. G. Bury. Cambridge, Massachusetts, Harvard University Press.
_____. *Theaetetus.* Loeb Classical Library. Translated by H. N. Fowler. Cambridge, Massachusetts, Harvard University Press.
Plotinus. *The Enneads.* Translated by Stephen Mackenna. Burdett, N.Y., Larson Publications, 1992.

Poma de Ayala, Felipe Huaman. *La Nueva Chrónica y Buen Gobierno.* Kingston, Jamaica, University of the West Indies, 1968.
_____. *La Nueva Chrónica y Buen Gobierno*, facsimile edition of original, Paris, Insitute d'ethnologie, 1936.

Porphyry, *On the Cave of the Nymphs.* Translated by Thomas Taylor. Grand Rapids, Michigan, Phanes Press, 1991.

Prasad, R. C. *The Upanayama: the Hindu ceremonies of the sacred thread*. Translated and edited from the Sanscrit by the author. Delhi, Motilal Banarsidass, 1997.

Pullan, J. M. *The History of the Abacus*. New York, Praeger, 1969.

Raglan, Lord. *The Hero*. London, Methuan & Co. Ltd., 1936.
____. *The House and the Temple*. London, Routledge and Kegan Paul, 1964.
____. *The Origins of Religion*. London, Watts and Co., 1949.

Raymond, Louis C. *Spindle Whorls in Archaeology*. Greeley, Colorado, Katunob, Occasional Publications in Mesoamerican Anthropology, No. 30, 1984. Department of Anthropology, University of Northern Colorado.

G. Reichel-Dolmatoff. *The Sacred Mountain of Columbia's Kogi Indians*. Leiden, E. T. Brill, 1990.
Roaf, Michael. *Cultural Atlas of Mesopotamia and the Ancient Near East*. New York, Facts on File Limited, 1990.

Rykwert, Joseph. *The Idea of a Town*. Princeton, NJ., Princeton University Press, 1976.
____. *The Dancing Column: On Order in Architecture*. Cambridge, MA. MIT Press, 1996.

Santillana, Giorgio and Von Dechend, Hertha. *Hamlet's Mill*. Boston, David R. Godine, 1999.

Saxo Grammaticus. *The First Nine Books of the Danish Histories*. Translated by Oliver Elton. London, Norroena Society, 1907.

Scholem, Gershom. *Major Trends in Jewish Mysticism*. New York, Schocken Books, 1946.

Seiler-Baldinger, Annemarie. *Textiles. A Classification of Techniques*. Washington D.C. Smithsonian Institution Press, 1994.

Serra y Boldú, Valerio. *Llibre d'Or del Rosari a Catalunya*. Privately printed, Barcelona, 1925.

Shakespeare, William. *The Tragedy of Macbeth*. Edited by Wakkins and Lemmon. London, Oxford University Press, 1964.

Siegel, Lee. *Net of Magic*. Chicago, University of Chicago Press, 1991.

Simpson, William. *The Buddhist Praying-Wheel*. MacMillan and Co., London, 1896.

Snell, Bruno. *The Discovery of the Mind*. New York, Dover Publications, 1982.

Schnitger, Frederic Martin. *Forgotten Kingdoms in Sumatra*. Leiden, E.J. Brill, 1939.

Snodgrass, Adrian. *The Symbolism of the Stupa*. Ithaca, New York, Studies on Southeast Asia, Cornell University Press, 1985.

Speck, Frank. *Naskapi*. Norman, University of Oklahoma Press, 1935.

Storer, Thomas F. *String Figure Bibliography* (Second Edition). ISFA Press, Pasadena, California.

Tanner, Clara Lee. *Prehistoric Southwestern Craft Arts*. Tucson, University of Arizona Press, 1976.

Tax, Sol, ed. *Indian Tribes of Aboriginal America*. University of Chicago Press, 1952.

Thompson, Stith. *Motif Index of Folk Literature*. Bloomington, Indiana, Indiana University Press, 1932-36.

Turner, J. C. and van de Griend, Peter. *History and Science of Knots*. London, World Scientific, 1996.

Vergil. *The Aeneid*. Translated by W. F. Jackson Knight. London, Penguin, 1956.
____. *The Eclogues*. Translated by John Dryden. London, Mills, Jowett and Mills.

Voorhoeve, P. *Catalogue of Indonesian Manuscripts*. Part 1: Batak Manuscripts. With a contribution by Carl Shuster. The Royal Library, Copenhagen, 1975.

Werner, Alice. *Mythology of All Races*, Boston, 1925, vol. 7, "African Mythology."

Weule, Dr. Karl. *Native Life in East Africa*. Translated by Alice Werner. Chicago, IL., Afro-Am Press, 1969.

Williamson, Ray A. and Farrer, Claire R., eds. *Earth & Sky. Visions of the Cosmos in Native American Folklore*. Albuquerque, University of New Mexico Press, 1992.

Winston-Allen, Anne. *Stories of the Rose. The Making of the Rosary in the Middle Ages*. University Park, Pennsylvania, the Pennsylvania State University Press, 1997.

Wirz, Paul. *Der Totenkult auf Bali*. Stuttgart, Strecker und Schroder, 1928.

Wunderlich, Hans George. *The Secret of Crete*. Translated by Richard and Clara Winston. New York, Macmillan, 1974.

ARTICLES, MUSEUM CATALOGS, AND MISCELLANEA

Banks, M. M. "Tangled-Thread Mazes." *Folk-Lore*, vol. 46 (1935), p. 78.

Barbeau, Marius. "The Old-World Dragon in America." *Indian Tribes of Aboriginal America*, pp. 115-122. Edited by Sol Tax, University of Chicago Press, 1952.

Benveniste, E. "Un Emploi du nom du 'Genou' en Vieil-Irlandais et en Sogdien." *Bulletin de la Société de Linguistique de Paris*, vol. 27 (1926), pp. 51-53.

Birket-Smith, Kaj. "The Circumpacific Distribution of Knot Records," *Folk*, vol. 8-9, (1966-67), pp. 15-24, Copenhagen, Denmark.

Blackman, W. S. "Rosaries." *Hastings Encyclopedia of Religion and Ethics*, pp. 847-856. Edinburgh, T & T Clark, 1908-27.

Boas, Franz. "The Eskimos of Baffin Land and Hudson Bay." *Bulletin of the American Museum of Natural History*, vol. 15 (1901), pp. 35-37.

Bunker, Emma, Chatwin, Bruce, and Farkas, Anne. *"Animal Style"Art from East to West*. Exhibition catalogue of The Asia Society, 1970.

Cahen, Maurice. "'Genou', 'Adoption' et 'Parente' en Germanique." *Bulletin de la Société de Linguistique de Paris*, vol. 27 (1926), pp. 56-67.

Chen, Hsia-Sheng. *The Art of Chinese Knotting*. New York, Exhibition Catalog of China Institute in America, July 29 – September 12, 1981.

Christensen, Antje. "The Peruvian Quipu." In Turner, J. C. and van de Griend, Peter, *History and Science of Knots*. London, World Scientific, 1996, pp. 71-88.

Coomaraswamy, Ananda K. "The Tree of Jesse and Indian Parallels or Sources." *Art Bulletin* 11, (1929), pp. 217-220.
____. "Angel and Titan: An Essay in Vedic Ontology." *American Oriental Society Journal*, LV (1935) pp. 373-419.

_____. "The Symbolism of Archery." *Ars Islamica*, vol. 10 (1943), pp. 105-119.

_____. "A Note on the Stickfast Motif." *Journal of American Folklore*, vol. 57 (1944), pp. 128-131.

_____. "The Iconography of Durer's Knots and Leonardo's Concatenation." *Arts Quarterly*, vol. 7 (1944), pp. 109-128.

_____. Unpublished manuscript on reincarnation, Firestone Library, Princeton University.

Conklin, William J. "The Information System of Middle Horizon Quipus." *Annals of the New York Academy of Sciences*, vol. 385, pp. 261-281.

Deacon, Arthur Bernard. "Geometrical Drawings from Malekula and Other Islands of the New Hebrides," *Journal of the Royal Anthropological Institute of Great Britain and Ireland*, 64/1 (1934), p. 129-175.

_____. "The Regulation of Marriage in Ambrym," *Journal of the Royal Asiatic Institute* (JRAI), LVII (July–December, 1927).

de Beauclair, Inez. "Three Genealogical Stories from Botel Tobago: A Contribution to the Folklore of the Yami," Academica Sinica Web site, http://www.sinica.edu.tw/~dlproj/article.html.

Dilling, W. J. "Knots." *Hastings Encyclopedia of Religion and Ethics*, vol. 7.

Eames, Ray and Charles. *The Films of Ray and Charles Eames* (on DVD), Image Entertainment, Inc., 1998.

Eis, Ruth. *Ornamental Bags for Tallit and Tefillin of the Judah L. Magnes Museum.* Catalog of the Judah L. Magnes Museum, Berkeley, California, 1984.

Elderkin, Kate. "Jointed Dolls in Antiquity." *American Journal of Archeology*, vol. 34 (1930), pp. 455-479.

Feldman, Jerome. *Arc of the Ancestors. Indonesian Art from the Jerome L. Joss Collection at UCLA.* Fowler Museum of Cultural History, University of California, Los Angeles, 1994.

Gandz, S. "The Knot in Hebrew Literature or From the Knot to the Alphabet." *Isis*, vol. 14 (1930).

Gaster, M. Correspondence in *Folklore*, vol. XXV (1914), pp. 254-258.

Glory, Abbot. "Debris de corde paleolithique à la Grotte de Lascaux." *Memoires de la Société Préhistorique Française* 5 (1959), pp. 135-169.

Hooper, Lucille. *The Cahuilla Indians.* University of California Publications in American Archeology and Ethnology, Vol. 16 (6), pp. 315-380.

Jensen, Alfred. "Beziehungen zwischen dem alten Testament und der nilotischen Kultur in Afrika." *Culture in History, Essays in Honor of Paul Radin*, pp. 449-466, New York, 1960.

Klein, Cecilia F. "Snares and Entrails: Mesoamerican Symbols of Sin and Punishment." *Res*, vol. 19/20 (1990/1991), pp. 81-103.

_____. "Woven Heaven, Tangled Earth: A Weaver's Paradigm of the Mesoamerican Cosmos." *Annals of the New York Academy of Sciences*, vol. 385, pp. 1-35.

Larsen, Helge. "The Ipiutak Culture: Its Origins and Relationiships," pp. 22-34, in *Indian Tribes of Aboriginal America*, edited by Sol Tax, University of Chicago Press, 1952.

Layard, John. "Maze Dances and the Ritual of the Labyrinth in Malekula." *Folk-Lore*, vol. 47 (1936), pp. 123-170.

_____. "Labyrinth Ritual in South India: Threshold and Tattoo Designs." *Folk-Lore*, vol. 48 (1937), pp. 115-182.

_____. "The Labyrinth in the Megalithic Areas of Malekula, the Deccan, Scandinavia, and Scotland: With Special Reference to the Malekulan Geometric Drawings Collected by Deacon." *Man*, 35/10, London.

Lorm, A. J. de. "Bataksche Maskers in de Haagsche Volkenkundige Verzameling." *Cultureel Indië*. Eerste Jaargang, 1939, pp. 48-53, Leiden, E.J. Brill.

Loth, J. "Le Mot Désignant Le Genou au Sens de Génération Chez les Celtes, les Germains, Les Slaves, Les Assyriens." *Revue Celtique*, vol. 40 (1923), pp. 143-152.

Maude, H. E. and H. C. "String Figures from the Gilbert Islands." Aukland, *Polynesian Society (Memoir No. 13)* (1958).

Meillet, A. "LAT. genuinus." *Bulletin de la Société de Linguistique de Paris*, vol. 27, (1926), pp. 54-55.

Nelson, Edward William. "The Eskimo About Bering Strait." *Eighteenth Annual Report of the Bureau of American Ethnology* (BAE), (1896-97), part 1. Washington D.C., Government Printing Office, 1899.

Onians, Richard. "On the Knees of the Gods." *Classical Review* (Feb., 1924).

Ott, Sandra. "Aristotle Among the Basques: 'The Cheese Analogy' of Conception." *Man*, vol. 14, no. 4, pp. 699-711.

Reichel-Dolmatoff, G. "The Loom of Life: A Kogi Principle of Integration." *Journal of Latin American Lore*, vol. 4:1 (1978), University of California at Los Angeles.

Richter, G. M. A. "Description of Attic Greek Vase (c. 560 B.C.) with scenes of spinning and weaving." *Metropolitan Museum of Art Bulletin* (Dec., 1931).

Roth, H. Ling. "Ancient Egyptian and Greek Looms." *Bankfield Museum Notes*, series 2, no. 2, (1913).

Schuster, Carl. "An Archaic Form of Chess in Chinese Peasant Embroidery." *Man* (Sept., 1936), pp. 148-151.
_____. "A Prehistoric Symbol in Modern Chinese Folk Art" *Man*, vol. XXXVI (270-292), (Dec., 1936), pp. 201-203.
_____. "A Comparative Study of Motives in Western Chinese Folk Embroideries" *Monumenta Serica*, vol. 2, fasc. 1, (1936), Peking.
_____. "Peasant Embroideries of China" *Asia* (Jan., 1937), pp. 26-31.
_____. "The Triumphant Equestrian," *Monumenta Serica*, vol. II, fasc. 2 (1937), Peking, pp. 437-440.
_____. "Joint Marks: A Possible Index of Cultural Constact Between America, Oceania, and the Far East." *Koninklijk Instituut Voor de Tropen*, Amsterdam, 1951.
_____. "A Survival of the Eurasiatic Animal Style in Modern Alaskan Eskimo Art." *Indian Tribes of Aboriginal America*, edited by Sol Tax, pp. 35-45, University of Chicago Press, 1952.
_____. "Genealogical Patterns in the Old and New Worlds." *Revista Do Museu Paulista, Nova Série*, vol. X (1956/58), Sao Paulo, Brazil. This article was also printed separately as a booklet under the same title.
_____. "Observations on the Painted Designs of Patagonian Skin Robes." *Essays in Pre-Columbian Art and Archaeology*, Samuel Lothrop, ed. Harvard University Press, Cambridge, MA., 1961, pp. 421-447.
_____. "Skin and Fur Mosaics in Pehistoric and Modern Times," in Festschrift für Ad. E. Jensen, Munich, (1964), pp. 559-610.
_____. "Incised Stones from Nevada and Elsewhere." *The Nevada Archaeological Survey Reporter*. Vol. II, No. 5 (May, 1968). University of Nevada, Reno, NV.
_____. "Relations of a Chinese Embroidary Design: Eastern Europe and Western Asia, Southeast Asia (the Dongson Culture) and Melanesia." *Early Chinese Art and its Possible Influence in the Pacific Basin*, edited by Noel Barnard and Douglas Fraser, vol. II, pp. 243-290, N.Y., 1972.
_____. "Comparative Observations on Some Typical Designs in Batak Manuscripts." *Catalog of Indonesian Manuscripts, Part 1 Batak Manuscripts,* edited by P. Voorhoeve, pp. 52-85, The Royal Library, Copenhagen, 1975.

Sherman, Claire Richter. *Writing on Hands. Memory and Knowledge in Early Modern Europe.* Catalog of an exhibition at the Trout Gallery, Dickinson College, Carlisle, Pennsylvania (Sept. 8, 2000– Nov. 25,

217

2000) and the Folger Shakespeare Library, Washington D.C. (Dec. 13, 2000–March 4, 2001). Distributed by University of Washington Press, Seattle, Washington.

Simon, Edmund. "Uber Knotenschriften und ahnliche Knotenschnure der Riukiu-Inseln." *Asia Major II*, 1924, pp. 657-667.

Small, Audrey. "Selected String Figures, Myths and Mythmakers." *Bulletin of the International String Figure Society*, vol. 1 (1994), p. 15.

Stanner, W. E. H. "Aboriginal Modes of Address and Reference in the North-West of the Northern Territory." *Oceania*, vol. 7 (1937), pp. 300-315, Sydney, Australia.

Steinberg, Leo. "The Sexuality of Christ in Renaissance Art and in Modern Oblivion." *October*, no. 25 (Summer, 1983), MIT Press.

Travis, James. "Old Celtic Design Music." *Miscellanea Musica Celtica, Musicological Studies*, vol. XIV. The Institute of Medieval Music, Ltd., Brooklyn, N.Y.

Wilbert, Johannes. "The Thread of Life. Symbolism of Miniature Art from Ecuador." *Studies in Pre-Columbian Art and Archeology*, vol. 12 (1974). Dumbarton Oaks, Washington, D.C.

ILLUSTRATION SOURCES

The author has attempted to obtain permissions for the use of all the images reproduced in this book.

FORWARD / MAGIC KNOTS

F1. Reconstruction of paleolithic cord from a fossil imprint in clay. Three two-ply cords. Lascaux, France, 15,000 B.C. Abbot Glory, "Debris de corde paleolithique à la Grotte de Lascaux." Memoires de la Société Préhistorique Française 5 (1959), pp. 135-169.

F2. Külko basketry technique. *Handbook of South American Indians*, volume 2, p. 714. BAE, Washington D.C. After Claude Joseph, 1931.

F3. Huichol calendar. Lumholtz, *Symbolism of the Huichol Indians*, p. 188. Courtesy of the American Museum of Natural History.

1. Fisherman's knot. Day, *Quipus' and Witches' Knots*, p. 83, no. 11. Images from this book are reproduced with permission of the University of Kansas Press.

2. Fisherman's knot. Day, *Quipus' and Witches' Knots*, p. 130, top.

3. Roman bride with Hercules knot. Day, *Quipus' and Witches' Knots*, p. 55, no. 3.

4. Square knot. Day, *Quipus' and Witches' Knots*, p. 83, no. 3.

5. Goddess at Lucknow, *Quipus' and Witches' Knots*, p. 55, no. 5.

6. Caduceus, *Quipus' and Witches' Knots*, p. 56, no. 2.

7. Statue of Juno Lucina, Musuem of Capua, Italy, *Priests of Lucina.*

8. Statue of Varuna, Patna Museum, India, *Encyclopedia of Hindu Gods*, p. 1595. Courtesy of the American Institute of Indian Studies.

9. Wind knots, Magnus Olaus, *Historia de Gentibus Septentriorialibus*, liber tertius. Images from this book are reproduced with the permission of Rosenkilde & Bagger A/S.

10. Four winds, Magnus Olaus,. *Historia de Gentibus Septentriorialibus*, liber primus.

MNEMONIC KNOTS

1. G. Reichel-Dolmatoff. *The Sacred Mountain of Columbia's Kogi Indians*. Leiden, E. T. Brill, 1990. Plate XXXVII. Man using mnemonic device.

2. Carpenter, Edmund, and Carl Schuster. *Materials for the Study of Social Symbolism in Ancient and Tribal Art*, 3 volumes. New York, Rock Foundation, 1986-1988, vol. 2, bk. 1, p. 223. Maori *whakapapa*. All material reproduced from the work of Carl Schuster courtesy of the Rock Foundation.

3. Edmund, and Carl Schuster. *Materials for the Study of Social Symbolism in Ancient and Tribal Art*, 3 vols. New York, Rock Foundation, 1986-1988, vol. 2, bk. 1, p. 227. Bamboo tally stick, Burma.

4. Birket-Smith, Kaj. "The Circumpacific Distribution of Knot Records," *Folk*, Vol. 8-9, p. 17, 1966-67, Copenhagen, Denmark. Courtesy of the Danish Ethnographic Society. Map of knot record distribution in North and South America.

5. Birket-Smith, Kaj. "The Circumpacific Distribution of Knot Records," *Folk*, Vol. 8-9, p. 19, 1966-67, Copenhagen, Denmark. Courtesy of the Danish Ethnographic Society. Map of knot record distribution in Asia and Pacific.

6. Pick one of the three available. Simon, Edmund. "Uber Knotenschriften und ahnliche Knotenschnure der Riukiu-Inseln." *Asia Major II*, 1924, pp. 657-667. Knot records from the Ryukyu Islands.

7. Locke, L. L. *The Ancient Quipu or Peruvian Knot Record*. New York, American Museum of Natural History, 1923. Quipu number 5 from Medialima. Courtesy of the American Museum of Natural History.

8. Poma de Ayala, Felipe *Huaman. La Nueva Chrónica y Buen Gobierno*. Quipu keeper with long quipu and counting board.

9. Poma de Ayala, Felipe Huaman. *La Nueva Chrónica y Buen Gobierno*. Quipu keeper with two small quipus.

10. Locke, L. L. *The Ancient Quipu or Peruvian Knot Record*. New York, American Museum of Natural History, 1923. Quipu number 4 from Chancay. Courtesy of the American Museum of Natural History.

11. Locke, L. L. *The Ancient Quipu or Peruvian Knot Record*. New York, American Museum of Natural History, 1923. p. 13. Methods of tying knots in the quipu. Courtesy of the American Museum of Natural History.

12. Eis, Ruth. Ornamental Bags for Tallit and Tefillin of the Judah L. Magnes Museum. Catalog of the Judah L. Magnes Museum, Berkeley, California, 1984. Phylacteries of the hand and head. Courtesy of the Magnes Musuem.

13. Kaplan, Aryeh. *Tzitzith: A Thread of Light*. NCSY/Orthodox Union, New York, 1984, p. 10. Fringes (*tzitzith*).

14. Moon, Parry. *The Abacus*. London, Gordon & Breach, 1971, p. 31. Modern chinese abacus (*suan-pan*). Courtesy of Gordon & Breach.

15. Pullan, J. M. *The History of the Abacus*. New York, Praeger, 1969. . Salamis counting board. Courtesy of the Random House Group.

16. Pullan, J. M. *The History of the Abacus*. New York, Praeger, 1969. Darius Vase. Courtesy of the Random House Group.

17. Pullan, J. M. *The History of the Abacus*. New York, Praeger, 1969. Portable handheld abacus Courtesy of the Random House Group.

18. Moon, Parry. *The Abacus*. London, Gordon & Breach, 1971. Dame arithmetic. Courtesy of Gordon & Breach.

19. Ifrah, Georges. *From One to Zero*. Translated by Lowell Bair. New York, Viking Penguin, 1985, p. 37.

20. Counting by twenty. Ifrah, Georges. *From One to Zero*. Translated by Lowell Bair. New York, Viking Penguin, 1985, p. 18. Counting by fives.

21. Ifrah, Georges. From One to Zero. Translated by Lowell Bair. New York, Viking Penguin, 1985, p. 65. Counting by twelves.

22. Leupold, Jacob. *Theatrum Arithmetico-Geometricum*. Leipzig, C. Zunkel, 1727. Finger reckoning.

23. Ifrah, Georges. *From One to Zero*. Translated by Lowell Bair. New York, Viking Penguin, 1985, p. 75.

Bedes' method of finger reckoning (units).

24. Ifrah, Georges. *From One to Zero*. Translated by Lowell Bair. New York, Viking Penguin, 1985, p. 75. Bedes' method of finger reckoning (tens).

25. Ifrah, Georges. *From One to Zero*. Translated by Lowell Bair. New York, Viking Penguin, 1985, p. 75. Bedes' method of finger reckoning (hundreds).

26. Ifrah, Georges. *From One to Zero*. Translated by Lowell Bair. New York, Viking Penguin, 1985, p. 75. Bedes' method of finger reckoning (thousands).

27. Ifrah, Georges. *From One to Zero*. Translated by Lowell Bair. New York, Viking Penguin, 1985, p. 62. Bedes' method for counting the solar cycle.

28. Bedes' method for counting the lunar cycle. Ifrah, Georges. *From One to Zero*. Translated by Lowell Bair. New York, Viking Penguin, 1985, p. 62.

29. Ifrah, Georges. *From One to Zero*. Translated by Lowell Bair. New York, Viking Penguin, 1985, p. 62. Counting by twelves using the joints.

30. Carpenter, Edmund, and Carl Schuster. *Materials for the Study of Social Symbolism in Ancient and Tribal Art*, 3 vols. New York, Rock Foundation, 1986-1988. vol. 3, bk. 2, p. 387. Division of major body joints.

31. *Serra y Boldú, Valerio. Llibre d'Or del Rosari a Catalunya*. Privately printed, Barcelona, 1925. Buddhist monk and Balinese priest with rosaries.

32. *Serra y Boldú, Valerio. Llibre d'Or del Rosari a Catalunya*. Privately printed, Barcelona, 1925. Rosary from St. James of Galicia.

33. Winston-Allen, Anne. *Stories of the Rose. The Making of the Rosary in the Middle Ages*. The Pennsylvania State University Press, University Park, Pennsylvania, 1997. p. 90.

34. *Das Hausbuch der Mendelschen Zwölfbrüderstiftung zu Nürnberg*. Facsimile of the original. Two volumes. Bruckmann, Munich, 1965.

35. Serra y Boldú, Valerio. *Llibre d'Or del Rosari a Catalunya*. Privately printed, Barcelona, 1925, p. 8. Charles V with rosary.

36. Ifrah, Georges. *From One to Zero*. Translated by Lowell Bair. New York, Viking Penguin, 1985, p. 64. Moslem *subha*.

37. Ifrah, Georges. *From One to Zero*. Translated by Lowell Bair. New York, Viking Penguin, 1985, p. 64. Moslem method of counting.

38. Cargill, John. *The Celtic Cross and Greek Proportion*. Chicago, Charles G. Blake Co., 1930. Picture of John Cargill.

39. *The Celtic Cross and Greek Proportion*. Chicago, Charles G. Blake Co., 1930. Figures 5/6. Measurements of stone.

40. Carpenter, Edmund, and Carl Schuster. *Materials for the Study of Social Symbolism in Ancient and Tribal Art*, 3 volumes. New York, Rock Foundation, 1986-1988. vol. 3, bk. 1, p. 100. Celtic standing stone.

41. Carpenter, Edmund, and Carl Schuster. *Materials for the Study of Social Symbolism in Ancient and Tribal Art*, 3 volumes. New York, Rock Foundation, 1986-1988. vol. 3, bk. 1, p. 101. Music in stone.

42. Sherman, Claire Richter. "Writing on Hands. Memory and Knowledge in Early Modern Europe." Catalog of an exhibition at the Trout Gallery, Dickinson College, Carlisle, Pennsylvania (Sept. 8, 2000–Nov. 25, 2000) and the Folger Shakespeare Library, Washington D.C. (Dec. 13, 2000–March 4, 2001). Distributed by University of Washington Press, Seattle, Washington. Method of teaching music using the hands.

SUTRATMAN

1. L'Orange, Hans Peter. *Studies on The Iconography of Cosmic Kingship in the Ancient World*. New Rochelle, New York, Caratzas Brothers, 1982, p. 159.

2. L'Orange, Hans Peter. *Studies on The Iconography of Cosmic Kingship in the Ancient World*. New Rochelle, New York, Caratzas Brothers, 1982, p. 98.

3. Bateson, Gregory, and Mead, Margaret. *Balinese Character*. New York, New York Academy of Sciences, 1942, p. 98, fig. 7. Images from this book are reproduced with the permission of the New York Academy of Sciences.

4. Nelson, Edward William. "The Eskimo About Bering Strait." *Eighteenth Annual Report of the Bureau of American Ethnology (BAE)*, (1896-97), Part 1. Washington D.C., Government Printing Office, 1899. Page 844. Eskimo mechanical doll.

5. *Crepereia Tryphaena*. Milan, Italy, Gruppo Editoriale Fabbri, 1983, p. 13 and p. 17. Roman doll.

6. Wirz, Paul. *Der Totenkult auf Bali*. Stuttgart, Strecker und Schroder, 1928, fig. 10, *Ukur-kèpèng*, Bali.

7. Lorm, A. J. de. "Bataksche Maskers in de Haagsche Volkenkundige Verzameling." *Cultureel Indië*. Eerste Jaargang, 1939, pp. 48-53, Leiden, E.J. Brill. plate 12, mechanical doll (*sigalegale*).

8. Schnitger, Frederic Martin. *Forgotten Kingdoms in Sumatra*. Leiden, E.J. Brill, 1939, p. 108. Head of *sigalegale*.

9. Snell, Bruno. *The Discovery of the Mind*. New York, Dover Publications, p. 7. Ancient Greek depiction of the human body.

10. Bateson, Gregory, and Mead, Margaret. *Balinese Character*. New York, New York Academy of Sciences, 1942, p. 86, fig. 8. Balinese dance teacher instructing student.

11. Bateson, Gregory, and Mead, Margaret. *Balinese Character*. New York, New York Academy of Sciences, 1942. Page 98, fig. 4. Girl in courtship dance.

12. Bateson, Gregory, and Mead, Margaret. *Balinese Character*. New York, New York Academy of Sciences, 1942, p. 90, fig. 3. Balinese *sangiang deling* ritual.

13. Bateson, Gregory, and Mead, Margaret. *Balinese Character*. New York, New York Academy of Sciences, 1942. Page 94, figs. 4 and 5. Balinese protective spirit (Multiple Soldier) and shadow puppets of graveyard spirits.

14. Mercante, Anthony. *Encyclopedia of World Mythology and Legend*. Facts on File, New York, 1988, p. 396. The Three Fates (*morae*).

15. Carpenter, Edmund, and Carl Schuster. *Materials for the Study of Social Symbolism in Ancient and Tribal Art*, 3 vols. New York, Rock Foundation, 1986-1988, vol. 2, bk. 2, p. 320. Drawing of a Samoyed woman making clothing.

16. Coomaraswamy, Ananda. "The Iconography of Durer's Knots and Leonardo's Concatenation." Arts Quarterly, Vol. 7 (1944), fig. 16. Greek Geometric double-spiral fibula.

17. The Face of Christ on the Sudary. Engraving by the French artist, Claude Mellan (1649).

18. Richter, G. M. A. Attic Greek Vase (c. 560 B.C.) with scenes of spinning and weaving. Attributed to the Amasis Painter. Metropolitan Museum of Art Bulletin, Dec. 1931. Photograph reproduced with the permission of the Metropolitan Museum of Art.

19. Seiler-Baldinger, Annemarie. *Textiles. A Classification of Techniques*. Washington D.C. Smithsonian Institution Press, 1994, p. 82. Backstrap loom. Image reproduced with the permission of the Museum der Kulturen Basel.

20. *Handbook of South American Indians*. Seven volumes. Washington, D.C., Bureau of American Ethnology Bulletin 143, US Government Printing Office, 1946-1959. Vol. 5, p. 109, Chiriguano bandloom.

21. Seiler-Baldinger, Annemarie. *Textiles. A Classification of Techniques*. Washington D.C. Smithsonian Institution Press, 1994, p. 81. Horizontal ground loom. Image reproduced with the permission of the Museum der Kulturen Basel.

22. Carpenter, Edmund, and Carl Schuster. *Materials for the Study of Social Symbolism in Ancient and Tribal Art*, 3 vols. New York, Rock Foundation, 1986-1988, vol. 1, bk. 1, p. 244, fig. 283. Cast bronze plaque, Merovingian, Linz, Austria.

23. Carpenter, Edmund, and Carl Schuster. *Materials for the Study of Social Symbolism in Ancient and Tribal Art*, 3 volumes. New York, Rock Foundation, 1986-1988, vol. 1, bk. 1, p. 243, fig. 279. Neolithic steatite figurine of crossed bodies, from Nicosia, Cyprus.

24 Carpenter, Edmund, and Carl Schuster. *Materials for the Study of Social Symbolism in Ancient and Tribal Art*, 3 vols. New York, Rock Foundation, 1986-1988, vol. 3, bk. 3, p. 505, fig. 549. Inverted figure on gravestone. Tombstone of William Walker, Bella Coola Indians, British Columbia, Canada.

25. G. Reichel-Dolmatoff. *The Sacred Mountain of Columbia's Kogi Indians*. Leiden, E. T. Brill, 1990, p. 9. Kogi man weaving a cloth. Permission courtesy of Latin American Center publications, UCLA.

26. G. Reichel-Dolmatoff. *The Sacred Mountain of Columbia's Kogi Indians*. Leiden, E. T. Brill, 1990, p. 7. Drawing of a Kogi spindle. Permission courtesy of Latin American Center publications, UCLA.

27. G. Reichel-Dolmatoff. *The Sacred Mountain of Columbia's Kogi Indians*. Leiden, E. T. Brill, 1990, p. 7. Drawing of framework of a Kogi loom. Permission courtesy of Latin American Center publications, UCLA.

28. G. Reichel-Dolmatoff. *The Sacred Mountain of Columbia's Kogi Indians*. Leiden, E. T. Brill, 1990, plate XXVIII. Kogi ritual posture of listening. Permission courtesy of Latin American Center publications, UCLA.

29. G. Reichel-Dolmatoff. *The Sacred Mountain of Columbia's Kogi Indians*. Leiden, E. T. Brill, 1990, plate VII. Main Kogi temple at Takina, Columbia. Permission courtesy of Latin American Center publications, UCLA.

30. *Handbook of South American Indians*. Seven volumes. Washington, D.C., Bureau of American Ethnology Bulletin 143, US Government Printing Office, 1946-1959, vol. 3, p. 868. Rucuyen woman spinning.

31. G. Reichel-Dolmatoff. *The Sacred Mountain of Columbia's Kogi Indians*. Leiden, E. T. Brill, 1990, plate XXXIV. Kogi spindle. Permission courtesy of Latin American Center publications, UCLA.

32. Wilbert, Johannes. "The Thread of Life. Symbolism of Miniature Art from Ecuador." *Studies in Pre-Columbian Art and Archeology*, vol. 12 (1974), Dumbarton Oaks, Washington, D.C., p. 27. Spindle whorl types. Permission courtesy of Dumbarton Oaks publications.

33. Carpenter, Edmund, and Carl Schuster. *Materials for the Study of Social Symbolism in Ancient and Tribal Art*, 3 vols. New York, Rock Foundation, 1986-1988, vol. 3, bk. 1, p. 75, fig. 45. Churning of the Sea of Milk. 12th century bas-relief, Ankor Wat, Cambodia.

34. Simpson, William. *The Buddhist Praying-Wheel.* MacMillan and Co., London, 1896, frontispiece and p. 7. Large and small prayer-wheels, India.

35. Carpenter, Edmund, and Carl Schuster. *Materials for the Study of Social Symbolism in Ancient and Tribal Art*, 3 vols. New York, Rock Foundation, 1986-1988, vol. 3, bk. 1, p. 70, figs. 40 and 41. Bow drill and pump drill, Chuckchee, Siberia.

36. Carpenter, Edmund, and Carl Schuster. *Materials for the Study of Social Symbolism in Ancient and Tribal Art*, 3 vols. New York, Rock Foundation, 1986-1988, vol. 3, bk. 1, p. 71, fig. 42. Eskimo with bow drill making sled part, Baker Lake, N.W.T., Canada.

37. Carpenter, Edmund, and Carl Schuster. *Materials for the Study of Social Symbolism in Ancient and Tribal Art*, 3 vols. New York, Rock Foundation, 1986-1988, vol. 3, bk. 1, p. 72, figs. 43a, b, c. Maritime Koryak fire boards and drill, Siberia.

38. Carpenter, Edmund, and Carl Schuster. *Materials for the Study of Social Symbolism in Ancient and Tribal Art*, 3 vols. New York, Rock Foundation, 1986-1988, vol. 1, bk. 2, p. 661, fig. 1164. Hopi Indian painted pottery buzzer. Moki, Arizona.

39. Wilbert, Johannes. "The Thread of Life. Symbolism of Miniature Art from Ecuador." *Studies in Pre-Columbian Art and Archeology*, Vol. 12 (1974). Dumbarton Oaks, Washington, D.C., fig, 133. Spindle whorl with hocker. Permission courtesy of Dumbarton Oaks publications.

40. Carpenter, Edmund, and Carl Schuster. *Materials for the Study of Social Symbolism in Ancient and Tribal Art*, 3 vols. New York, Rock Foundation, 1986-1988, vol. 1, bk. 1, p. 231, fig. 261. Micronesian house gable with hocker, Palau, Caroline Islands.

41. Furst, Peter and Jill. *North American Indian Art.* New York, Rizzoli International Publications, 1982, plate 127. Salish spindle whorl with human/toad figure, 19th century.

42. Carpenter, Edmund, and Carl Schuster. *Materials for the Study of Social Symbolism in Ancient and Tribal Art*, 3 vols. New York, Rock Foundation, 1986-1988, vol. 3, bk. 1, p. 239, fig. 266. Wooden disk (spindle whorl) from Barreales culture, province of St. Juan, Argentina.

43. Donovan, Claire. *The Wincester Bible.* London, British Library, 1993, p. 43, fig. 172. *Ofannim* in the Book of Ezekial.

44. Carpenter, Edmund, and Carl Schuster. *Materials for the Study of Social Symbolism in Ancient and Tribal Art*, 3 vols. New York, Rock Foundation, 1986-1988, vol. 1, bk. 2, p. 613, fig. 1017. Perforated and drilled amber disk, Germany, middle Neolithic.

45. Crewe, Lindy *Spindle Whorls.* Jonsered, Sweden, Paul Aströms Förlag, 1998, app. 2, fig. A2.19. Designs on spindle whorls from Cyprus, Central Plain, Dhenia Kafkalla. Drawings by Lindy Crewe.

46. Carpenter, Edmund, and Carl Schuster. Materials for the Study of Social Symbolism in Ancient and Tribal Art, 3 vols. New York, Rock Foundation, 1986-1988, vol. 1, bk. 2, p. 601, fig. 992. Araucanian shamans with drums, Machis, Cautin, Chile.

47. *Animals.* New York, Dover Publishing, 1979. Silk spider from Malaysia of the genus *Nephila* (male above, female below).

48. Harris, Joel Chandler. *Uncle Remus his Songs and Sayings.* Illustrations by Frederick Church and James

H. Moser. New York, Appleton & Co., 1886, p. 23, Tar-Baby and Brer Rabbit.

49. "The Iconography of Durer's Knots and Leonardo's Concatenation." Arts Quarterly, vol. 7 1944, p. 111, fig 1. One of Durer's "Sechs Knoten".

50. "The Iconography of Durer's Knots and Leonardo's Concatenation." Arts Quarterly, vol. 7 1944, p. 111, fig. 2. Leonardo's "Concatenation".

51. Carpenter, Edmund, and Carl Schuster. *Materials for the Study of Social Symbolism in Ancient and Tribal Art*, 3 vols. New York, Rock Foundation, 1986-1988, vol. 3, bk. 2, p. 268, fig. 276. Coin with labyrinth from Crete, 3rd century B.C.

52. Carpenter, Edmund, and Carl Schuster. *Materials for the Study of Social Symbolism in Ancient and Tribal Art*, 3 vols. New York, Rock Foundation, 1986-1988, vol. 3, bk. 2, p. 350, fig. 392. Miniature from the Farhi Bible, copied in Spain or Provence, 14th century.

53. Carpenter, Edmund, and Carl Schuster. *Materials for the Study of Social Symbolism in Ancient and Tribal Art*, 3 vols. New York, Rock Foundation, 1986-1988, vols. 3, bk. 1, p. 88, fig. 64. Quioco bird design, Angola.

54. Carpenter, Edmund, and Carl Schuster. *Materials for the Study of Social Symbolism in Ancient and Tribal Art*, 3 vols. New York, Rock Foundation, 1986-1988, vol. 3, bk. 1, p. 84, fig. 61. Exorcism of snakes by means of a serpentine diagram drawn around dots on the ground, South India.

55. Bain, George. *Celtic Art. The Methods of Construction*. New York, Dover, 1973, p. 49, plate 10. Celtic knotwork design.

56. Carpenter, Edmund, and Carl Schuster. *Materials for the Study of Social Symbolism in Ancient and Tribal Art*, 3 vols. New York, Rock Foundation, 1986-1988, vol. 3, bk. 1, p. 76, fig. 48. Sand drawing of a turtle, Malekula, New Hebrides Islands.

57. Carpenter, Edmund, and Carl Schuster. *Materials for the Study of Social Symbolism in Ancient and Tribal Art*, 3 vols. New York, Rock Foundation, 1986-1988, vol. 3, bk. 1, p. 87, fig. 63. Malekulan sand drawing from Seniang, New Hebrides Islands, called *Nahal*.

58. Carpenter, Edmund, and Carl Schuster. *Materials for the Study of Social Symbolism in Ancient and Tribal Art*, 3 vols. New York, Rock Foundation, 1986-1988, vol. 3, bk. 2, p. 408, fig. 58. Sand-drawn turtle effigy, Lambumbu, New Hebrides Islands. This is the road along which the ghosts pass to Iambi.

59. Carpenter, Edmund, and Carl Schuster. *Materials for the Study of Social Symbolism in Ancient and Tribal Art*, 3 vols. New York, Rock Foundation, 1986-1988, vol. 3, bk. 1, p. 239, fig. 266. Wooden disk (spindle whorl) from Barreales culture, province of St. Juan, Argentina.

60. Carpenter, Edmund, and Carl Schuster. *Materials for the Study of Social Symbolism in Ancient and Tribal Art*, 3 vols. New York, Rock Foundation, 1986-1988, vol. 3, bk. 1, p. 85, fig. 62. Hindu woman drawing threshold design, South India.

61. Carpenter, Edmund, and Carl Schuster. *Materials for the Study of Social Symbolism in Ancient and Tribal Art*, 3 vols. New York, Rock Foundation, 1986-1988, vol. 3, bk 1, p. 92, fig. 74. *Rangoli* design of bird, 19th century, India.

62. Gerdes, Paulus. *Une Tradition Géométrique En Afrique. Les Dessins Sur Le Sable*. Three vols. Paris, L'Harmattan, 1995, vol. 1, p. 62, fig 66 (pangolin), and p. 63, fig. 67 (chimba). Images reproduced with the permission of Harmattan Press.

63. Gerdes, Paulus. *Une Tradition Géométrique En Afrique. Les Dessins Sur Le Sable*. Three vols. Paris, L'Harmattan, 1995, vol. 3, p, 488, fig, 6. Snake drawing, Mesopotamia, 3rd millennium.

64. Carpenter, Edmund, and Carl Schuster. *Materials for the Study of Social Symbolism in Ancient and Tribal Art*, 3 vols. New York, Rock Foundation, 1986-1988, vol. 3, bk. 1, p. 94, fig 77. Greek vase, proto-Corinthian, end of 8th century B.C.

65. Jayne, Caroline Furness. *String Figures and How to Make Them*. New York, Dover, 1962, p. 15, fig. 21. Method of constructing a string figure.

66. Jayne, Caroline Furness. *String Figures and How to Make Them*. New York, Dover, 1962, p. 247, fig. 563. String figure called "Teepee" or "Tent".

67. Carpenter, Edmund, and Carl Schuster. *Materials for the Study of Social Symbolism in Ancient and Tribal Art*, 3 vols. New York, Rock Foundation, 1986-1988, vol. 3, bk. 1, p. 83, figs. 58 and 59. String figure and Malekulan turtle drawing.

68. P. Voorhoeve, *Catalogue of Indonesian Manuscripts*, Part 1: Batak Manuscripts. The Royal Library, Copenhagen, 1975, p. 62, fig. 12. Shang inscription from China, 13th century B.C.

69. P. Voorhoeve, *Catalogue of Indonesian Manuscripts*, Part 1: Batak Manuscripts. The Royal Library, Copenhagen, 1975, p. 62, figs. 13 and 14. Copper plates from Mohenjo-Daro, 13th century B.C.

70. Rykwert, Joseph. *The Idea of a Town*. Princeton, N.J., Princeton University Press, 1976, p. 144. Greek kylix depicting Theseus killing the minotaur.

71. Maiuri, Amadeo. *The Phlegraean Fields: from Virgil's tomb to the grotto of the Cumaean sibyl.* Translated by V. Priestly. Rome, Instituto poligrafico dello Stato, 1947, p. 114. Grotto of the Sibyl. Courtesy of the Instituto Poligrafico e Zecca dello Stato, Rome, Italy.

72. Carpenter, Edmund, and Carl Schuster. *Materials for the Study of Social Symbolism in Ancient and Tribal Art*, 3 vols. New York, Rock Foundation, 1986-1988, vol. 3, bk. 2, p. 408, fig. 441. Sand-drawing from the New Hebrides.

73. Carpenter, Edmund, and Carl Schuster. *Materials for the Study of Social Symbolism in Ancient and Tribal Art*, 3 vols. New York, Rock Foundation, 1986-1988, vol. 3, bk. 2, p. 288, fig. 306. Labyrinth from an anonymous pattern-book of *rangoli* or threshold designs, first-half of 19th century, India.

74. Carpenter, Edmund, and Carl Schuster. *Materials for the Study of Social Symbolism in Ancient and Tribal Art*, 3 vols. New York, Rock Foundation, 1986-1988, vol. 3, bk. 2, p. 289, fig. 308. Labyrinth drawing from a postcard, circa 1950, India.

75. Carpenter, Edmund, and Carl Schuster. *Materials for the Study of Social Symbolism in Ancient and Tribal Art*, 3 vols. New York, Rock Foundation, 1986-1988, vol. 3, bk. 2, p. 425, fig. 463. Maze engraved on a stela, Bryne Celli Ddu, Ireland.

76. Carpenter, Edmund, and Carl Schuster. *Materials for the Study of Social Symbolism in Ancient and Tribal Art*, 3 vols. New York, Rock Foundation, 1986-1988, vol. 3, bk. 2, p. 271, fig. 282. Etruscan vase, 7th century B.C., Tragliatella, Italy.

77. Carpenter, Edmund, and Carl Schuster. *Materials for the Study of Social Symbolism in Ancient and Tribal Art*, 3 vols. New York, Rock Foundation, 1986-1988, vol. 3, bk. 2, p. 388, fig. 265. Hypothetical plan of the *Lusus Troiae* and one method of drawing the labyrinth.

78. Knight, W. F. Jackson. *Vergil. Epic and Anthropology*. Norman, Barnes & Noble, New York, 1967, p. 232, Babylonian tablets with spiral patterns connected with entrail divination.

79. Carpenter, Edmund, and Carl Schuster. *Materials for the Study of Social Symbolism in Ancient and Tribal Art*, 3 vols. New York, Rock Foundation, 1986-1988, vol. 3, bk. 2, p. 269, fig. 278. Labyrinth on a

Linear B tablet, Minoan-Mycenean period (circa 1200 B.C.), Pylos, Greece.

80. Carpenter, Edmund, and Carl Schuster. *Materials for the Study of Social Symbolism in Ancient and Tribal Art*, 3 vols. New York, Rock Foundation, 1986-1988, vol. 3, bk. 2, p. 268, figs 276 and 277. Coins with square and round labyrinths, 3rd century B.C., Crete.

81. Carpenter, Edmund, and Carl Schuster. *Materials for the Study of Social Symbolism in Ancient and Tribal Art*, 3 vols. New York, Rock Foundation, 1986-1988, vol. 3, bk. 2, p. 412, fig. 363. Petroglyph of labyrinth, Camonica Valley, Italy.

82. Carpenter, Edmund, and Carl Schuster. *Materials for the Study of Social Symbolism in Ancient and Tribal Art*, 3 vols. New York, Rock Foundation, 1986-1988, vol. 3, bk. 2, p. 281, fig. 296. Bowl from clay spoon or ladle, jabbed decoration, Ober-Jersdal, Amt Hadersleben, Denmark. Found together with Neolithic pottery.

83. Carpenter, Edmund, and Carl Schuster. *Materials for the Study of Social Symbolism in Ancient and Tribal Art*, 3 vols. New York, Rock Foundation, 1986-1988, vol. 3, bk. 2, p. 347, fig. 389. Debased labyrinth carved on a bed-board, 18th century, Iceland.

84. Carpenter, Edmund, and Carl Schuster. *Materials for the Study of Social Symbolism in Ancient and Tribal Art*, 3 vols. New York, Rock Foundation, 1986-1988, vol. 3, bk. 2, p. 286, fig. 303. Stone labyrinth at St. Agnes in the Scilly Islands, England.

85. Carpenter, Edmund, and Carl Schuster. *Materials for the Study of Social Symbolism in Ancient and Tribal Art*, 3 vols. New York, Rock Foundation, 1986-1988, vol. 3, bk. 2, p. 308, fig. 325. Sandstone carving from corral wall, Hopi village of Old Oraibi, Arizona.

86. Carpenter, Edmund, and Carl Schuster. *Materials for the Study of Social Symbolism in Ancient and Tribal Art*, 3 vols. New York, Rock Foundation, 1986-1988, vol. 3, bk. 2, p. 410, fig. 442. Labyrinth with figure in center, church fresco beneath 15th century painting, Sippo, Finland.

87. Carpenter, Edmund, and Carl Schuster. *Materials for the Study of Social Symbolism in Ancient and Tribal Art*, 3 vols. New York, Rock Foundation, 1986-1988, vol. 3, bk. 2, p. 413, fig. 448. Detail of woven mat with labyrinth, Sri Lanka.

88. Carpenter, Edmund, and Carl Schuster. *Materials for the Study of Social Symbolism in Ancient and Tribal Art*, 3 vols. New York, Rock Foundation, 1986-1988, vol. 3, bk. 2, p. 418, fig. 452. Drawing titled "Seneca Legend of Bare Hill," Ernie Smith, Seneca Indian, 1930s, Rochester, New York.

89. Carpenter, Edmund, and Carl Schuster. *Materials for the Study of Social Symbolism in Ancient and Tribal Art*, 3 vols. New York, Rock Foundation, 1986-1988, vol. 3, bk. 2, p. 415, fig. 450. Bronze wine bucket (*you*) depicting T'ao-tieh (Glutton), end of Shang dynasty, China.

90. Carpenter, Edmund, and Carl Schuster. *Materials for the Study of Social Symbolism in Ancient and Tribal Art*, 3 vols. New York, Rock Foundation, 1986-1988, vol. 3, bk. 2, p. 420, fig. 455. Pictograph of Warombi, Wailbri tribe, N'Gama Cave, Mt. Doreen Station, Australia.

91. Carpenter, Edmund, and Carl Schuster. *Materials for the Study of Social Symbolism in Ancient and Tribal Art*, 3 vols. New York, Rock Foundation, 1986-1988, vol. 3, bk. 2, p. 264, fig. 269. Hypothetical method for drawing the labyrinth using the cross-arc-dots method.

92. Carpenter, Edmund, and Carl Schuster. *Materials for the Study of Social Symbolism in Ancient and Tribal Art*, 3 vols. New York, Rock Foundation, 1986-1988, vol. 3, bk. 2, p. 274, fig. 286. Boulder with incised labyrinth, Hollywood, County Wicklow, Ireland.

93. Carpenter, Edmund, and Carl Schuster. *Materials for the Study of Social Symbolism in Ancient and*

Tribal Art, 3 vols. New York, Rock Foundation, 1986-1988, vol. 3, bk. 2, p. 382, fig. 427. Letter from William Denton illustrating the two-line method for drawing the labyrinth.

94. Carpenter, Edmund, and Carl Schuster. *Materials for the Study of Social Symbolism in Ancient and Tribal Art*, 3 vols. New York, Rock Foundation, 1986-1988, vol. 3, bk. 2, p. 385, fig. 428. Hypothetical method for drawing the labyrinth without arcs, using only a cross, four dots, and four lines.

95. Carpenter, Edmund, and Carl Schuster. *Materials for the Study of Social Symbolism in Ancient and Tribal Art*, 3 vols. New York, Rock Foundation, 1986-1988, vol. 3, bk. 2, p. 430. Abbreviated form of labyrinth found on many rings and amulets in the Near East and Central Asia.

96. Carpenter, Edmund, and Carl Schuster. *Materials for the Study of Social Symbolism in Ancient and Tribal Art*, 3 vols. New York, Rock Foundation, 1986-1988, vol. 3, bk. 2, p. 386, fig. 429. Hypothetical method for drawing the labyrinth with a cross, twelve dots, and four lines.

97. Carpenter, Edmund, and Carl Schuster. *Materials for the Study of Social Symbolism in Ancient and Tribal Art*, 3 vols. New York, Rock Foundation, 1986-1988, vol. 3, bk. 2, p. 387. Illustrations of joint-marked mythical ancestors (human, reptilian, avian).

98. Carpenter, Edmund, and Carl Schuster. *Materials for the Study of Social Symbolism in Ancient and Tribal Art*, 3 vols. New York, Rock Foundation, 1986-1988, vol. 3, bk. 2, p. 407, fig. 439. Yakut peg-calendar, Siberia, Russia, 1871.

99. Carpenter, Edmund, and Carl Schuster. *Materials for the Study of Social Symbolism in Ancient and Tribal Art*, 3 vols. New York, Rock Foundation, 1986-1988, vol. 3, bk. 1, p. 151, fig. 151. Medieval astrological chart, Germany.

THE WORK OF CARL SCHUSTER

1. Carpenter, Edmund, and Carl Schuster. *Materials for the Study of Social Symbolism in Ancient and Tribal Art*, 3 vols. New York, Rock Foundation, 1986-1988, vol. 1, bk. 1, p. 12. Carl Schuster collecting embroideries in Western China, 1935.

2. Carpenter, Edmund, and Carl Schuster. *Materials for the Study of Social Symbolism in Ancient and Tribal Art*, 3 vols. New York, Rock Foundation, 1986-1988, vol. 1, bk. 4, p. 941. Schuster archives in Basel, Switzerland.

3. Baker, Muriel, and Lunt, Margaret. *Blue and White. The Cotton Embroideries of Rural China*. Charles Scribner and Sons, New York, 1977, p. 53. Two bed valences with medallions, Pachow, China.

4. Baker, Muriel, and Lunt, Margaret. *Blue and White. The Cotton Embroideries of Rural China*. Charles Scribner and Sons, New York, 1977, p. 98. Child's embroidered dress, China.

5. "A Comparative Study of Motives in Western Chinese Folk Embroideries" *Monumenta Serica*, vol. 2, fasc. 1, Peking, 1936, p. 48, fig. 9. The Triumphant Scholar (*chuang yüan*) motif on a Chinese embroidery.

6. "A Comparative Study of Motives in Western Chinese Folk Embroideries" *Monumenta Serica*, vol. 2, fasc. 1, Peking, 1936, p. 49, fig. 11a. Scene from a Sassanian cliff-sculpture, (A.D. 618–907).

7. Carpenter, Edmund, and Carl Schuster. *Materials for the Study of Social Symbolism in Ancient and Tribal Art*, 3 vols. New York, Rock Foundation, 1986-1988, vol. 1, bk. 3, p. 822, fig. 1326. Paddle blade, probably Kenyah, upper Redjang River, Sarawak, Borneo.

8. Carpenter, Edmund, and Carl Schuster. *Materials for the Study of Social Symbolism in Ancient and Tribal Art*, 3 vols. New York, Rock Foundation, 1986-1988, vol. 1, bk. 3, p. 812, fig. 1313. Tocorón pottery bowl, La Mata-Tocorón mound-fields, Venezuela.

9. Carpenter, Edmund, and Carl Schuster. *Materials for the Study of Social Symbolism in Ancient and Tribal Art*, 3 vols. New York, Rock Foundation, 1986-1988, vol. 1, bk. 3, p. 794, fig. 1277. Carved and painted interior screen, Eagle House crest, Haida, Howkan, Long Island, Alaska.

10. Carpenter, Edmund, and Carl Schuster. *Materials for the Study of Social Symbolism in Ancient and Tribal Art*, 3 vols. New York, Rock Foundation, 1986-1988, vol. 1, bk. 3, p. 795, fig. 1278. Interior house-screen, Tlingit, Wrangell, Alaska.

11. Carpenter, Edmund, and Carl Schuster. *Materials for the Study of Social Symbolism in Ancient and Tribal Art*, 3 vols. New York, Rock Foundation, 1986-1988, vol. 1, bk. 4, p. 925, fig. 1472. Flat relief decoration, Chinese bronze vessel, Huai or Late Chou style, China.

12. Carpenter, Edmund, and Carl Schuster. *Materials for the Study of Social Symbolism in Ancient and Tribal Art*, 3 vols. New York, Rock Foundation, 1986-1988, vol. 1, bk. 4, p. 920, fig. 1466. Gold plaque, originally with inlay, Scythian, Siberia, 5th to 4th century B.C.

13. Carpenter, Edmund, and Carl Schuster. *Materials for the Study of Social Symbolism in Ancient and Tribal Art*, 3 vols. New York, Rock Foundation, 1986-1988, vol. 1, bk. 4, p. 915, fig. 1441. Design painted on the interior of a wooden bowl, Eskimo, Alaska.

14. Carpenter, Edmund, and Carl Schuster. *Materials for the Study of Social Symbolism in Ancient and Tribal Art*, 3 vols. New York, Rock Foundation, 1986-1988, vol. 1, bk. 4, p. 915, fig. 1455. Painting of sea-monster, *pal-rai-yûk* on *umiak*, Eskimo, Alaska.

15. Carpenter, Edmund, and Carl Schuster. *Materials for the Study of Social Symbolism in Ancient and Tribal Art*, 3 vols. New York, Rock Foundation, 1986-1988, vol. 1, bk. 4, p. 913, fig. 1447. Cast metal plaque, Minusinsk basin of the upper Yenisei, eastern Siberia.

16. Carpenter, Edmund, and Carl Schuster. *Materials for the Study of Social Symbolism in Ancient and Tribal Art*, 3 vols. New York, Rock Foundation, 1986-1988, vol. 1, bk. 4, p. 913, fig. 1456. Dragon design incised on black pottery vessel, northwestern Argentina. Barreales period, circa A.D. 500.

17. Carpenter, Edmund, and Carl Schuster. *Materials for the Study of Social Symbolism in Ancient and Tribal Art*, 3 vols. New York, Rock Foundation, 1986-1988, vol. 1, bk. 4, p. 921, fig. 1442. Design engraved on an ivory tobacco pipe, Eskimo, Alaska.

18. Carpenter, Edmund, and Carl Schuster. *Materials for the Study of Social Symbolism in Ancient and Tribal Art*, 3 vols. New York, Rock Foundation, 1986-1988, vol. 1, bk. 3, p. 798, fig. 1284. Aztec earth-goddess, Coatlicue, early post-conquest codex, Florence, Italy.

19. Carpenter, Edmund, and Carl Schuster. *Materials for the Study of Social Symbolism in Ancient and Tribal Art*, 3 vols. New York, Rock Foundation, 1986-1988, vol. 1, bk. 3, p. 800, fig. 1287. Aztec earth-goddess *Tlaltecuhtli* from *Codex Borgia*, p. 32.

20. Carpenter, Edmund, and Carl Schuster. *Materials for the Study of Social Symbolism in Ancient and Tribal Art*, 3 vols. New York, Rock Foundation, 1986-1988, vol. 1, bk. 3, p. 779, fig. 1254. Carved plank, Maori, New Zealand.

21. Carpenter, Edmund, and Carl Schuster. *Materials for the Study of Social Symbolism in Ancient and Tribal Art*, 3 vols. New York, Rock Foundation, 1986-1988, vol. 1, bk. 3, p. 778, fig. 1253. Wood carving of two bowls with connecting human figure, shell inlaid, Hawaii.

22. Carpenter, Edmund, and Carl Schuster. *Materials for the Study of Social Symbolism in Ancient and Tribal Art*, 3 vols. New York, Rock Foundation, 1986-1988, vol. 1, bk. 3, p. 774, fig. 1251. Tattooed Marquesan male.

23. Carpenter, Edmund, and Carl Schuster. *Materials for the Study of Social Symbolism in Ancient and Tribal Art*, 3 vols. New York, Rock Foundation, 1986-1988, vol. 1, bk. 3, p. 783, fig. 1261. Scarified male, Sepik, Papua/New Guinea.

24. Carpenter, Edmund, and Carl Schuster. *Materials for the Study of Social Symbolism in Ancient and Tribal Art*, 3 vols. New York, Rock Foundation, 1986-1988, vol. 1, bk. 3, p. 856, fig. 1396. Wooden figure, Vooanderbeeld, Irian Jaya.

25. Carpenter, Edmund, and Carl Schuster. *Materials for the Study of Social Symbolism in Ancient and Tribal Art*, 3 vols. New York, Rock Foundation, 1986-1988, vol. 1, bk. 3, p. 849, fig. 1381. Human figure of wood, *korwar*, Wardo, Wiak, Irian Jaya.

26. Carpenter, Edmund, and Carl Schuster. *Materials for the Study of Social Symbolism in Ancient and Tribal Art*, 3 vols. New York, Rock Foundation, 1986-1988, vol. 1, bk. 3, p. 855, fig. 1393. Chief's chair, Bamum, Cameroon Grasslands.

27. Carpenter, Edmund, and Carl Schuster. *Materials for the Study of Social Symbolism in Ancient and Tribal Art*, 3 vols. New York, Rock Foundation, 1986-1988, vol. 1, bk. 3, p. 899, fig. 1435. Fragmentary stone leg with greave, from statue of Ares, classical Greek.

28. Carpenter, Edmund, and Carl Schuster. *Materials for the Study of Social Symbolism in Ancient and Tribal Art*, 3 vols. New York, Rock Foundation, 1986-1988, vol. 1, bk. 1, p. 48. Conventionalized human figures used in the construction of genealogical patterns.

29. Carpenter, Edmund, and Carl Schuster. *Materials for the Study of Social Symbolism in Ancient and Tribal Art*, 3 vols. New York, Rock Foundation, 1986-1988, vol. 1, bk. 1, p. 49. Figures linked diagonally to depict genetic descent.

30. Carpenter, Edmund, and Carl Schuster. *Materials for the Study of Social Symbolism in Ancient and Tribal Art*, 3 vols. New York, Rock Foundation, 1986-1988, vol. 1, bk. 1, p. 54. Figures linked horizontally to depict relationship in a single generation.

31. Carpenter, Edmund, and Carl Schuster. *Materials for the Study of Social Symbolism in Ancient and Tribal Art*, 3 vols. New York, Rock Foundation, 1986-1988, vol. 1, bk. 1, p. 55, fig. 3. Design incised on a club, Byron Strait Islands, northern New Ireland.

32. Carpenter, Edmund, and Carl Schuster. *Materials for the Study of Social Symbolism in Ancient and Tribal Art*, 3 vols. New York, Rock Foundation, 1986-1988, vol. 1, bk. 1, p. 50, fig. 1. Cotton ikat, tie-dyed warp, pall for coffin, Toradjas, Galumpang, Central Celebes.

33. Carpenter, Edmund, and Carl Schuster. *Materials for the Study of Social Symbolism in Ancient and Tribal Art*, 3 vols. New York, Rock Foundation, 1986-1988, vol. 1, bk. 1, p. 51. Member of the social group depicted within the structure of ancestors and descendants. The split indicates the juncture of two moieties within the individual.

34. Carpenter, Edmund, and Carl Schuster. *Materials for the Study of Social Symbolism in Ancient and Tribal Art*, 3 vols. New York, Rock Foundation, 1986-1988, vol. 1, bk. 1, p. 61. Headless human figures in an all-over pattern.

35. Carpenter, Edmund, and Carl Schuster. *Materials for the Study of Social Symbolism in Ancient and Tribal Art*, 3 vols. New York, Rock Foundation, 1986-1988, vol. 1, bk. 1, p. 279, fig. 337. Open-work matting, pandanus, Tonga. Collected by John Weber on Cook's third voyage.

36. Carpenter, Edmund, and Carl Schuster. *Materials for the Study of Social Symbolism in Ancient and Tribal Art*, 3 vols. New York, Rock Foundation, 1986-1988, vol. 1, bk. 1, p. 71, figs. 18 and 19. Two drums from Hawaii.

37. Carpenter, Edmund, and Carl Schuster. *Materials for the Study of Social Symbolism in Ancient and Tribal Art*, 3 vols. New York, Rock Foundation, 1986-1988, vol. 1, bk. 1, p. 105, fig. 75. Pottery vessel, Bamoum, Cameroon.

38. Jayne, Caroline Furness. *String Figures and How to Make Them*. New York, Dover, 1962, pp. 150 and 156.

39. Stamp from The Republic of Nauru, Micronesia, depicting a string figure called "Holding Up the Sky".

40. Carpenter, Edmund, and Carl Schuster. *Materials for the Study of Social Symbolism in Ancient and Tribal Art*, 3 vols. New York, Rock Foundation, 1986-1988, vol. 1, bk. 1, p. 284. Pattern excerpted from an over-all pattern of connected human bodies (ancestors).

41. Carpenter, Edmund, and Carl Schuster. *Materials for the Study of Social Symbolism in Ancient and Tribal Art*, 3 vols. New York, Rock Foundation, 1986-1988, vol. 1, bk. 1, p. 287, fig. 350. Incised object of bone or antler, Maglemose, Denmark.

42. Jyotsna, Maurya. *Distinctive Beads of Ancient India*. Archaeopress, British Archaeological Reports International, Series 864, Oxford, England, 2000, p. 91, bead number 24.

43. Carpenter, Edmund, and Carl Schuster. *Materials for the Study of Social Symbolism in Ancient and Tribal Art*, 3 vols. New York, Rock Foundation, 1986-1988, vol. 1, bk. 1, p. 56, fig. 5. Design carved around bamboo tube, Simbuap, Toricelli, Aitape, Sepik, Papua/New Guinea.

44. Carpenter, Edmund, and Carl Schuster. *Materials for the Study of Social Symbolism in Ancient and Tribal Art*, 3 vols. New York, Rock Foundation, 1986-1988, vol. 1, bk. 1, p. 57, fig. 6. Design incised on an antler axe, Lammefjord, Zealand, Denmark (circa 5000 B.C).

45. Carpenter, Edmund, and Carl Schuster. *Materials for the Study of Social Symbolism in Ancient and Tribal Art*, 3 vols. New York, Rock Foundation, 1986-1988, vol. 1, bk. 2, p. 604, fig. 996. Painted pottery cup from burial, Vykhvatintsy burial mound, Moldavia, near Odessa, Ukraine.

46. Carpenter, Edmund, and Carl Schuster. *Materials for the Study of Social Symbolism in Ancient and Tribal Art*, 3 vols. New York, Rock Foundation, 1986-1988, vol. 1, bk. 2, p. 524. Vertically split genealogical pattern emphasizing dual parentage.

47. Carpenter, Edmund, and Carl Schuster. *Materials for the Study of Social Symbolism in Ancient and Tribal Art*, 3 vols. New York, Rock Foundation, 1986-1988, vol. 1, bk. 2, p. 526. Diagram illustrating the symbolism of split patterns.

48. Carpenter, Edmund, and Carl Schuster. *Materials for the Study of Social Symbolism in Ancient and Tribal Art*, 3 vols. New York, Rock Foundation, 1986-1988, vol. 1, bk. 2, p. 526. Examples of split patterns.

49. Carpenter, Edmund, and Carl Schuster. *Materials for the Study of Social Symbolism in Ancient and Tribal Art*, 3 vols. New York, Rock Foundation, 1986-1988, vol. 1, bk. 2, p. 524. A common split pattern.

50. Carpenter, Edmund, and Carl Schuster. *Materials for the Study of Social Symbolism in Ancient and Tribal Art*, 3 vols. New York, Rock Foundation, 1986-1988, vol. 1, bk. 2, p. 525. Another common split pattern.

51. Carpenter, Edmund, and Carl Schuster. *Materials for the Study of Social Symbolism in Ancient and Tribal Art*, 3 vols. New York, Rock Foundation, 1986-1988, vol. 1, bk. 2, p. 420, fig. 578. Spear decoration, Asmat, Irian Jaya.

52. Carpenter, Edmund, and Carl Schuster. *Materials for the Study of Social Symbolism in Ancient and Tribal Art*, 3 vols. New York, Rock Foundation, 1986-1988, vol. 1, bk. 2, p. 552, fig. 908. Incised pebble, Grotta Romanelli, Otranto, Italy, Paleolithic.

53. Carpenter, Edmund, and Carl Schuster. *Materials for the Study of Social Symbolism in Ancient and Tribal Art*, 3 vols. New York, Rock Foundation, 1986-1988, vol. 1, bk. 2, p. 556, fig. 914. Interior of Delaware Big House, Oklahoma, circa 1932.

54. Carpenter, Edmund, and Carl Schuster. *Materials for the Study of Social Symbolism in Ancient and Tribal Art*, 3 vols. New York, Rock Foundation, 1986-1988, vol. 1, bk. 2, p. 560. Diagram illustrating quartering.

55. Carpenter, Edmund, and Carl Schuster. *Materials for the Study of Social Symbolism in Ancient and Tribal Art*, 3 vols. New York, Rock Foundation, 1986-1988, vol. 1, bk. 2, p. 562, fig. 923. Painted decoration on a house-post, Uanana (Tukanoan group), Carurú, Rio Caiary-Uaupés, northwestern Amazon Basin, Brazil.

56. Carpenter, Edmund, and Carl Schuster. *Materials for the Study of Social Symbolism in Ancient and Tribal Art*, 3 vols. New York, Rock Foundation, 1986-1988, vol. 1, bk. 2, p. 570, fig. 929. Sand-painting, Navaho, Arizona.

57. Carpenter, Edmund, and Carl Schuster. *Materials for the Study of Social Symbolism in Ancient and Tribal Art*, 3 vols. New York, Rock Foundation, 1986-1988, vol. 1, bk. 2, p. 602, fig. 995. Wind chart, *Speculum Virginum*, mid-12th century.

58. Carpenter, Edmund, and Carl Schuster. *Materials for the Study of Social Symbolism in Ancient and Tribal Art*, 3 vols. New York, Rock Foundation, 1986-1988, vol. 1, bk. 2, p. 574, fig. 934. *Kapkap*, Roviana, New Georgia.

59. Carpenter, Edmund, and Carl Schuster. *Materials for the Study of Social Symbolism in Ancient and Tribal Art*, 3 vols. New York, Rock Foundation, 1986-1988, vol. 1, bk. 2, p. 612, fig. 1016. Circular lid, perforated for thongs; grave-find from Kampen, Tonder, Denmark, Maglemose style.

60. Carpenter, Edmund, and Carl Schuster. *Materials for the Study of Social Symbolism in Ancient and Tribal Art*, 3 vols. New York, Rock Foundation, 1986-1988, vol. 1, bk. 2, p. 613, fig. 1020. Perforated and engraved bone disk, Denmark, late Bronze Age. Type generally found in graves and associated with garments.

61. Crewe, Lindy *Spindle Whorls*. Jonsered, Sweden, Paul Aströms Förlag, 1998, app. 2, fig. A2.25, Central Plain, Marki *Alonia*, Crete.

62. Carpenter, Edmund, and Carl Schuster. *Materials for the Study of Social Symbolism in Ancient and Tribal Art*, 3 vols. New York, Rock Foundation, 1986-1988, vol. 1, bk. 2, p. 447. Stacked figures (ramiforms).

63. Carpenter, Edmund, and Carl Schuster. *Materials for the Study of Social Symbolism in Ancient and Tribal Art*, 3 vols. New York, Rock Foundation, 1986-1988, vol. 1, bk. 2, p. 450, fig. 628. One of four identical "cloud men" (in four different colors) painted on a buckskin used in curative ceremonies. Navaho, Arizona/New Mexico.

64. Carpenter, Edmund, and Carl Schuster. *Materials for the Study of Social Symbolism in Ancient and Tribal Art*, 3 vols. New York, Rock Foundation, 1986-1988, vol. 1, bk. 2, p. 655, fig. 642. Sketch made in 1829 by a Beothuck Indian, Newfoundland. Said to represent a six-foot staff, *Ash-u-meet*, interpreted by William Dawson as a family crest, "corresponding with armorial bearings of civilized persons."

65. Carpenter, Edmund, and Carl Schuster. *Materials for the Study of Social Symbolism in Ancient and*

Tribal Art, 3 vols. New York, Rock Foundation, 1986-1988, vol. 1, bk. 2, p. 451, fig. 630. Painted sherd, Neolithic, Tepe Moussian, Iran, circa 3500-3200 B.C.

66. Carpenter, Edmund, and Carl Schuster. *Materials for the Study of Social Symbolism in Ancient and Tribal Art*, 3 vols. New York, Rock Foundation, 1986-1988, vol. 1, bk. 2, p. 510, fig. 834. Pictographs in rock-shelter, Murron del Pino, Ciudad Real, south-central Spain.

67. Carpenter, Edmund, and Carl Schuster. *Materials for the Study of Social Symbolism in Ancient and Tribal Art*, 3 vols. New York, Rock Foundation, 1986-1988, vol. 1, bk. 2, p. 511, fig. 837. Painted pebble, red oxide of iron, Mas d'Azil, Ariège, France.

68. Carpenter, Edmund, and Carl Schuster. *Materials for the Study of Social Symbolism in Ancient and Tribal Art*, 3 vols. New York, Rock Foundation, 1986-1988, vol. 2, bk. 1, p. 253, fig. 353. Notched post from funeral house, Metoko tribe, Lualaba, Zaire.

69. Carpenter, Edmund, and Carl Schuster. *Materials for the Study of Social Symbolism in Ancient and Tribal Art*, 3 vols. New York, Rock Foundation, 1986-1988, vol. 2, bk. 1, p. 261, fig. 364. Model of an anthropomorphic ladder, collected in 1920, Tura, Garo Hills, Assam, India.

70. Carpenter, Edmund, and Carl Schuster. *Materials for the Study of Social Symbolism in Ancient and Tribal Art*, 3 vols. New York, Rock Foundation, 1986-1988, vol. 2, bk. 1, p. 285, fig. 399. Mapuche (Araucanian) shaman's ladder (*rewe*), Cholchol, Chile.

71. Carpenter, Edmund, and Carl Schuster. *Materials for the Study of Social Symbolism in Ancient and Tribal Art*, 3 vols. New York, Rock Foundation, 1986-1988, vol. 2, bk. 1, p. 262, fig. 366. Moi anthropomorphic ladder, Vietnam.

72. Carpenter, Edmund, and Carl Schuster. *Materials for the Study of Social Symbolism in Ancient and Tribal Art*, 3 vols. New York, Rock Foundation, 1986-1988, vol. 3, bk. 1, p. 199, fig. 222. Hopscotch diagram, West Africa.

73. Carpenter, Edmund, and Carl Schuster. *Materials for the Study of Social Symbolism in Ancient and Tribal Art*, 3 vols. New York, Rock Foundation, 1986-1988, vol. 2, bk. 1, p. 233, fig. 323. Door-post from the Council Chambers, Pematang, Raja, Toba Lands, east coast of Sumatra, Indonesia.

74. Carpenter, Edmund, and Carl Schuster. *Materials for the Study of Social Symbolism in Ancient and Tribal Art*, 3 vols. New York, Rock Foundation, 1986-1988, vol. 1, bk. 1, p. 185. Examples of excerpted figures.

75. Carpenter, Edmund, and Carl Schuster. *Materials for the Study of Social Symbolism in Ancient and Tribal Art*, 3 vols. New York, Rock Foundation, 1986-1988, vol. 1, bk. 1, p. 185 (bottom figures). Excerpted figures elaborated with clothing.

76. Carpenter, Edmund, and Carl Schuster. *Materials for the Study of Social Symbolism in Ancient and Tribal Art*, 3 vols. New York, Rock Foundation, 1986-1988, vol. 1, bk. 1, p. 187. Cut-out figures forming new patterns.

77. Carpenter, Edmund, and Carl Schuster. *Materials for the Study of Social Symbolism in Ancient and Tribal Art*, 3 vols. New York, Rock Foundation, 1986-1988, vol. 1, bk. 1, p. 205. Fig. 226, bronze pendant, Hungary. Fig. 227, ivory figurine, Susa, Iran. Fig. 228, alabaster figure, Tepe Hissar, Damghan, Iran.

78. G. Reichel-Dolmatoff. *The Sacred Mountain of Columbia's Kogi Indians.* Leiden, E. T. Brill, 1990, p. 8, fig. 2. Framework of a Kogi loom.

79. Wilbert, Johannes. "The Thread of Life. Symbolism of Miniature Art from Ecuador." *Studies in Pre-Columbian Art and Archeology*, Vol. 12 (1974). Dumbarton Oaks, Washington, D.C., p. 99, fig. 133. Spindle whorl with hocker.

80. Carpenter, Edmund, and Carl Schuster. *Materials for the Study of Social Symbolism in Ancient and Tribal Art*, 3 vols. New York, Rock Foundation, 1986-1988, vol. 2, bk. 2, p. 338, fig. 434. Painted design on an upright of a dolmen at Côta (Pedralta, province of Beira Alta), Portugal.

81. Carpenter, Edmund, and Carl Schuster. *Materials for the Study of Social Symbolism in Ancient and Tribal Art*, 3 vols. New York, Rock Foundation, 1986-1988, vol. 2, bk. 2, p. 304, fig. 409. Fur side of a vicuna robe, Tehuelche Indian, Patagonia, Argentina.

82. Carpenter, Edmund, and Carl Schuster. *Materials for the Study of Social Symbolism in Ancient and Tribal Art*, 3 vols. New York, Rock Foundation, 1986-1988, vol. 2, bk. 2, p. 344. Method for constructing an interlocking, bichromatic skin-fur mosaic.

83. Carpenter, Edmund, and Carl Schuster. *Materials for the Study of Social Symbolism in Ancient and Tribal Art*, 3 vols. New York, Rock Foundation, 1986-1988, vol. 2, bk. 2, p. 302, fig. 409. Fur side of a guanaco robe, Tehuelche Indian, Patagonia, Argentina.

84. Carpenter, Edmund, and Carl Schuster. *Materials for the Study of Social Symbolism in Ancient and Tribal Art*, 3 vols. New York, Rock Foundation, 1986-1988, vol. 2, bk. 2, pp. 456-7, figs. 537 and 537a. Stone ceremonial axe, Neuquén, Argentina.

85. Carpenter, Edmund, and Carl Schuster. *Materials for the Study of Social Symbolism in Ancient and Tribal Art*, 3 vols. New York, Rock Foundation, 1986-1988, vol. 2, bk. 2, p. 315, fig. 410. Drawing of the skin side of a guanaco robe, Tehuelche Indian, Patagonia, Argentina. Shows the sinew-stitched seams by which the component skins are joined, as well as painted borders, two painted vertical stripes, and a portion of the painted all-over pattern (upper-right). The wrinkled triangular pieces of skin in the upper corners serve as grips for the wearer.

86. Carpenter, Edmund, and Carl Schuster. *Materials for the Study of Social Symbolism in Ancient and Tribal Art*, 3 vols. New York, Rock Foundation, 1986-1988, vol. 2, bk. 2, p. 308, fig. 411. Buffalo robe, painted and ornamented with porcupine quills and tin pendants, Pawnee Indian, Plains.

87. Carpenter, Edmund, and Carl Schuster. *Materials for the Study of Social Symbolism in Ancient and Tribal Art*, 3 vols. New York, Rock Foundation, 1986-1988, vol. 2, bk. 2, p. 310, fig. 412. Blanket strip, 'pony-beaded,' probably Arapaho, Central Plains.

88. Carpenter, Edmund, and Carl Schuster. *Materials for the Study of Social Symbolism in Ancient and Tribal Art*, 3 vols. New York, Rock Foundation, 1986-1988, vol. 2, bk. 2, p. 310, fig. 414. Petroglyph, Site 202, Yerington, Nevada.

89. Carpenter, Edmund, and Carl Schuster. *Materials for the Study of Social Symbolism in Ancient and Tribal Art*, 3 vols. New York, Rock Foundation, 1986-1988, vol. 2, bk. 2, p. 396, fig. 472. Tehuelche Indian of Patagonia wearing a native robe, *quillango*, of guanaco skins with painted decoration.

90. Carpenter, Edmund, and Carl Schuster. *Materials for the Study of Social Symbolism in Ancient and Tribal Art*, 3 vols. New York, Rock Foundation, 1986-1988, vol. 2, bk. 2, p. 397, fig. 475. Pottery vessel from Catamarca, northwestern Argentina. Barreales or 'Draconian' culture. Presumably 1st half of the 1st millennium, A.D.

91. Schuster, "Observations on the Painted Designs of Patagonian Skin Robes," pp. 430 and 431, fig. 10, Tehuelche woman painting a skin robe, and fig. 11, Australian family from New South Wales.

92. Carpenter, Edmund, and Carl Schuster. *Materials for the Study of Social Symbolism in Ancient and Tribal Art*, 3 vols. New York, Rock Foundation, 1986-1988, vol. 2, bk. 3, p. 526, fig. 534. Robe of opossum skins with scratched decoration, Hunter River, New South Wales, Australia. Collected by Horatio Hale (1839-1840).

93. Carpenter, Edmund, and Carl Schuster. *Materials for the Study of Social Symbolism in Ancient and Tribal Art*, 3 vols. New York, Rock Foundation, 1986-1988, vol. 2, bk. 3, p. 526, fig. 534. Detail of opossum skin robe showing shadow system of human figures within figures. Hunter River, New South Wales, Australia. Collected by Horatio Hale (1839-1840).

94. Carpenter, Edmund, and Carl Schuster. *Materials for the Study of Social Symbolism in Ancient and Tribal Art*, 3 vols. New York, Rock Foundation, 1986-1988, vol. 2, bk. 2, p. 385, fig. 464. English tabard blazoned with the arms of England and Scotland, reign of Queen Anne (1665-1714).

95. Carpenter, Edmund, and Carl Schuster. *Materials for the Study of Social Symbolism in Ancient and Tribal Art*, 3 vols. New York, Rock Foundation, 1986-1988, vol. 2, bk. 2, p. 386, fig. 465. Painted hide shield, East Africa.

96. Carpenter, Edmund, and Carl Schuster. *Materials for the Study of Social Symbolism in Ancient and Tribal Art*, 3 vols. New York, Rock Foundation, 1986-1988, vol. 2, bk. 2, p. 369, fig. 448. Definition and illustration of the heraldic 'vair,' from *Webster's New International Dictionary*, 1923. *The New English Dictionary*, Oxford, 1933, has *s.v.* vair, 1: 'A fur obtained from a variety of squirrel with gray back and white belly, much used in the 13th and 14th centuries as a trimming or lining for garments. Now only archaic.' Then, under 3: *Heraldry*: 'One of the heraldic furs, represented by bell- or cup-shaped spaces of two (or more) tinctures, usually azure and argent, disposed alternately (in imitation of small skins arranged in a similar manner and sewn together).' In his novel, *Pnin*, 1957, p. 191, Nabokov suggests a different etymology for 'vair': 'not from *varius*, variegated, but from *veveritsa*, Slavic for certain beautiful, pale, winter-squirrel fur, having a bluish…shade."

97. Carpenter, Edmund, and Carl Schuster. *Materials for the Study of Social Symbolism in Ancient and Tribal Art*, 3 vols. New York, Rock Foundation, 1986-1988, vol. 2, bk. 2, p. 375, fig. 450. Engraved stela, Ellenberg, Schwalm-Eder-Kreis, Germany. Found in a burial mound of the Beaker Culture, circa 2800-2400 B.C.

98. Carpenter, Edmund, and Carl Schuster. *Materials for the Study of Social Symbolism in Ancient and Tribal Art*, 3 vols. New York, Rock Foundation, 1986-1988, vol. 2, bk. 3, p. 565, figs. 632 and 633. Dendoglyph, New South Wales, Australia, and one of four dendroglyphs around a grave on Yarrabundi Creek, Trundle, New South Wales, Australia.

99. Carpenter, Edmund, and Carl Schuster. *Materials for the Study of Social Symbolism in Ancient and Tribal Art*, 3 vols. New York, Rock Foundation, 1986-1988, vol. 2, bk. 2, p. 370, fig. 449. Iberian painted schist 'idols' selected from 42 examples assembled and illustrated by Henri Breuil.

100. Carpenter, Edmund, and Carl Schuster. *Materials for the Study of Social Symbolism in Ancient and Tribal Art*, 3 vols. New York, Rock Foundation, 1986-1988, vol. 2, bk. 2, p. 318, fig. 417. Tavgi-Samoyed (Nganasan) woman cutting a fur mosaic. Northern Siberia.

101. Carpenter, Edmund, and Carl Schuster. *Materials for the Study of Social Symbolism in Ancient and Tribal Art*, 3 vols. New York, Rock Foundation, 1986-1988, vol. 2, bk. 2, p. 321, fig. 418. Sewing bag of a Vogul woman, western Siberia.

102. Carpenter, Edmund, and Carl Schuster. *Materials for the Study of Social Symbolism in Ancient and Tribal Art*, 3 vols. New York, Rock Foundation, 1986-1988, vol. 2, bk. 2, p. 321, fig. 420. Basic design element of Obugrian fur mosaic, western Siberia.

103. Carpenter, Edmund, and Carl Schuster. *Materials for the Study of Social Symbolism in Ancient and Tribal Art*, 3 vols. New York, Rock Foundation, 1986-1988, vol. 2, bk. 2, p. 333, fig. 423. Neolithic pottery rim sherd, Danilo, near Sibenik, Dalmatia, Croatia.

104. Carpenter, Edmund, and Carl Schuster. *Materials for the Study of Social Symbolism in Ancient and Tribal Art*, 3 vols. New York, Rock Foundation, 1986-1988, vol. 2, bk. 2, p. 332, fig. 431. Pottery support or base for a vessel, with painted decoration in red and black on buff, Trusesti, Moldavia, Romania. Cucuteni A, (Neolithic).

105. Carpenter, Edmund, and Carl Schuster. *Materials for the Study of Social Symbolism in Ancient and Tribal Art*, 3 vols. New York, Rock Foundation, 1986-1988, vol. 2, bk. 2, p. 327, fig. 422. Neolithic black pottery sherd, Butmir, Bosnia.

106. Carpenter, Edmund, and Carl Schuster. *Materials for the Study of Social Symbolism in Ancient and Tribal Art*, 3 vols. New York, Rock Foundation, 1986-1988, vol. 2, bk. 2, p. 327, fig. 425. Neolithic pottery sherd, Bükk type, Rakamaz, Hungary.

107. Carpenter, Edmund, and Carl Schuster. *Materials for the Study of Social Symbolism in Ancient and Tribal Art*, 3 vols. New York, Rock Foundation, 1986-1988, vol. 1, bk. 1, p. 55, fig. 3. Design incised on a club, Byron Strait Islands, northern New Ireland.

108. Carpenter, Edmund, and Carl Schuster. *Materials for the Study of Social Symbolism in Ancient and Tribal Art*, 3 vols. New York, Rock Foundation, 1986-1988, vol. 1, bk. 3, p. 903, fig. 1440. Detail from amphora, circa 410 B.C., Greek.

109. Carpenter, Edmund, and Carl Schuster. *Materials for the Study of Social Symbolism in Ancient and Tribal Art*, 3 vols. New York, Rock Foundation, 1986-1988, vol. 1, bk. 1, p. 163, fig. 155. Textile, Paiwan tribe, Taiwan.

110. Carpenter, Edmund, and Carl Schuster. *Materials for the Study of Social Symbolism in Ancient and Tribal Art*, 3 vols. New York, Rock Foundation, 1986-1988, vol. 1, bk. 1, p. 162, fig. 154. Petroglyph, Waraputa cataract, Essequibo River, Guiana.

111. Carpenter, Edmund, and Carl Schuster. *Materials for the Study of Social Symbolism in Ancient and Tribal Art*, 3 vols. New York, Rock Foundation, 1986-1988, vol. 1, bk. 3, p. 901, fig. 1437. Abraham and Lazarus, miniature, 12th century manuscript, Mount Athos, Greece.

112. Carpenter, Edmund, and Carl Schuster. *Materials for the Study of Social Symbolism in Ancient and Tribal Art*, 3 vols. New York, Rock Foundation, 1986-1988, vol. 1, bk. 3, p. 742, fig. 1223. Wooden figure of Tangaroa Upao Vahu, Polynesian sea-god, Ruruni, Austral Islands.

113. Carpenter, Edmund, and Carl Schuster. *Materials for the Study of Social Symbolism in Ancient and Tribal Art*, 3 vols. New York, Rock Foundation, 1986-1988, vol. 1, bk. 3, p. 750, fig. 1226. Woodcut from Hans Staden's *Wahrhafige Historia* (True History).

114. Carpenter, Edmund, and Carl Schuster. *Materials for the Study of Social Symbolism in Ancient and Tribal Art*, 3 vols. New York, Rock Foundation, 1986-1988, vol. 1, bk. 3, p. 885, fig. 1422. Feast dishes representing *Dzonokwa*, Cannibal Woman. Kwakiutl Indians, British Columbia, Canada.

115. Carpenter, Edmund, and Carl Schuster. *Materials for the Study of Social Symbolism in Ancient and Tribal Art*, 3 vols. New York, Rock Foundation, 1986-1988, vol. 1, bk. 3, p. 872, figs. 1412, 1413, and 1414. Tattooed hands, Taiwan (2) and design on the hand of a Skapan chief, tattooed in the Kayan manner, Sarawak, Borneo.

116. Carpenter, Edmund, and Carl Schuster. *Materials for the Study of Social Symbolism in Ancient and Tribal Art*, 3 vols. New York, Rock Foundation, 1986-1988, vol. 1, bk. 3, p. 873, fig. 1417. Shaman's wooden ornament, carved to represent a hand with spirits coming out of the knuckles, Tlingit, Alaska.

117. Sherman, Claire Richter. "Writing on Hands. Memory and Knowledge in Early Modern Europe," p. 154. Illustration from *Schatzbehalter der wahren Reichtümer des Heils* (The Treasure Chest of Salvation).

118. Carpenter, Edmund, and Carl Schuster. *Materials for the Study of Social Symbolism in Ancient and Tribal Art*, 3 vols. New York, Rock Foundation, 1986-1988, vol. 1, bk. 3, p. 756, fig. 1231. Assemblage of images of mutilated hands, Paleolithic, France.

119. Carpenter, Edmund, and Carl Schuster. *Materials for the Study of Social Symbolism in Ancient and Tribal Art*, 3 vols. New York, Rock Foundation, 1986-1988, vol. 1, bk. 3, p. 757, fig. 1234. Petroglyphs, Rio de las Pinturas, Canadón de las Cuevas, Santa Cruz, Patagonia.

120. Carpenter, Edmund, and Carl Schuster. *Materials for the Study of Social Symbolism in Ancient and Tribal Art*, 3 vols. New York, Rock Foundation, 1986-1988, vol. 1, bk. 3, p. 764, fig. 1243. Pictograph, Canyon de Chelly, Arizona.

121. Carpenter, Edmund, and Carl Schuster. *Materials for the Study of Social Symbolism in Ancient and Tribal Art*, 3 vols. New York, Rock Foundation, 1986-1988, vol. 1, bk. 3, p. 868, figs. 1404a and 1404b. Genealogical chart (*Verwandtschaftsbild*) 14th century German, from the Wolfenbüttel *Sachsenspiegel.*

122. Carpenter, Edmund, and Carl Schuster. *Materials for the Study of Social Symbolism in Ancient and Tribal Art*, 3 vols. New York, Rock Foundation, 1986-1988, vol. 1, bk. 3, p. 870, fig. 1410. Genealogical chart, Dogon, Mali. Redrawn from Marcel Griaule.

123. Wirz, Paul. *Der Totenkult auf Bali*. Stuttgart, Strecker und Schroder, 1928, fig. 10. *Ukur-kèpèng, Bali.*

124. Carpenter, Edmund, and Carl Schuster. *Patterns That Connect*, p. 28, Tree of Jesse. Pen and ink drawing, Antwerp artist, circa 1520.

125. Coomaraswamy, Ananda K. *Yaksas: Essays in the Water Cosmology*. Edited by Paul Schroeder. New Delhi, Oxford University Press, 1993, fig. 70a. Birth of Brahma from a lotus springing from the navel of Narayana, Dasavatara. Elura, India, 8th century A.D.

126. Coomaraswamy, Ananda K. *Yaksas: Essays in the Water Cosmology*. Edited by Paul Schroeder. New Delhi, Oxford University Press, 1993, fig. 53c. Rhizome with flowers, buds and leaves, rising from the mouth of a *yaksa*. Amaravati, about A.D. 200 or earlier.

127. Coomaraswamy, Ananda K. *Yaksas: Essays in the Water Cosmology*. Edited by Paul Schroeder. New Delhi, Oxford University Press, 1993, fig. 51a. Full vase (*purna kalasa*). Amaravati, about A.D. 200 or earlier.

128. Schuster, "A Prehistoric Symbol in Modern Chinese Folk Art," *Man*, vol. XXXVI (270-292), Dec., 1936, pp. 201-203. Cover illustration of water pots with 'W' markings.

129. Carpenter, Edmund, and Carl Schuster. *Materials for the Study of Social Symbolism in Ancient and Tribal Art*, 3 vols. New York, Rock Foundation, 1986-1988, vol. 1, bk. 2, p. 466. Columns of W's and M's; headless hockers (ancestors) with multiple bodies used to represent generations.

130. Coomaraswamy, Ananda K. *Yaksas: Essays in the Water Cosmology*. Edited by Paul Schroeder. New Delhi, Oxford University Press, 1993, fig. 64c. Design of over-flowing vases, built up from the common Sumerian symbol of the vase plus two rivers.

131. Carpenter, Edmund, and Carl Schuster. *Materials for the Study of Social Symbolism in Ancient and Tribal Art*, 3 vols. New York, Rock Foundation, 1986-1988, vol. 1, bk. 1, p. 176, figs. 179a and 179b. Pictographs, Los Letreros cave, Velez Blanco, Almeria, Spain. Neolithic or Chalcolithic period (4000-3000 B.C.).

132. Carpenter, Edmund, and Carl Schuster. *Materials for the Study of Social Symbolism in Ancient and Tribal Art*, 3 vols. New York, Rock Foundation, 1986-1988, vol. 1, bk. 3, p. 724, fig. 1201. Representation of human figures carved in the earth at an initiation cerermony. Kamilaroi tribe, New South Wales, Australia.

133. Carpenter, Edmund, and Carl Schuster. *Materials for the Study of Social Symbolism in Ancient and Tribal Art*, 3 vols. New York, Rock Foundation, 1986-1988, vol. 1, bk. 3, p. 724, fig. 120. Panel of an Australian opossum-skin robe with scratched design. Collected by Charles Wilkes (1839-41).

134. Carpenter, Edmund, and Carl Schuster. *Materials for the Study of Social Symbolism in Ancient and Tribal Art*, 3 vols. New York, Rock Foundation, 1986-1988, vol. 1, bk. 1, p. 234, fig. 263. Pictograph, Cerron Carbón, between Barioche and Río Nireco, Nacional del Río Négro, Argentina.

135. Carpenter, Edmund, and Carl Schuster. *Materials for the Study of Social Symbolism in Ancient and Tribal Art*, 3 vols. New York, Rock Foundation, 1986-1988, vol. 3, bk. 1, p. 236, fig. 264. Painting on a Patagonian rock wall, (detail of a larger composition), Huemul peninsula, Lake Nahuel Huapi, Territorio Nacional del Neuquen, Argentina.

136. Carpenter, Edmund, and Carl Schuster. *Materials for the Study of Social Symbolism in Ancient and Tribal Art*, 3 vols. New York, Rock Foundation, 1986-1988, vol. 3, bk. 1, p. 238, fig. 265. Hypothetical method for drawing the labyrinth, based on Petrikovits. See chapter 3 in this work.

137. Carpenter, Edmund, and Carl Schuster. *Materials for the Study of Social Symbolism in Ancient and Tribal Art*, 3 vols. New York, Rock Foundation, 1986-1988, vol. 3, bk. 1, p. 238, fig. 58. Sand-drawn turtle effigy, Lambumbu, New Hebrides. Road along which the ghosts pass to *Iambi*.

138. Carpenter, Edmund, and Carl Schuster. *Materials for the Study of Social Symbolism in Ancient and Tribal Art*, 3 vols. New York, Rock Foundation, 1986-1988, vol. 3, bk. 1, p. 239, fig. 266. Wooden disk (spindle whorl) from Barreales culture, province of St. Juan, Argentina.

139. Carpenter, Edmund, and Carl Schuster. *Materials for the Study of Social Symbolism in Ancient and Tribal Art*, 3 vols. New York, Rock Foundation, 1986-1988, vol. 2, bk. 2, pp. 457, figs. 537 and 537a. Stone ceremonial axe with detail of fret-style design, Neuquén, Argentina.

INDEX

A

abacus 1, 30-31, 34-38, 48, 56, 213-214, 220
    Chinese *suan-phan* (calculating plate) 34, 36-37, 220
    counting board 23, 30, 34-35, 37-38, 220
    origin of word 35
    Roman hand-held abacus 36, 220
    sand tray 34
Abbé Breuil 160, 196, 201, 235
Adam 81, 82, 177, 185, 201
Adam Kadmon 121
aither (ether) 67, 78-79
Alcmena (Greek goddess) 7
American Museum of Natural History (AMNH) 29, 139, 212, 215, 219-220
amulets 1, 4, 8, 10, 11, 13, 119, 228
Animal Style art 141-142, 200, 215, 217
Aristotle 61, 64, 89, 126, 128, 217
articulus (L. joint) 37-38, 124
Assyrian 9, 13, 183, 217
atomic now (Gr. *atomos nun*) 89
axis mundi 65, 78-79, 83, 87, 89-90, 92-93, 128-129, 157, 161
Aztec 112-113, 143, 187, 229

B

Babylonian 9-10, 13-14, 34-35, 37, 43, 46, 56-57, 103, 113, 127, 226
Balder (Norse god) 13
Bali 47, 69, 126, 193, 215, 223, 237
Balinese 66, 69, 71-73, 209-210, 221-222
    dancing 66, 71-73, 222
    puppet-complex 65, 72, 78, 125
    sangiang deling ritual 72, 222
    ukur-kepeng 69, 193, 237
    ukur-mas 69
Barber, Elizabeth 18, 79, 87, 127, 128, 209
basketry viii, ix, x, 18, 116, 127, 129, 197, 207, 212, 219
Bateson, Gregory 71, 126, 205-206, 209, 222
Beowulf 74, 127, 209
Bhagavad Gita 96
Bible iii, 10, 21, 26, 32-34, 94, 127, 201, 210, 213, 224-225
    New Testament
        John 66, 78, 120, 193
        Luke 19
        Mark 66
        Matthew 19, 78, 163
    Old Testament
        Deuteronomy 32, 57
        Ecclesiastes 78
        Ezekiel 56, 68, 94, 129, 224

Genesis 27, 33, 57, 63, 128, 167, 177, 183, 201-202
Hebrews 181, 202
Hosea 33
Isaiah 19, 33, 68
Jeremiah 25, 168
Numbers 18, 33, 56-57
Proverbs 32, 56
Psalms 13, 19
birth 3, 7-8, 18, 64, 73-74, 76, 81, 87, 89, 93, 96, 108, 121, 126, 130, 159, 177-178, 180-181, 184-185, 194, 201-202, 237
    rituals connected with untying 7, 8
    umbilical cord 96, 108, 130
birth from the knee 177-184
    derived from genealogical iconography 148, 177
    Dionysius 120, 177, 180
    in folklore 177-182
    in Grail motif 180-181
    knee as generative organ 182
    origin of child in the father 177-184
blanket strip 169, 234
Boas, Franz 140, 215
body as kinship chart 188, 191-193
bonds 7-8, 12, 68, 70, 78, 177, 193-199
    analogy to plants 126, 194-197, 206
    death 11-12
    kinship 124
    life 10, 14, 61, 68, 70, 73-74, 78
Buddha 89, 193, 205
Buddhist 6, 46-47, 50, 80, 96, 126, 128-129, 210, 214, 221, 224
Burnett, John 52, 57, 126, 209
Burns, Robert 8-9, 19, 209

C

caduceus 6, 89, 219
Camonica Valley (Italian Alps) 114, 131, 209, 227
cannibalism 120, 123, 185-187, 236
Cargill, John 52-54, 57, 210, 221
    Cross at Canna 52-53
Carpenter, Edmund v, 18, 111, 127-131, 136, 146, 161, 164, 197, 200-203, 210, 219, 221-238
    Materials for the Study of Social Symbolism in Ancient and Tribal Art 210, 219, 221-238
    Patterns That Connect 130, 137, 146, 201-203, 210, 237
cat's cradles (see string figures)
Celtic 40, 52-54, 57, 100, 121, 130, 183, 202-203, 209-210, 218, 220-221, 225
    knotwork 100, 130, 209, 225
    musical notation 52-54, 57, 210, 218, 220-221

Christ 13, 47-48, 53, 57, 73, 76-78, 120-121, 193, 203, 218, 223
Christian 74, 96, 117, 120-121, 126, 201, 203, 210
Churning of the Sea of Milk 88, 89, 92, 128, 224
clashing rocks (Gr. *symplegades*) 94, 131
continuous-line drawings 76, 94, 97-106, 117-119, 124, 197-199, 203
    Celtic 100, 225
    Dürer's Knots 60, 97, 125, 127, 129, 216, 222, 224
    in Africa 103, 211, 225
    in ancient Greece 103, 226
    in ancient Near East 103, 113, 225-226
    in India 102, 225
    in modern art 99, 130
    in Scotland 103
    in the New Hebrides 100-101, 107, 130, 198, 210, 216, 225-226, 238
    Leonardo's Concatenation 97-98, 125, 127, 129, 216, 222, 225
    principles of construction 97, 99, 118-120
    relation to labyrinth 118-120
Coomaraswamy, Ananda K. v, vii, 3, 8, 19, 61-62, 64-65, 70, 73, 76, 78-79, 97-99, 125-129, 131, 135-136, 161, 180, 193, 195, 200-203, 206-207, 210, 215, 222, 237
couvade 184, 187, 203, 210
    origin of child in the father 177-184
crossed figures 81, 127, 157, 223

D

Dalyell, J. G. 10, 18, 19, 210
Dante 63, 68, 98, 126, 129, 211
Darius Vase 35, 220
Da Vinci, Leonardo 97-98, 125, 127, 129, 216, 222, 225
Day, Cyrus 11, 18-19, 29, 56, 210, 219
death 7-8, 10-12, 19, 46, 61, 64, 68, 73-76, 78, 85-87, 89, 93, 97, 101-102, 104-105, 107-108, 110, 113, 117, 121, 123-124, 126, 131, 136, 143, 156, 191, 206
    unstringing 68
    with noose 11-12
De la Vega, Garcilaso 29-30, 56, 211
Delphi 14, 108, 130
Demetrius (Greek physician) 14
Dionysius (Greek god) 46, 120, 177, 180
dismemberment 46, 72, 120-122, 124, 131, 185-187, 201
    symbolic meaning in religion 120
dolls 69-70, 124, 126, 193, 216, 222
drills 90-91, 128-129, 157, 224
Dürer, Albrecht 60, 97-98, 125, 127, 129, 216, 222, 225

T

U

V

W

Y

Z